D0897615

Society and History
in English Renaissance Verse

The Social World of the Florentine Humanists *(1963)*

Lawyers and Statecraft in Renaissance Florence *(1968)*

Violence and Civil Disorder in Italian Cities,
1200—1500, *Editor (1972)*

Not In God's Image: Women in History from the Greeks
to the Victorians, *with Julia O'Faolain (1973)*

Power and Imagination: City-States in Renaissance Italy *(1979)*

Society and History
in English Renaissance Verse

❧

LAURO MARTINES

Basil Blackwell

© Lauro Martines 1985
First published 1985

Basil Blackwell Ltd
108 Cowley Road, Oxford OX4 1JF, UK

Basil Blackwell Inc.
432 Park Avenue South, Suite 1505,
New York, NY 10016, USA

British Library Cataloguing in Publication Data

Martines, Lauro
Society and history in English Renaissance verse.
1. English poetry—Early modern, 1500—1700
2. Literature and society—Great Britain—
History
I. Title
821'.3   PR531
ISBN 0-631-14115-4

Library of Congress Cataloging in Publication Data

Martines, Lauro.
Society and history in English Renaissance verse.
Bibliography: pp. 163—81
Includes index.
1. English poetry—Early modern, 1500—1700—History
and criticism.   2. Literature and history—Great Britain.
3. Literature and society—Great Britain.
I. Title.
PR535.H5M37   1985   831'.3'09358   84—28249
ISBN 0-631-14115-4

Typeset by Pioneer, East Sussex
Printed in Great Britain by
Page Bros Ltd., Norwich.

Contents

Acknowledgements		vi
Foreword		vii
1	Theory	1
2	Strategies: from poem to world	18
	Action and direct reference	18
	Ideas and subject-matter	21
	Diction and figurative language	25
	Style, tone, viewpoint	37
	Genre and indirect reference	44
3	Strategies: from world to poem	53
	Patronage, occasions, readers	53
	Biography, class, milieu	61
	Politics, period, historical change	68
4	Reconsiderations	73
	Action, direct reference, ideas	73
	Diction and imagery	76
	Style	86
	Genre	93
5	A new discourse: needs and prospects	97
	A new discourse	97
	Needs and prospects	107
6	Against specialization: history, poetry, milieu	128
	Notes	150
	Bibliography	163
	Index	183

Acknowledgements

The National Endowment for the Humanities, based in Washington, DC, funded the beginnings of this book in 1978—9, though I set out in fact, and promised, to do a socio-historical study of poetry in Renaissance Italy. This may yet come. I trust, meanwhile, that the Endowment will forgive my breach of contract.

I am grateful to the University of California, whose research funds, year after year, have been a source of encouragement both tangible and semiotic.

Worthy to be remembered always is the kind assistance of the staff of the British Library, particularly in that haven, the North Library. I must record good conversations with a friend and colleague, Albert Braunmuller, and thank Sue Phillpott at Basil Blackwell for a superior job of copy-editing. My first love of English Renaissance poetry goes back many years, to a time when I studied with Kenneth Burke, E. L. Mayo, Theodore Stroud, Thomas F. Dunn, and the philosopher, William Reese. To them, my gratitude indeed.

Lauro Martines

Foreword

> but we worldly men
> Have miserable, mad, mistaking eyes.
> *Titus Andronicus,* V, ii, 65

The coupling of history and poetry will seem a strange pairing to historians, who stay away from poetry as if by a strict professional rule. They hold the common view that verse is the utterance of fine sentiments in fancy words and so has little to do with reality. They are mistaken.

Ranging over the period from about 1580 to the 1660s, this book is about the ties between non-dramatic poetry of the English Renaissance and the social world of its composition. Historical and literary method are at the focus: questions of theory, strategies of analysis, and the nature of relations between Renaissance poetry and its society. I use two terms throughout: 'world' and 'poem'. The former refers to the historical and social setting of the poem: for example, reading audiences, patronage, politics, milieu, religious matters, and social groups. 'Poem' means any particular poem and its parts — diction, figurative language, tone, generic conventions, and rhetorical or semiotic features. As envisaged in this book, the supreme task of social literary analysis is to hurdle the gap between poem and social world so as to bring the two together. And though analysis may proceed from the poem *or* from the world, scholarly practice usually begins with texts rather than worldly contexts, as any text will always have more order and infinitely less variety than the world.

Renaissance poetry deals with attestable experience and strives to get at it in ways that may not interest the writer of prose.* This means that it is

---

*Though in the sixteenth and seventeenth centuries poetry and prose stood closer together than most historians suspect: K. G. Hamilton, *The Two Harmonies: Poetry and Prose in the Seventeenth Century* (Oxford, 1963), chs 1–2.

likely to be the chief gateway to certain zones in experience. Yet no study now exists that tells historians how as historians to read Renaissance verse, nor has anyone outlined a method to assist literary scholars in *their* search for the traces of society and history in the verse of the sixteenth and seventeenth centuries.

I shall be accused of wishing to 'reduce' poetry to social history. On the contrary, I argue for its large scope by striving to show that it belongs to a wider experience: it gives voice to historical and social realities, in addition to having the rhetorical and semiotic structures discerned by formalist critics.

The mode of analysis to be presented here has been gleaned and pieced together from the pertinent literary scholarship and criticism of the past half-century. In reading poetry, no one critic has evolved a method of social literary analysis, a set of considered procedures for studying the relations between poem and world, but many critics have had fragments of such a method.

The strongest argument against reading any literary text in its historical and social context rests on the claim that art is an 'independent semantic unity', not at all in line with 'reality' and not even in sensible touch with it. In our day, the 'semiotic' version of this claim holds (see pp. 126—7) that literature is the free play of signs within a system of signification (language). Break up the parts of the poem — any given text — with an eye to exiting from that system, so as to make contact with the historical world of its composition, and you also shatter the meaning assembled there. This is to say that the alleged ties between poem and world are a mere invention, for in converting his experience of the world (and of language) into a poem, the poet so transforms it as to destroy all traceable ties between poem and world.

The following pages challenge this claim; they present a method for unlocking the poem and getting at the ties. Though Renaissance poetry is neither a mirror nor a window to its world, it drew contemporary experience into an engagement so important and substantial as to make the historian's neglect of it astonishing.

1

Theory

The singling out of relations between English Renaissance verse and its socio-historical world is so common an exercise in criticism and literary scholarship as to seem venerable practice. Whether we go back to Renaissance theorists, to the eighteenth century, or the 1970s, we find large numbers of critics making observations about the ties between poetry and its social world. But social analysis — as I shall call such observation — has always been done in a hit-and-miss fashion by critics of nearly all schools and tempers. And nearly always their procedure has been to relate some part or aspect of the poem to some part of the world: a piecemeal, broken, impressionistic approach.

These adjectives imply criticism, when in fact I mean none, for the approach has been rich in analytic strategies. Piecemeal and impressionistic, the very nature of traditional analysis has made for some of its strengths. Critics who work in this vein go their preferred ways, free to bend with personal talents or to develop insights in accordance with subject-matter and private inclination.

Chapters 2, 3, and 4 go through the different steps of social analysis with a view to outlining a method. But theory is my point of departure in this chapter because the method relies on a wide variety of strategies and these depend, in turn, upon a core of unspoken assumptions.

The following numbered propositions do a double job: they sum up the guidelines of social literary analysis and state its basic assumptions.

1 Poets, like all people, belong to a time and place, and therefore any act of creative writing on their part is likely to bear the marks of a milieu.

2 Emphasis on the individuality of experience must be balanced by the observation that the diversity of any man's experience has all first been socially prepared — 'processed' and endowed with a given range of potential meanings by his upbringing, by language and values, codes and customs: that is to say, by his society's ways of doing things and seeing the world. Thus our first proposition — namely, that all people belong to a time and a place and so are social phenomena.[1]

3 Renaissance poetry enlists the whole of the poet's experience because of its linguistic and associative resources, above all as contained in simile, metaphor, image, symbol, wordplay, and lexical ambiguity. A poet says one thing — e.g., Shakespeare in the *Sonnets* — and straightway he is saying other things as well because of the tentacular possibilities of his medium. This ease of association is what reaches into the whole of his experience to draw out meanings and corruscations that catch something of the elusive coherence in consciousness.

Coda The stricter a set of verse conventions — as in pastoral, the sonnet, or the epigram — the more likely the poet is, in using them, to give expression to the social (i.e., the more impersonal) voices of his age; and therefore his own experience will enter more glancingly, more covertly and irregularly, into his manipulation of the given code. To misuse or violate a generic code may issue in a personal statement, but by rejecting certain parts of the genre (and hence the attendant social voices) he also turns it into a social statement.

4 Renaissance poetry comes out of experience of the world and of literature, but in the distinction between direct experience of the world and indirect (literary) experience, direct experience is prior and primary. This is to say that of the two, to court a woman and to read a sonnet, the first has existential and historical priority.

Coda Drawing on his literary experience (reading), a man may write a sonnet before he courts a woman. In this exercise, he gives us in some sense the stored-up experience of others. And if the sonnet be a vital genre for his time and place, then his very use of the form is a response to social solicitations and is thus a social response.

5   Renaissance poetry does not seek on the whole to escape the world but to engage it, to comment on it, or in some fashion — as in political poetry — to change it. Even at its most realistic, however, it cannot reflect the world in the sense of mirroring some hard and fast fact or reality 'out there'. Poetry transforms what is given in experience; but what is given is also itself in process of transformation, most especially in an expanding society, where social reality and social relations gain and lose, shift or turn, being in a continual process of change.

   Coda   So far as Cavalier poetry has 'escapist' strains, these appear in the theme of 'retirement', espoused by many a disappointed royalist, and in the fetishistic verse of amorous dalliance; yet even these — dalliance and retirement — were modes of survival in a grim time.

6   In making verse out of his experience, the Renaissance poet, though seeking to engage the world, 'rewrites' his experience and makes something of it (art) which is different from life. Let no historian, however, be diverted or repelled; he is not, after all, repelled by political thinkers. Hobbes, Filmer, and Locke do not reproduce or represent the life of politics. They approach this reality only in the way in which a generalization approaches the particular. The poet, on the contrary, moves in the opposite direction: he offers us the particular, a whole impasto of particulars. His poetry is as close to 'life' — historical reality — from one side (particularly) as is the political treatise from the other (generality). Poet and political thinker are opposites. But just as the social historian must know what to discount in political ideas, what to readjust or pare away, in order to move them closer to political and social life, so must he also know what to bring to poetry to find its alignments with life, with social experience.

7   The burden of social analysis is to find the different lines of connection between poem and world. Since the poem is not a mirror held up to the world, the connecting lines are not direct and do not make for one-to-one relationships. They are devious, unsteady, and perplexing, because the poet rewrites the experience which the world has written in him. Accordingly, social analysis must be devious and probing, a breaker of codes, for poetry is not

— and yet is — what it seems. Renaissance love poetry often turns love into a metaphor for other things, just as religious verse may rely heavily on the locutions and conventions of profane love. The poetry of complaint and of wooing for favor and patronage may, when addressed to Queen Elizabeth, turn into a poetry of love. Petrarchan love verse could be parodied and turned into out-and-out political verse.[2] The metaphysics of praise in Jacobean verse (John Donne) may be, in addition, an elaborate plea for patronage, just as bread-and-butter poems of patronage may turn into brilliant ideological statements, rich and resonant, bewitching and honest (Ben Jonson's 'To Penshurst'). A love lyric may flicker with feudal, legal, or commercial terms and thus be saying things of capital interest, albeit obliquely, about its social world; and a poem of religious meditation may also be a plea for the divine right of kings.

Again, in poetry things are, and yet are not, what they seem, for poetry enlists the whole of the poet's experience and any man's experience is likely to catch something of the world's diversity.

8 If Propositions 1, 2, 3, and 7 add up to anything at all, it is that history holds nothing in airtight compartments. Social life — society — is a vital whole or unity of some kind. The truth of this is measured in the innumerable interconnections among the diversities of individual, group, community, and national experience. In semiotic terms, this suggests that meaning can be 'transcoded' — transposed from one network of signs to another.

9 The preceding assumptions issue in the obligation to make a statement of purpose — my concluding proposition. The ultimate aim of social literary analysis is a double one: to throw light on poetry and to throw light on history — that is, to use the light of social and historical analysis to find the traces of society in poetry, and to use social literary analysis to bring the light of poetry to the mysteries of the historical world. Each aim already contains the other, just as in the process of analysis movement from the poem to the world already signifies the possibility of movement from the world to the poem.

The nine propositions seek to avoid literary and social-science terminology in order to sidestep the gigantic body of pertinent current theory, although interested readers should take note of pages 126—7 and be on the lookout for commentary in my notes. The ends of this study are attainable with little recourse to technical vocabularies. Even avoiding these, the method to be X-rayed here will be wide-ranging and complex enough. And in any case, I have sought to base my propositions on the predominant practice of literary scholarship and criticism: a practice founded on rule-of-thumb strategies rather than on a corpus of systematic rumination.

The overarching vision of social analysis may be described in a sentence. If the social world is some kind of living whole which engages all who live in it, and if the poem belongs to a socio-historical world by virtue of the poet's contact with his contemporary readers, then however ingenious or fanciful the poem, we must assume that it has relations with that world. Our task is to find and describe them.

One 'meta' problem confronts us at the outset. In the act of reading a Jacobean or Caroline poem, the twentieth-century critic bears something of his own world back into the seventeenth century. There can be no doubt of this; and if such 'interference' invalidates the enterprise of social analysis, this is no more than to say that the study of history and the whole historical discipline are humbug. It is also to say that the moment we begin to make sense of any historical artefact — be it pottery, parchment, or poem — our eyes turn it mainly into a twentieth-century object, so that in so-called historical matters the perceiving subject seems to overwhelm the object. From a philosophical viewpoint this may be so; yet 'instinct' and good sense rebel. For various reasons, involving the very history we have lived, we seem destined to study the past, and this puts both historian and critic before the same task: that of reading texts in their historical time. That any serious critic is pressed to read verse in its historical time is attested by the fact that he makes a fool of himself whenever, in discussing a Jacobean poem, he fails to give words their early seventeenth-century values. This part at least of his labor is historical; and of course the moment he says anything at all about poetic conventions, genre, patronage, or the education of the poet, let alone 'schools' of poetry or Jacobean reading publics, he passes fully over to an historical vantage point. Much of the job of editing a seventeenth-century poem is historical: as in the collating of manuscripts and comparisons with the first printed edition, lexical emendations in line with seventeenth-century usage, the identification of topical allusions, the clarification of verbal obscurities, and a statement about the situation, if known, leading up to the composition of the poem.

In associating the critic and the historian, I raise a question designed to lead us directly to the main problems connected with the nine propositions.

We cannot turn a prose document into a poem of the period, but we can turn a poem into an historical document — and yet not quite. We cannot turn a poem into an historical document if we mean by this that we can distil it into a statement in prose. Some *part* of the poem can be thus reduced, but not the poem. This warns us against trying to read Renaissance poems as prose documents, the besetting sin in the work of many critics who emphasize ideas, political poetry, and the prosy content of verse. To convert a poem into prose is to shear it of everything that makes it a poem: its associative powers and the results of glancing forays, made during the composition of the poem, into the wider experience of the poet, wider than anything suggested by the mere theme of the poem. The critic who does such shearing cuts away parts of consciousness and expressed experience in order to make the poem manageable, to bring it into line with an interpretation, or simply to enable him to write and present a clear argument. This is all perfectly acceptable, so long as he realizes that in the process of shearing he is being true neither to his own experience nor to that of others.

Ben Jonson claimed — in what some scholars have deemed classical practice — that he did the first version of poems in prose; he began with a statement of the poem's intentional content. Drawing instruction from their classical mentors, Jonson and other Renaissance literati put poetry with the best prose and assigned both to the art of rhetoric. Yet Jonson's claim says nothing about the changes wrought in the prose version, the allusions introduced, by the process of versification.[3] And what about his 'ineffable cadence'? How did this work on readers and what did it communicate? Answers to these questions would undermine Jonson's disarming conception of the prose content of verse.

The difference between an historical document and a poem is the difference between ordinary written expression and literary art. This distinction brings us at once to the essential problems posed by the nine propositions.

I have suggested (Proposition 1) that poetry reveals something of its time and place. But poems are not historical documents in prose. Hence they do not and cannot ordinarily reveal a milieu in the fashion of conventional historical documents. This, again, is because art is different from prosaic expression.

What happens however when, in considering historical documentation, we compare poetry with 'artistic' prose? Sidney's *Astrophel and Stella* with the essays of Bacon or Montaigne? Or Donne's amatory verse with Machiavelli's *The Prince,* with Lord Herbert of Cherbury's *Autobiography,* or with the letters of a highly cultivated man such as Pascal? The answer lies clearly in the ordinary practice of historians. They reject poetry but they study and use artistic, literary prose. They turn to the latter for 'hard' evidence when writing intellectual history, the history of religion, political history, or even social history. It is enough to mention the use, admittedly sporadic, of the nineteenth-century novel by certain social historians.

The conclusion is that *all* prose qualifies for treatment as some kind of historical documentation, however artistic, fictional, or brainspun it may be.[4] For a piece of writing to count as history there is one requirement only: that it not be poetry. For poetry — thus the inescapable implication in the common practice of historians — is so special ('arty?') an art form, it works over the material of experience so thoroughly, that it removes itself far enough from 'real' life, or distorts it enough, to be untrustworthy as history.[5]

This very odd view has wide-ranging implications, only three of which I shall consider at this point.

(a)   Poetry does not reveal its milieu; poetry may reveal it but cannot be trusted to do so; poetry reveals its milieu in such mad or mysterious ways that the historian is well advised to stay away from it.

The reply to these warnings is this book as a whole.

(b)   The second implication is that 'literature' has two orders, prose and poetry. Literary prose — whatever its somersaults or castles in the air — is related to historical reality, but poetry's relation to the same reality is not verifiable.

This distinction, if stated thus, is so fraught with problems that it scarcely merits a reply.

(c)   The art of poetry holds so dubious a place relative to reality that the relationship is best seen in terms of a split, such as poem — world, art — nature, unreal — real, and imagination — reason or fancy — moderation.

This implication, with its dualistic overtones, touches the core of social literary analysis by raising the problem of the connection between poetry on the one side and experience, consciousness, or reality on the other. The implication — indisputably present, I say, in the historian's refusal to draw upon poetry as evidence — is the more serious in having the support of aestheticians and critics who hold that poetry, far from being looked at contextually, should be considered 'in and for itself'. For a poem is 'a work of art' and art occupies a realm apart, different from life and different from 'nature'. A poem departs from reality because it is made by an independent mind which, in so performing, creates an autonomous world of relations and meanings.[6]

How the reader, when 'producing' the poem by his reading, strips himself of his experience of the world, in order to rise transcendently with the poem, makes for a massive epistemological problem. Yet the conception of poetry as denizen of a transcendent world must be taken seriously for a moment because it has a surprising ally in the everyday practice of historians and bears directly on three of the propositions (3, 6, 7) in our range of assumptions.

As a working historian writing in the apposite mode, I have no obligation to define poetry for all times and places or to make a universal statement about art and experience. This is the lunatic office of the philosopher. And anyway such statements often hinge on tacit assumptions about 'human nature' — a notion which can do the historian no good.

That there is a difference between art and life no one denies, just as there is a difference between a formal garden and a wild heath, though this analogy is already misleading because the Renaissance poet began with pen and paper, not with material, like the sculptor, to be reshaped with his hands. The appropriate question here is whether or not the English Renaissance poet, in the act of composing a poem, or working his experience into art, altered personal contacts with reality so completely as to expunge all traces of the poem's origins in his experience and in a specific time and place?

Poets of the period did no such thing. They knew too much about the art of rhetoric, were too interested in their intended readers, took poetry too seriously, and loved it too much to divorce it from 'life'. In fact, they *used* it in letter writing, in prayer, to express gratitude, to celebrate occasions, to curry favor, to praise friends and patrons, and to win friends or influence people. Poetry, as we shall see, was action *in* the world. Life and poetry were not one, but they were closely joined.

These observations do not and cannot refute the claims of the aesthetician who argues that a poem is a self-contained mobile of relations and meanings, though he faces a formidable epistemological problem in having to deal with the act of reading, and therefore with readers and their relations both to their own world and to the poem. But neither can the poem as transcendent entity extinguish the other manifestation of the poem as action in the world, and it is this we look for in social analysis, not for the poem's transcendent ghost.

Holding that the worldly poem — as opposed to the transcendent one — has temporal relations with the world (i.e., with life, experience, 'reality'), we come next to the trickiest of all questions: what is the nature exactly of the poem's relation to its historico-social world? Cast in this abstract form, the question is too philosophical and so is wrongly put from the standpoint of the historical discipline. What we want, instead, is a more humble and practical question or, rather, several questions that tilt closer to some particular reality. Thus, in the period between about 1580 and the 1660s, how do the varieties of English poetry reveal their milieu, what do they reveal, and how reliable are the revelations?

We have seen that prose, however belletrist, poses no paralyzing problems for the historian. He invokes prose of all sorts as historical evidence, on the supposition that all prose not only makes contact with its society but also has something to say about it. This supposition makes for all the authority we need to extend the same status to poetry. It cannot be that Renaissance verse cuts itself off from social reality, thereby dropping out of history, by its reliance not on more imagination but on metaphor, meter, genre, rhyme, or regular verse forms. This is not to say that verse and literary prose necessarily occupy the same ground relative to historical experience and social change, although I have no doubt that this could be argued for the period from the sixteenth to the eighteenth centuries. But to hold that verse has no reliable contact with its social world is nonsense, unless *literary* prose (including, e.g., essays, familiar letters, and polished sermons) is also denied that contact.

On the assumption that Renaissance verse and prose make contact with their social world, and do so in different ways and from different angles, what might the essential differences be?

Historians ordinarily take for granted that their prose sources refer to things going on in the world or in the mind (or both): acts of government, riots, wars, harvesting, plague, industrial activity, attending a Catholic rather than a Protestant church, thinking as a Calvinist, or having feelings and thoughts about government, society, trade, farming, colonies, prayer, women, the family, science, and philosophical matters. Renaissance verse may refer to all these things, but seldom in a sustained or flatly descriptive fashion, and consequently it is not prose's rival for the same office. Verse has different ends. It touches everything in the above list and more, much more, for it aims to be suggestive, to teach, move and delight, to take in a wider radius of experience, to convey thought as well as feeling and halfway stages between the two, but yet to do all this by means of discipline in the craft, so as to produce a unity of expression ('art'), be it sonnet, epic, satire, elegy, panegyric, epigram, verse letter, religious ode, or whatnot. And here, therefore, one wants to exclaim: it is not up to Renaissance poetry to prove that it carries within it part of the world it came from; it's up to the historian to find ways of deciphering poetry's social code, to learn how to take meaning from it and how to organize what is taken.

I state in Proposition 6 that the poet rewrites and transforms the experience inscribed in him by the world. But whatever his individual stamp, since he is a social phenomenon (Proposition 2), aspects of his social world cannot fail to pervade his verse. There is no invitation here to blot out the individual. On the contrary, the historian's social interest requires that he also go in quest of the individual, the better to pick out what is representative or typical from what is not, what belongs to a school, a movement, or a time and place, and what belongs to the individual and to idiosyncrasy. In other words, social analysis is called upon to take notice of individuals as well as groups, of deviations and also norms, or it risks confusing the quirky with the common, the eccentric with the conventional, the individual with the class, group, or coterie. Social analysis looks for the individual, but mainly, it is true, for the sake of getting at his society. There cannot be a society of one, unless that one have two or more voices, and in this case he will already have been through the social mill. Savage boys do not have alter egos.

I can almost imagine an individual so peculiar and fantastic that he would seem not to have been touched at all by society. For all practical purposes such a man has not lived in history and so is not, in our terms, of the party of humanity. But I cannot imagine a Renaissance poem so queer that nothing in it belongs to the sixteenth and seventeenth centuries. What would make it a *Renaissance* poem? Or to broach the matter another way: any poem of the period has been cast onto the stage of history by the poet's simple decision to convey a message or signal, since he could do this only by trying to make contact with another being like himself, an operation wholly dependent on the social (and hence historical) process. Although knowing themselves to be of a time and place, Renaissance poets often longed for immortality through their verse and wished to be read forever. The fact that we can make sense of their verse is proof enough that something about it transcends time and place. The means of this 'escape' lies in our common humanity with the writers of that verse. Their verse reaches us by what they share with us, and we are able to enter their times by what we share with them. But this is not, after all, so strange and we need not even be talking about art. If we are able to read and understand the plainest sixteenth-century diary, kept by a cobbler or a baker, then it too transcends its times and nowadays would be greatly prized as a source for social historians intent on reconstructing the sixteenth-century world.

The truth is that the simplest statement in prose can reach beyond its period, to convey meaning across the ages, more easily than any poem. Poetry is more problematic but it is no exotic dwarf or oddity relative to its society, even though it may not be a cobbler or a baker. Paradoxically indeed, poetry's success in transcending its times — as in the case of simple prose — is the very mark of its historicity. It is because Ben Jonson lived and loved in time that, catching elements of this experience in verse, he is able to communicate them to me, who has also lived and loved in time. I understand something about him and have his 'feel', up to a point at any rate, *because* of my time-bound experience and his; but I am also able to make the effort of mind to reconstitute his milieu, if need be even in his verse, and to try to restore him to it.

The question of how Renaissance poems fit into their milieu is the question of what they reveal about it and how reliably so. Also involved here is the question of how we approach such poems, and in this operation no student can afford to be innocent. For being steeped in the secondary literature and having usually worked in the field for years, skilled critics and historians, when doing a particular reading or tackling a particular problem, ordinarily take a milieu for granted; they *begin* with an idea of the appropriate milieu, although this idea may change in the course of research. What we have, then, is a 'knowing' observer putting the poem or document into its time and place, both by bringing a certain preparation to it and by striving to tease hitherto unknown matters from it, matters that may alter his understanding of the milieu.

In the sixteenth and seventeenth centuries, much political, satiric, and occasional verse openly touches its milieu by frank references to happenings there. The contact with the world seems immediate, though it may not be. More often, however, Renaissance poetry's relations to its milieu seem oblique, discontinuous, or veiled. This is because *we* impose the conditions. That is, we define 'milieu' in terms of socio-economic groups, basic values, social attitudes, often politics, and more or less clear ideas; whereas poetry may be centered on the themes and shapes of love, destructive time, religious meditation, praise, complaint, offbeat description, or pastoral fantasy. But even where the contact with milieu is more direct, as in satire or political verse, the poem's 'excesses' (hyperbole, metaphor), veiled allusions, fictions, and select language will seem to distance it from the world of social reality as generally conceived by historians. The simple document in prose is made the measure of historical authenticity and poetry can find no foothold here. However, if we define milieu so as to take in a larger or more subtle circle of experience and consciousness (and why shouldn't we?), then poetry rightly enters into the historical canon. If we grant that despite their art and polish, poetic expressions of love, fantasy and religiosity may also be filters for other themes and feelings; if we concede that experience anyway is rarely one-dimensional (i.e., purely religious, purely economic, or purely amatory) but is rather, in the wholeness and complexity of consciousness, mixed and disjointed, yet somehow coherent; and if we see that culture, however we define it in relation to consciousness, is a social web of interconnected meanings, reaching from cooking to the gods, then we shall need poetry to help us reconstitute social milieux.[7]

In trying to grasp the theoretical problems raised by our nine opening propositions, I have underlined various points: our need of historical study, a working difference between verse and prose, the different ways in which these record experience and reality, the element of poetic 'transcendence' (attained by a commitment to experience and milieux), and something of what verse can give to historians. Now let it be noted that just as critic and literary scholar need some historical knowledge to understand poetry, so historians need poetry to understand parts of history and especially to help them grasp the broad lineaments of culture and consciousness. It cannot be, in logical terms, that the critic *needs* an historical preparation to understand poetic texts, unless these are locked into the historical process. This means that they can tell us something about it, and therefore the historian's professional neglect of verse is 'a trained incapacity'.

My fleeting brush with the nature of 'experience' requires that I return to Proposition 4, which distinguishes the poet's experience of the world from his experience of literature (reading, writing, and submission to literary influence). The proposition holds that experience of the world is primary, the other secondary. So simple-sounding and reasonable on the face of it, this claim is problematic, yet social literary analysis cannot proceed without it.[8]

If I write a best-selling novel by working to formula, having first carefully extracted a recipe from the leading best-sellers of the past five years, have I produced a novel from life or from 'literature'? The obvious answer would seem to be from literature — that is, from secondary, vicarious, or imagined experience. But queries and qualifications spring up at once.

(a)   Is my novel 'literature'? Is it 'popular' literature? If we study it, is it to be a study of 'privileged' or of 'popular' literature?

(b)   Despite recipes, how much and what parts of my own primary experience of the world were filtered into the novel, into its diction, tone, figurative language, characters, or something else?

(c)   If the novel says nothing at all about me, will it not say something about the taste of my society, the taste of a large reading public?

(d)   And if it does say a thing or two about general taste, have I not, in writing to formula, caught something of my time and place, even though having short-circuited my primary experience? Indeed, how much of the guiding or monitoring parts of my experience (my evaluating consciousness) did I truly block out? The chances are that I share in that general taste.

(e)   Apparently, then, my primary as well as my literary experience went into the making of the novel. And though we shall want to keep the theoretical distinction between the two, practical analysis will rarely be able to disentangle them.

(f)   It follows that literary conventions and formulae — validated in some sense too by my own primary experience of the world — are able to catch or give a voice to milieux. The wand of imagination translates ordinary experience — my own and that of my readers — into fanciful scenes and characters, but the translation is coded with the values, velleities, wish—dreams, and aversions of experience.

(g)   Once we consent to the direction of the preceding points and queries, the way is open for social analysis. Its essential job will be to break up 'general taste' (c, d) into its component parts: namely, to decode the novel's fanciful scenes, characters, themes, and story (f) by tracking these out to the reading public's values, social attitudes, fixations, fears, and hopes. In short, our business will be to search for all the parts of a socially anchored view of the world.

My parable of the best-seller refers of course to English Renaissance verse, much of which keeps to the rules and conventions of the different kinds (genres). Renaissance society, culture, and readers were, however, so different from the like in our own world that we shall need a realignment.

Intent on making contact with their readers and guided by a sense of poetry's public—social mission, Renaissance poets were often content to observe genre, in the knowledge that the established forms and conventions were the vessels of immediate communication. Heroic poem, hymn, sonnet, epithalamion, pastoral, verse letter, panegyric: these were known ways of addressing the literate community. When a poet had something special — something of his own — to say, he worked it into one of the kinds or modes. But new departures within the genre, as in Shakespeare or Donne, were noticed at once, for it could be manipulated to make more personal or telling statements; and parody used genre for saying things unconventional. The sonnet form, for instance, was flouted when filled with the wrong content, but the intended message went out thereby with a sharper point.

The strength of the kinds and modes — making for a community idiom — was a comment on the cohesiveness of educated society in Renaissance England, not a statement about its servility to classical or later genres. Poets and readers turned to certain forms in Virgil, Horace, Martial, Juvenal, Pindar, and the great *trecentista* Petrarch because some vital matter there engaged the primary experience of the leading social groups in the sixteenth and seventeenth centuries. One social connection is evident at once: the kinds were arrayed in a hierarchy, with the epic and hymn at the top, and at this level the poet spoke to God or sang of princes, heroes, and noblemen. At the bottom — not actually a part of the literary (highbrow) canon — was the popular ballad. Society thus sketched out its anatomy in the very forms and purposes of its poetry. In this prospect, a decline or a change in genre was necessarily keyed to social change, as in the rise of mock heroic or the decline of the country-house poem.[9]

Below epic came the ode, ceremonious and reflective, fit for lofty matters public or religious. The sonnet, steeped in the pastime of love, belonged first to the social psychology of the Court and of aristocratic circles. Donne, Jonson, Daniel, and others introduced the verse epistle to converse with friends and patrons, thus using this genre to circumscribe the elect. Education itself, with its emphatic literary and classical bias, fostered allegiance to the kinds, though let it always be recalled that the 'educational revolution' of the Elizabethan Age hinged on the aims and ideals of pushy new groups and the most ambitious parts of the gentry.

The conclusion to be drawn is that the conventions and formulae of genre and mode were vehicles for social need and social realities. Whatever the experience of poets, genre and mode canalized the primary experience and ideals of dominant or enterprising social groups. Here, all at once, we see the need for the theoretical distinction between primary (direct) and secondary (literary) experience, despite the fact that social analysis is rarely able to disentangle the two. For literary conventions — sonnet, couplet, pastoral, verse epistle, etc. — live and are renewed by the primary experience of groups, classes, or communities. Thus whatever *his* primary experience, a poet may lend his voice to a social current or a mode of social consciousness by simply adopting the accepted and valued literary conventions. These are kept vital by a responding readership and hence by a section of the community. Because the poet lives in that milieu, we must suspect that some part of his primary experience — as summed up, for instance, in his way of judging and discriminating — enters into his specific use of literary convention. But we shall not need to nag at this, having a prior assurance in the theoretical claim concerning the primacy of group or community experience.

The distinction between primary and secondary experience has a corollary: it is that the first sustains the second. This is nothing more than a commonplace — literature depends upon life — but a commonplace which also implies, in its demotion of the art—life dualism, that the history of literature cannot be wrenched away from the larger history of society, unless it be to posit a transcendent and autonomous 'realm of art'. And in this case we can no longer pretend to offer *historical* accounts of change within the literary tradition (though what is a tradition if not an historical increment?). Art as autonomy refers to itself, not to life in society. The history of literature becomes a self-producing discourse. Once swift changes in poetic style, content and outlook — as recorded in the 1590s and the Restoration — have been cut away from their lifeline in society, they become numinous phenomena, often guided by a mechanical notion of action and reaction or by the force of powerful personalities (Donne, Jonson, Dryden), but personalities which must be divorced from everything in time and space except the literary tradition. To be consistent and true to itself, this aesthetic view of literary history has no business talking about the impact of Puritanism on Jacobean drama, of the Court on the poetry of courtly love, of religion on the religious lyric, of politics on political satire, or of the Civil War on poetry.

As the remote past comes into being through the science and labor of historians (otherwise we look upon monuments empty of all meaning), so poems exist through the activity of readers; and the resolution to despoil readers of their experience so as to keep poems pure is fated to end in utopia.

The theoretical distinction between primary and secondary experience takes for granted that the two are vitally related. And if practical analysis, in the detailed discussion of any poem, is unable to sort out the poet's primary and secondary experience, this is no more than an indicator of the close relations between the two. So long as literary convention shows a vigorous persistence whether in genre or mode, an active readership is obviously continually endorsing it, and the input of the community is here guaranteed. Let readers turn away from a convention — epic verse, for example — and its vitality must cease, however lofty and captivating its earlier prestige. Such a demise — *why* readers and poets turn away — can only be explained by an account which breaks out of the literary tradition into social history and the amplitudes of consciousness.

In these musings, I have brought poet and Renaissance reader close together for two reasons: (a) to help explain the energy of genre, mode, and convention in the poetry of the age; and (b) to indicate that the individual experience of the poet may fall easily into line with what is called for in literary formulae. I shall restate this in a different way so as to make a theoretical point for my claims about figurative language and style in the following chapter.

Social analysis deemphasizes the imprint and signs of the individual, but this is not tantamount to demoting individual experience. There is no paradox here. For all my being very much like other men around me, it is as an individual that I must experience the world; I must know it through my own nervous system, if I am to be like them. Therefore, just as individual experience works to make me unlike others, so it also works to make me like them. The root of my sameness with others is an individuality.

2

Strategies: from poem to world

Owing to the wealth of its resources for making associations (Proposition 3, p. 2), Renaissance poetry, I have suggested, was in a unique position to probe variously into contemporary experience, to listen to its resonances, to highlight new meanings, to delineate shifting social identities, to try for new perceptions while reshuffling old ones, and in a word to find the contours of upper-class consciousness. This it did not by airy means but by a search for meaning and significance in the themes of self-awareness, of love and worship, time and death, youth and beauty, power and destitution, nobility and low estate. Poets used these themes as occasions for looking out upon the whole landscape of life: at religion, politics, and 'the social system', and at disgrace, plague, ostentation, or even at ways of avoiding unpleasant realities. The resulting *aperçus* and meanings do not, however, leap out and strike the eye (neither does 'history' in conventional historical documents): they go out to the trained reader. They are oblique or coded: stored up in poetry's grammar and figurative language, in lexical or syntactic ambiguities, in the mode of its rhetoric, in tone and style, in genre, ironies, and conventions, or in something else. This is to say that the historical and social world does appear in poetry but in disguise, as a kind of cipher, and we need an assortment of strategies to fetch it out: some up-to-date version of the ancient practice of reading between the lines, though with the demystifying eyes of the social historian.

ACTION AND DIRECT REFERENCE

We take for granted, generally, that poetry and society belong to two different orders of being: one is 'art', the other is the whole fabric of social

18

reality. In the study of English Renaissance verse, this distinction immediately breaks down, for many poems were so much a part of the world — of the Court or great-house world, for instance — and crystallized so many of its mental features, that it makes sense to regard these poems as actions in the world. They could make things happen.

Nothing better illustrates this than Sir Philip Sidney's sequence of 108 sonnets, *Astrophel and Stella* (c. 1582), where there is much of Sidney in the speaking poet, Astrophel (starlover, Phil), and where Stella (star), his beloved, is a well known beauty of the time, Penelope Rich née Devereux. The sequence circulated among intimates but then passed beyond, and was not printed until the incomplete, pirated edition of 1591. It is not just a record of real and imagined experience; it is also a display of courtliness, a gambit in the serious game of love, possibly the unfolding of an attempted seduction, and a conversation with Stella and friends. It is a form of self-inquiry, both behavior and a handbook or code of behavior. Moreover, some of the early sonnets of the sequence (1,3,6,15) offer at once a statement and an enactment of sonnet theory. So we may say that *Astrophel and Stella* belonged as much to the world as did the outlook, manners, and actions of courtiers and noblemen.[1]

Another action or incident in this world was the 'bread-and-butter' epistle,[2] Ben Jonson's 'To Penshurst' (before 1612?), an outstanding specimen of poetry of patronage. In addition to heaping praise on the lords of Penshurst, the Sidneys, the poem idealizes them and their place in rural society, thus exemplifying the view that 'One of the most important services a writer can render a patron is to provide his immediate social concerns with a metaphysical basis which transforms class values into an ideology.'[3] But like *Astrophel and Stella*, 'To Penshurst' is also action: in this case an acquittance of the debt imposed by patronage. Drawing its matter from the rank, life, and style of the Sidneys, the poem offers us a rich social vision, making a far more eloquent and forceful statement about the family than any they might have made about themselves. And so again, in being the payment of a debt, the articulation of a social vision, and the dressed-up mimesis of a way of life, 'To Penshurst' — composed by one of the keenest observers of contemporary affairs — is and was a part of the mental world of the Jacobean upper class. Poetry's public place and function in Renaissance England went to help poems be a force in the world in the act of their being read. Credited to eloquence (rhetoric), poetry was seen as a mode of speech intended to persuade people and even to move them to action in virtue, in amorous relations, in society, or in politics. Cleveland's political burlesques and Dryden's *Absalom and Achitophel* were forthright attacks in the political arena, far more effective than many a speech in the House of Commons. But poems of love and flattering poems of patronage also sought to make things happen in the world.

As action in the world, the poem aims to satisfy a patron, to fix an occasion in memory, to be a mode of behavior, or to procure something for the poet, such as money, employment, hospitality, a seduction, goodwill, or plaudits. We are in a world where poetry matters: where a new class of gentlemen, administrators, and clergymen is relentlessly on the make, where verbal skills are greatly prized, where the mighty also find use in poetry and are expected to esteem it, and where the upper-class occasions of a pre-industrial society are attended by ritual and deference. The chasm between rich and poor, between exalted rank and mean estate, is too great — and had been so since time out of mind — for the rich not to be flatteringly hemmed in by service and tribute. And 'the word', still associated with the educated clergy and with God, retains the color of some transcendency.[4]

In this world, poetry is easily turned into a form of practical action, so that Proposition 1 (p. 1), holding that poetry reveals its milieu, is more than verified: poetry itself is given the same ontological status as other social events in the world.

The natural starting point in the search for connections between poetry and its social world is the direct reference: any designation in the poem to something in the real world outside. If a poem has no such signifiers, then we must look for other links. Direct reference cannot include general allusions to 'nature' — to flowers, hills, trees, clouds, or stars — as these will rarely help to lodge the poem in a social contemporaneity. There is nothing spare, however, about the contrived landscapes in Sir John Denham's 'Cooper's Hill' or Andrew Marvell's 'Upon Appleton House': these flicker with calculated political and social commentary.[5]

In the strategy involving direct reference, the primary search is for pointers to people and to matters in the man-made world: to individuals (e.g., Sir Lucius Cary or Archbishop Laud), places (St Paul's, Penshurst), incidents (the assassination of the Duke of Buckingham), social groups (courtiers, Puritans, apprentices), events and topical affairs (war, religion, political scandal, a coronation), and social phenomena (ostentatious wealth, famine, social climbing). In all references of this kind, the poem itself forges a bond with the world and that bond validates our entering into the whole field of relations between text and historical context. Among the innumerable poems that pivot on direct reference, there are Waller's 'Of his Majesty Receiving News of the Duke of Buckingham's Death' (1628) and Cowley's 'On his Majesty's Return out of Scotland' (1633).

A vast quantity of English Renaissance verse was occasional in nature, written and given to mark a particular occasion. Tudor and Stuart society cherished the habit of making gifts, and the giving of occasional verse was ideally right for this atmosphere, where the performance of service had a high importance. Because such verse depended much on the incidence of direct reference, contemporaries came to expect references in all verse, whether in praise or dispraise. As a result, with the rise of political unease over the heirless Queen's old age, episcopal authority outlawed and burned verse satire in 1599. Reference and allusion to political matters became dangerous. London, the heart of literary traffic, was a nosey, clubby town. Some poets, such as Drayton and Greville, fearfully concealed certain of their works, while others — Jonson, Chapman, Daniel, Marston, Wither, John Day — were arrested or jailed for their audacities and indiscretions.[6] In 1605, some Scottish turns of phrase and mention of thirty-pound knights in the play, *Eastward Ho,* were taken to be slurs on King James I, and this meant immediate trouble for the authors: Marston fled from London, while Jonson and Chapman were thrown into jail, fearing that they might even have their noses slit. Samuel Daniel's 'Panegyricke Congratulatorie', written on the occasion of James I's accession to the throne (1603), is frankly political but shows nothing seditious. Its seventy-three octet stanzas are 'entirely devoted to exalting the union between Scotland and England, the benefits of peace, and the hopes inspired by the monarchy'.[7]

IDEAS AND SUBJECT-MATTER

Ideas as the way of contact with the world: in this strategy, the critic proceeds from the poem out to the world by way of the text's ideas and themes — an old and obvious route. If this approach alone is used, the poem is pared down to a mode of flat discourse and we may as well be reading prose. Allegorists like Spenser, Chapman, Milton, and Marvell are often studied this way; their works resonate with religious, political, and topical ideas. But the kind of poetry most easily reduced to its paraphrasable content is the 'poetry of public themes', which made up a good deal of the verse output of the late sixteenth and especially the seventeenth century. The classification includes political poetry, verse satire and much of its opposite (panegyric), some topographic poetry, some allegory, and a variety of occasional poems dealing with princes, powerful subjects, and state occasions. Moving from a presumptive sense of the poem's milieu, the literary scholar is able to use the poem's ideas as stepping stones out to the flanking social world, but only if the ideas are so much like what we assume to be out there that they function as near forms of direct reference. The preferred ideas are usually taken from politics, religion, social attitudes, and views of 'natural' or man-made hierarchies.

J. M. Wallace's book on Marvell is one of the best-known studies of this kind. He treats political poems as out-and-out historical documents. Thus 'The Last Instructions to a Painter' (1667) is alleged to throw light on a parliamentary debate slighted in other sources, while 'An Horatian Ode upon Cromwell's Return from Ireland' (1650) 'mirrors' a range of contemporary political uncertainties, attitudes, and ideas. The analysis recognizes no split between the political poem and its political world; the two are different aspects of a single reality. More exactly, the division between the poem and its political world is assumed to be similar to that which separates a sophisticated political analysis from its described setting. Therefore, to turn a political poem into an outright historical document is something best done in accordance with Wallace's procedures. He provides political and historical analyses of the immediate contexts of 'An Horatian Ode' and 'The Last Instructions'; he adduces state papers, pamphlets, and other contemporary sources, including variant editions of the poems; he looks for the views and values that bind the poems to the political world; and occasionally he also singles out ironies and imagery. In a word, he reads Marvell's political poetry much as historians read Machiavelli's *The Prince* or Locke's *Second Treatise of Civil Government.* Ideas, themes, ambiguities, and political viewpoints are seen in strict relation to their worldly setting: they *are* the political poem's bond with the world.

Suppose, however, that the poem's ideas point to nothing political or topical, to nothing ostensibly social? How then, if we depend chiefly on ideas, will contact with the world be made? Will the themes of love, religion, fleeting time, poetic immortality, or fragility and barbarity (as in Marvell's 'The Nymph Complaining for the Death of Her Faun'), have enough particularity, enough immediate rootedness, to enable the critic to pin the poem to its social milieu and not just to a moment in the literary tradition?

These questions expose the poverty of any overriding emphasis on ideas as the poem's prime link with the world. The strategy is valid but incomplete. If, by keeping chiefly to ideas, the critic is able to set the poem into nothing more concrete than, say, a general religious milieu, the approach is largely worthless from the standpoint of this study.

Social analysis does a job of negotiation with ideas. It examines the social situation around them, looking for their ways of adapting, for outside influences, and for valid passage from one zone of experience to another — from poem to world or world to poem. Ideas are not fixed lines or points, poetic themes even less so. Like poems, they are unstable 'occurrences' in the minds of readers and poets and even in a larger discourse such as 'social consciousness'. We approach ideas more or less. We sit down to read a Jacobean poem — which will be more unstable, of course, than a simple document in prose — and we have our own prejudices to beware of, as we grope for some seventeenth-century way of perceiving, feeling, and thinking. Here is something alive. How therefore, as historians, can we regard any idea in time as a fixity? We must bear the living tissue constantly in mind. The new astronomy was not a clump of ideas in Donne's mind, nor were the notions of kingship in Shakespeare's. Something moved and pulsated there, and so we are called upon to make fluid identifications. Indeed, thought is so twined with other urgencies and matters in consciousness — even in the heads of philosophers — that social analysis may momentarily depart from ideas as such and yet still be with them.

The theme of love in the sonnet has a background of literary influences leading back to Petrarch and other continental poets, or even to Plato. But once we observe it in a variety of specific historical contexts, we also begin to see its connections with the Court, the aristocracy, arranged marriage, ambitious courtiers, middle-class poets, patronage, posturing, social climbing, or a mode of social action.[8] Because there was so much ambiguity and resourcefulness in its poetic treatment, the love theme could serve a genuine variety of social situations. By comparison, the eternizing topos — immortality through poetry for mistress or patron — had fewer possibilities. Some critics have seen it as the function of an outright economic exchange: you grant me (the poet) favor or pension, I return fame and immortality. This reading is embarrassingly crude, but less so when approached in the context of patronage, of the prestige of poetry, of plague-ridden times, and of the beginnings of skepticism — whereupon the topic begins to look like a playful challenge to the Christian religion.

Though we must take for granted the directing mind of the poet, ideas are unstable in poetry precisely because, rather as in experience, they cling to or glide off other matters in motion, such as images, recollections, ambiguities, and sounds. In this circle of happening, an idea can have no fixed reality. It is subject to the stresses issuing forth, like everything else in the poem, from the living poet; thus the idea's membership — like the poem itself — in a world or discourse larger than the poem.

When, as in early Jacobean drama,[9] the theme of sexual lust or lechery is on the verge of being turned into the capital sin, so that it comes to be emblematic of virtually all other vices and crimes, we are compelled to pass beyond the theme of lust to an investigation of that drama's relation to its entire milieu, if we are to make satisfactory sense of what is going on there. The drama itself tells us something, but too many queries remain; no internalist, formalist, or rhetorical criticism can possibly account for the nature of the exaggeration involved. Again, the theme of retirement in much Cavalier verse of the 1640s and 1650s, with its stoical vision, love of the country, and anti-urban bias, may be traced back to Horace. In accenting literary influences, this approach takes ideas as fixities if it fails to note that the retirement theme rose to high fashion in tandem with the royalist débâcle of those years. Stricken and then resigned, the Cavaliers made a virtue of retirement to their rural estates, there to enjoy nature, study, contemplation, and friendship — the 'simple pleasures' — until such time as political order returned and the king was restored. In this angling, the novelty and force of the whole stoic ideal of self-sufficiency and rural retreat, as found in mid-century verse, are understood in the light of the social world of contemporary crisis politics.

Wherever themes and ideas do not work as forms of direct reference, the task of negotiating them across the obscure terrain between poem and world turns suddenly difficult, and now the other resources of social literary analysis must be called into play.

DICTION AND FIGURATIVE LANGUAGE

Any program resolved to sever Renaissance poetry from its historical and social moorings must capsize when faced with the aims of literary scholarship. As Dame Helen Gardner has noted, 'The critic today reads an author of the sixteenth and seventeenth century haunted by a sense that although what he reads is apparently written in the language which he himself speaks, in various, subtle ways it is not; and merely looking up the hard words in the *Oxford English Dictionary* does not help, because it is in the ordinary words that the traps lie.'[10] Much of the strain, then, goes into reading the poem in its semantic context. This enterprise calls for the study of words in the context of the poem, of that poem in the context of other contemporary poems, of the language of those poems in relation to the language of plays and the period's prose, and so on, until we take in the entire body of Elizabethan, Jacobean, and Caroline literature. But when this is done, we shall have circumscribed not only the literature but also the attitudes, values, obsessions, and indeed the consciousness of the age, or at least its literate, upper-class consciousness. The prospect is daunting and can be no more than a distant ideal.

The ways in which words as such disclose their ties to a time and place vary greatly, depending upon matters both in and outside the poem.

The Renaissance idea of verbal 'decorum' introduced the undisguised presence of society in matters of diction.[11] The so-called high and low styles called for appropriate vocabularies: an idiom for princes and an idiom for peasants, one for tragedy and another — peopled by 'lower' characters — for comedy. In heroic poetry, heroes could not 'trudge' — only beggars and lackeys do this — and 'Juno must not *tug* at Aeneas; it is a carter's word and connotes the pulling of oxen and horses.'[12] Nor could 'wet cloths' be described as blocking the rays of the sun — a diminishing of the sun's majesty in conventional poetic diction. Infractions of this kind were known in Renaissance poetics as 'tapinosis'.

In the last quarter of the sixteenth century, the exuberance and expansion of the language and of poetry stirred up a debate on the kinds of words suitable for poetry. Writers discussed archaisms, high and low expressions, inkhorn terms, words taken over from Latin and from Europe's vernaculars, new coinings, and dialect words. The discussion led to a direct connecting of poetry with the social world, for in matters of poetic diction there was no escaping the influence of London, of the Court, of educational backgrounds, group tastes, and reading audiences.

In his verse satires, John Marston uses 'words from popular speech' and 'from the seamy side of Elizabethan diction', evidently in the conviction that they would carry greater force by seeming to mirror the matter and scenes of his satiric attacks.[13] The leading theorist of the period, George Puttenham, held that the language of poetry should be confined to usage at Court and the vicinity of London. In fact, this was the customary practice. Power and milieu thus prove to be decisive even in supposed matters of the heart, the business of the sonnet form, whose diction was especially drawn from courtly conventions and the Court setting.

Beyond the Court lay a richer milieu, the urban setting, and this also had its effect. Roma Gill accepts Quintilian's definition of *urbanitas* as a perfect description of John Donne's language in the *Elegies*: it 'denotes language with a smack of the city in its words, accent and idiom, and further suggests a certain tincture of learning derived from associating with well educated men: in a word, it represents the opposite of rusticity.'[14] But in its influence on diction, the social scope — as noted apropos of the Court — may also be narrowed to include, say, only the Inns of Court (London's 'law schools' and social academies for rich or ambitious young men). The current of 'plain and vigorous and sometimes violent diction' to be found in Donne, Jonson, John Marston, Everard Guilpin, and John Davies is often closely associated with the life and temper of the Inns in the 1590s and early years of the seventeenth century.[15]

The language of Sidney's *Astrophel and Stella* indicates the existence of at least three reading audiences among his constituency of friends, relatives, acquaintances, and other Court people, including Stella herself (Penelope Rich): (1) readers schooled in the neo-Petrarchan diction of courtly love, (2) the more sophisticated readers who could follow Sidney's strictures against the weary lexical conventions of the Petrarchan line, and finally (3) those — no doubt including his closest associates — who could also detect the thread of sexual puns that courses through much of the sonnet sequence,[16] more difficult to recognize here than in Donne's *Elegies,* which 'certainly exploit the sexual puns so much enjoyed by Elizabethan readers'.[17]

Relations between diction and reading audiences make for an important moment in the poem's contact with the world, indicating one of the ways in which society got at the working mind of the poet. The bond must have been all the stronger when reader and patron were one and the same, for the poet was now likely to tailor the poem to a closer, more personal fit, as in the case of Drayton's sonnets for Lady Rainsford (Anne Goodere). The language of Donne's *Anniversaries* and verse epistles to great ladies (actual and potential patrons) has often struck critics — as it did certain contemporaries — by its extravagance, particularly in its flattery, which sometimes borders on peculiar forms of blasphemy. Sir Walter Raleigh and dozens of other poets showered verse on Queen Elizabeth that was rife with the locutions of love, worship, self-abasement, and complaint. But these are well known matters needing no commentary here. Patronage turned on relations between power and service, and in this give and take poetic diction was subject to the keenest stresses.

Our captivity in language and speech is a poem's true anchor in time and place, for poets, like all people, rely on a verbal algebra for turning their contact with the world into some kind of meaningful experience. In language poets are pinned to a grammar, in speech to a certain usage;[18] and therefore usage — being responsive to fashion and changing more rapidly — is likely to be our primary concern in the social analysis of poetic diction.

Visiting Bologna in the late thirteenth century, Dante detected local speech differences within the city, so marked was the character and vitality of its different neighborhoods.[19] Italy was a congeries of dialects and Dante was reflecting on the question of which of them would be best for Italian poetry. So English poetry too, facing a variety of dialects in the sixteenth century, had a similar question to resolve in practice. The victory went to the speech of London and its environs, particularly as heard from the mouths of people at Court and in the upper middle classes, but the victory was not apolitical. It was a victory over regional dialects and 'base' terms, thus adding up to a rejection of popular culture. Here was 'high' culture underwriting the power of the Crown and of London, as these sought to centralize authority and to bring the whole nation under their political and economic tutelage.

Having no tape recordings, we will never know what the colloquial speech of Shakespeare's London truly was; so that some recent scholarship has been right to dissent from critics of a generation ago who emphasized the element of colloquiality in much of Donne's verse. The suggestion now is that this was almost to claim something unknowable.[20] Yet in matters of language and diction, criticism has no choice but to rely on a sense of usage.

It is only by moving from the notion of a norm, of usage of some kind — even if the norm is never enunciated — that we are able to characterize a poet's diction: as when we say of a poem by Sidney, Spenser, Donne, or Waller, that its language is more or less 'polished' (select), more or less 'grand', more or less 'smooth', 'learned', 'Latinate', 'archaizing', or 'elliptical'. More or less in relation to what? Implicit comparisons and a tacit norm are at work here. The same *modus operandi* is used by historians when, in considering a treatise on government or a portrait by Van Dyck, they say that it is more or less idealized, realistic, topical, or pragmatic. Here, somewhere, a notion of reality is being taken for granted. Now in one sense, it is true, we cannot know what 'reality' was for the seventeenth century (no doubt it varied for the different social groups and geographic regions), and we would have trouble saying, with any exactitude, what it is for us. But we cannot work as historians without a sense of what reality was for the past. Only thus can we go about affecting to be able, in our historical writing, to reconstitute the economies, politics, institutions, creeds, and modes of behavior of past societies.

For the scholar who works on the diction and syntax of Renaissance verse, some notion of usage, of colloquiality, must have the same importance as does the tacit notion of reality for the historian. Usage is the verbal practice — conventions and all — that goes with everyday realities. We have some feeling of what this is for us. In historical and social analysis we must also have a sense of what usage was for the past.

The more a poet leans towards usage, the more realistic his idiom, and therefore the reverse. To cite five obvious examples: Donne, Raleigh, and Jonson employ a diction which is more realistic, hence closer to usage, than anything to be found in Chapman or Spenser, who favor an elevated poetic diction.

What is the point of tracking usage and realism in speech? What does social analysis seek in this? The simple answer is that the more realistic an idiom, the more suitable will it be for dealing with practical, ordinary, or everyday affairs and experience. So far as this is the case, diction alone may begin to suggest something about a poem's underlying social vision. This does not, however, follow of itself and is not automatic. The whole social and historical situation around the poem has to be considered. We have every reason to think, for instance, that despite their different and indeed conflicting dictions, Spenser and Donne were both deeply conservative in their political and social views, as was Ben Jonson. And all three came to depend upon royal patronage and favor. Nevertheless, the plainer diction of Donne and Jonson approaches the idiom of verse satire; it tallies with the rising critical mood of the Inns of Court; it is often used to flay and deride social posturing, to scoff at courtly love, and to strike out at vice, hypocrisy and trouble-making of all sorts, whether of Puritans, merchants, upstarts, or courtiers. Above all, down to the period of the Civil War, a plainer diction gives hostage to an anti-courtly stance because it is not slanted towards idealization or towards making things appear larger than life: it cannot easily elevate or amplify subject-matter in a world in which the Crown and the great men of the realm fully expect this and therefore seem to impose an idiom. Consequently, when Donne and Jonson depart decisively from their plainer diction, the likelihood is that they are either writing for the Court or in praise of a great patron.

Verse satire relies on a plainer diction and usage because it seeks a frank confrontation with the primary mode of historical reality — social phenomena. In this effort, satire is forced to look for a corresponding vocabulary and, in so doing, makes itself one of the key standards of colloquial usage, along with letters, diaries, and other plain testimonials. It is no accident that two of the age's 'plain stylists', Donne and Jonson, were also first-class satirists.

Regarding the ties between plain diction and social vision, it is now clear — given the pertinence of verse satire — that plain diction in verse was a species of language as social criticism in the Elizabethan and Jacobean setting. An interesting contradiction now begins to unwind. In using and fashioning a plainer diction, Donne and Jonson — despite sharing Spenser's deep conservatism — were helping to sharpen an anti-courtly instrument. This indicates that diction and style transcend the man. These belong as well to the age as to the poet, and he is not necessarily the master of what they mean in social terms.

That Donne and Jonson, manifest social conservatives, turned to an anti-courtly diction is action explainable on a social—biographical basis, and this more fully resolves the designated contradiction. The two were for a long time 'outsiders', although in very different ways. Donne was a Catholic, next an apostate (Carey), then alienated or kept far from the Court for years, while ever striving to impress his social superiors with the great Inns-of-Court taste of the 1590s — wit. In his detachment or alienation, he chose a plainer diction and a figured wit (any base professional could achieve a smooth and artificial diction), though in the poems of praise for the monied and mighty his labored reasoning alters the effects of his diction. Next Jonson: an outsider of lowly origins, rowdy ex-actor and bricklayer, irascible, envious, proud, suspicious, and touchy, an enemy to all affectation, hating to pay tribute to mere rank and blood, but possessor of great wit, imaginative swiftness, and a superior classical education. He also, for reasons different from Donne's, was more at home with an even plainer diction.

We have, then, two poets of the first rank who favor an anti-courtly idiom for personal and social reasons, while yet being staunchly royalist and conservative. All we need do is to imagine the force of their plain speech in verse, verse with a keen satiric edge turned fully against the Crown or the aristocracy, to realize how effective they would have been as critical observers of the politico-social scene; but they would have ended straightway in prison. The plain speakers, in short, could not speak out or could not publish;[21] and this means — hereby disqualifying both Donne and Jonson — that the truly political use of an anti-courtly tongue had to be indirect (in the allegorical or pastoral modes), a near impossibility. Besides, indirection disables political criticism; hence how anti-courtly could indirection be? The power of the preeminent groups in Renaissance England was such as to turn language to its service, at all events in highbrow culture. If you have to be indirect, you have already submitted your diction, tropes, and themes to the impress of power.

Spenser was another outsider of modest birth, but he went the other way in aiming for royal favor and for patronage from the mighty. He went the way of a grand, smooth, archaizing, unreal diction: a courtly tongue, but one moved by an ambiguous social vision in that it does double social service — courtly and 'bourgeois'. For his language elevates and idealizes the mighty; it enlarges their affairs and persons (as an heroic idiom should), thus supporting them in their view of themselves; but it also caters to the viewpoint of the aspiring yeoman or wealthy burgess, who looks up to and admires the Court and the aristocracy — his models and gods.

The study of diction — word choice — is part of a larger strategy which also includes the study of figurative language. By 'figurative language' I shall mean chiefly metaphor, simile, hyperbole, and personification. Clusters of these, in any particular poem, are often referred to as 'imagery'. In modern critical usage, however, the meaning of this term is so elastic as to include four different classes of things: (1) the word picture — e.g., 'Juliet is the sun' or 'keels plough air'; (2) the recurring visual motif — the sea, storms, the human body, animals, urban particulars, Cupid, gold, clothing, etc., or some specific activity emphasized by repetition or synonymic verbs (e.g., strike, hit, batter); (3) clusters of analogies or metaphors; and (4) thematic stress — 'nature', mutability, love, kinship ties, the body politic, and so on. I shall restrict my use to the first three of these.

Since the 1920s much criticism has supposed that unconscious influences have a part in fashioning the imagery and figurative language of poets. Be this as it may, the force of the individual consciousness — and therefore of its unconscious? — probably declines the farther back we go in time, owing to the greater coherence of community life in pre-industrial societies, the power of custom, the higher incidence of conventional usage in the composition of poetry, and the grasp of 'collective mentalities' in village, town, and Court. When the stock of literary conventions was far richer, as in the sixteenth and seventeenth centuries, and poets could more often draw on ready-to-hand locutions and associations, the fashioning of images and metaphors must have been more expressive of time and place (e.g., Elizabethan or Jacobean London) and of the changing outlines in local experience.

Scholars frequently point to the urban cast of imagery in Elizabethan and Jacobean comedy and verse satire. This is social analysis at the simplest level. But criticism has also gone well beyond jejune observation of this sort. Drayton, Barnes, and others provided grounds for social commentary when they slipped the imagery of the city into the courtly sonnet:[22] (1) they were deliberately violating sonneteering conventions; (2) they were introducing a new element of realism into the genre, at once updating and subverting it; (3) they were probably responding to a change in taste or fashion; and (4) when we consider that poets were suddenly fiddling around here with one of the most prized of all literary forms, then we begin to suspect that the new strains in 'literary experience' derived from changing stresses within the larger circumference of experience in the 1590s. Here — in a shadowy land between literary change on the one hand and changes in mood, outlook, and social balances on the other — we have at once the most difficult and the most important terrain for the social analysis of poetry.

In the poetry of the Cavaliers, the high incidence of the imagery of winter and storms is now often 'read' — in contrast with the themes of retirement and tranquility — as referring to political dissension, civil war, and the royalist disasters of the 1640s and 1650s.[23] Poets contrasted the implications of such imagery with an emphasis on friendship and warm hearths, with the belief that winter would pass, that the monarchy would be restored, and that all royalists in time would be returned to their estates as to their social dominance. In this fashion 'nature' — represented in the imagery of winter and storms — was deviously drawn into the poetic discourse to enhance Cavalier courage and to pick up spirits.

During the same troubled decades, again in Cavalier verse, the imagery of the country is often converted into a metaphor for property, order, and hierarchy, in opposition to the political turmoil of the unruly city, London.[24] Here, once more, the Cavaliers turned an imagistic cluster into a moral 'support system'. Similarly, 'Love poetry itself becomes a search for something to hold on to.'[25] The Cavaliers verge on turning love into a standard to be held up against intolerable strains. But is love truly so serious for them? Or do we face an embarrassing contradiction? For when profiled against the shadows of political crisis and civil war, the Cavalier theme of amatory dalliance has also seemed an evasive, escapist motif. This reading finds support in the mode's reliance upon fetishistic imagery, where love is no longer deeply serious or a journey through experience, and offers no manner of redemption (as in Shakespeare and Donne), but is instead both a way of escape and an erotic entertainment: a playing of hide-and-seek with ribbons, girdles, buckles, hair, gloves, and silks — charming and fun but picked clean of all moral commitment, except insofar as it is 'something to hold on to' in despairing times. The question arises, which of these contradictory accents shall we favor? In fact we must endorse both: the contradiction was lodged in the very experience of the Cavaliers and suggests much about their state of mind in the midst of crisis. Uneasy, indecisive, and morally on the run, they lacked any conviction strong enough to rival the passionate ideals of Puritans and Parliamentarians.

In all the foregoing examples, social and political strains surface as conciliatory images and metaphors — strategies for reorganizing unpleasant matters — and these then enable the poet to face up to a menacing worldly reality.

The social analysis of figurative language assumes that images are likely to reveal some connection with their social and literary worlds. Forms of comparison, correspondence, or contrast — e.g., in metaphor, personification, hyperbole, irony — are at the root of figures; and one of the binary terms usually refers to things in the social world *or* in the literary and cultural traditions, though these too have social sediments. The poet's immersion in a society ensures the contact between figures and the social dimensions of reality, unless he is writing mere imitations.

One line of criticism warns against treating imagery as an entry to biography, to the poet's personal experience and private life.[26] The claims of this line are dubious. In the best documented case, John Donne, we find that his imagery returns time and again to his years of intense study, to find its matter in science and learning — in geometry, astronomy, medicine, and theology. In accord with his more sensuous experience of the world, his verse also shows 'a stream of images' siphoned from 'commerce and money' as well as from 'sea travel, navigation, and exploration'.[27] Interestingly, though he was steeped in the most worldly of the Latin classics, he all but ignored classical mythology as a source for his imagery — 'the most convincing evidence of his revolt against that tradition'.[28] This is to say that the absence of a certain kind of image in Donne was a question of choice, in contrast to the practice of most other contemporary poets, who exploited mythologic allusion, hereby bearing one of the stamps of their age.

The caveat against the presumed link between imagery and biography is not, in any case, a stumbling block for social analysis, which holds no major brief for a pursuit of the unique and individual. Biographical profiles are important and occasionally critical in social inquiry, but they come forth in relation to and as a function of the more comprehensive analysis of milieux, groups, community values, movements of opinion, and the typical or representative. It should be emphasized that this is no call to slight the individual experience of the poet, for the genetic canal between the poem and the world *is* that experience. The poem's 'speech' makes contact with the world via the poet's individual experience, but much in that experience he shares with others of his place and time. Some part of this similitude, some part of all he knows and holds in common with other contemporaries, enters into the breadth of his figurative and connotative language: he takes it in by his talent for combining, comparing, and contrasting the *donnée* of experience in metaphor, ambiguity, hyperbole, and so forth.

But experience may be as wide as the world. So in our rummaging through imagery, what exactly are we in search of? We must have a sense of direction. Political and economic historians have one, as they move along their established, charted ways. This is clear. And just as clearly, we seek whatever will throw light on the social world of the poem or on the poem from the standpoint of its social world. We seek the lineaments and moving forces both of the society of the poet and of poetry in its society. In studying Renaissance verse, accordingly, we shall be open and attentive to all persistence and innovation: to recurring motifs, conventions, new forms, and patterns. For these transcend individuals by attracting the allegiance of many readers; they depend upon an active reading audience; and so they transmit — but also fudge and disguise — social voices. In another direction and more concretely, we shall be on the lookout for the imagery of kingship, of the Court, of trade, husbandry, social gradations, colonization, social climbing, maritime activity, the urban scene, social versus moral nobility, and all manner of domineering action and attitude. All these belong to important zones of social history, but all may also be linked to matter which is elusive, idealized, or seemingly universal, as in images drawn from pastoral, or from the heavens, the seasons, the Christian religion, courtly love, and classical mythology — all held on the screen, so to speak, of poetry's figurative language. When this more 'poetic' subject-matter is fused, by means of metaphor and ambiguity, with items from the different zones of social history, our task will be to study the fusions with a view to what they tell us about the poem's ties with the historical world.

As we study a given range of images, we shall aim to bring forth its underlying attitudes and values, but the ultimate purpose will be to try to identify the determining vision, world view, or social identity. When at last we are able to characterize the directing vision or identity, we shall also have treated the different aspects of style, as these too are shaped by the same social vision. The movement of social analysis is circular: from poem to world and world to poem. And if we are unable, in any given poem, to decipher the traces of its time and place in its figurative language, then we may turn to other stylistic features, such as tone or rhetorical ploys, and use these as the 'bridges' that lead from poem to world.

A series of hypothesized observations shows what may be done with figurative language. The putative texts are late sixteenth-century sonnets.[29]

(1)   If the poet sees himself as vassal, servitor, or slave, and assigns the lordship to his beloved, we see the signs here — however conventional the stance — of an enduring feudal psychology, yet in the context of a society whose feudal institutions have crumbled away. However, since deference, courtliness, and the ideal of service persist tenaciously in England's obsessively rank-conscious society (and where was this not so in Renaissance Europe?), the imagery of lord and servant remains vital and serviceable, though it may also show a tincture of nostalgia. Beyond this, in its

conventionality, the imagery puts the poem into a courtly or aristocratic setting. If produced by a poet from the middle classes, the 'imitation' — it being not his native idiom — is likely to adumbrate his aspirations, his social climbing, or his search for patronage. In fact, his imitative and creative talents may be so remarkable as to lead him to a new perfection (Spenser) or to a fecund violating of the idiom (Shakespeare). Again, in sifting through the lord—servitor imagery of love, the critic may find a studied or 'self-fashioning' posture in relation to power,[30] for the idiom of courtly love was evolved not only as a mode of entertainment but also as a way of dealing with gradations of power and favor in the close intimacy of the Court and its aristocratic circles, still powerful under Elizabeth and James.

(2) If the poet pictures his love in the imagery of Orient pearl or the gold of the Indies, he is doing so to amplify the blazon of her beauties, but he also means to convey conviction. It is revelatory that he should reach out in a moment of supposed love, be the moment conventional or felt, to the experience of oceanic navigation and the wealth of the Indies. Historically, here was one of the primary areas of sixteenth-century experience, and so to turn to it, whether in the courtly ritual or intimacy of love, is both to underwrite the glamor (and brute imperialism) of overseas trade and to claim some special authenticity for the love. For the sixteenth and early seventeenth centuries, the experience of distant and dangerous adventure in the name of wealth was fresh and luminous. This also goes to help explain — though the metaphor was Petrarchan too — the taste for sonnets wherein the condition of the lover was likened to a lost or storm-tossed vessel, such as Richard Lynche's 'Weary with serving where I nought could get', or E. C.'s 'My heart is like a ship on Neptune's back' (from *Emaricdulfe*).

(3) If the poet seals his relations to his mistress with egregious legal terminology, we shall look for fashion, for the voice of a coterie, for an Inns-of-Court milieu, or for derision and parody. Clues here as to where to look, or in which direction to lean, will come from the poem and from other contemporary sources.

(4) If the poet reckons his amatory travails in account-keeping terms, we shall look again for fashionable wit (hence to certain social circles), possibly for ironic winking, and certainly for a viewpoint which mimes or even parodies an urgent preoccupation of the day among the monied, many of whom were nagged by debt and frightening inflation.

(5)   If the poet envisages his ties to his lady in the guise of religious metaphor, as when she is the saint and he the worshipper, or her things are relics and he enshrines her, we will recognize at once that this is convention — a recognition based upon our grasp of the literary tradition, therefore on a knowledge of sources *outside* the poem: convention, *ergo* some degree of play. But vigorous poetic conventions bear social voices. What are they in this case? Shall we wonder about the challenge to religious belief? If composed by a Protestant, is there some mockery of Catholicism in such imagery? If by a Catholic, ought we to wonder about his 'blasphemy'? The age is still avowedly religious, a point always to be borne in mind (or have historians exaggerated this claim?). Later, among the Cavaliers, the religious—erotic metaphor will often have an element of play or serve to acknowledge loyalties by seeming to be a taunt to Puritans. But in the 1580s and 1590s? With Donne the wedding of religious and profane was strikingly felt: religious metaphors went to intensify his worldly love verse, just as later his religious verse was to carry more impact by enlisting the imagery of sensual love. What, if anything, can be made of this in larger social or historical terms?

Conclusion   We have raised a train of unanswered questions, worthy perhaps of sustained study.

The foregoing 'readings' and variations are anything but exhaustive, owing to the analytical need here to keep the models crystaline. If experience is as wide as the world, poetry cannot admit to running a mean second.

One influential modern assumption holds that 'the unconscious' has a major, even a decisive, input in metaphor (here for the moment taken as the paradigm for figurative language). I suspect that the claim is valid. A famous example is Shakespeare's association of sheets with scavenging kites, a link effected, it seems, by a personal experience with death.[31] Yet social analysis requires no theory of the unconscious. Its gaze is directed towards the public, the social, the community, the group; and it regards the individual within these perimeters, for individuality rises forth and only makes sense in a social framework.

Metaphor is the roping together of things, at times far apart, in the poet's experience. The couplings are made in the correspondences or comparisons that make up figurative language. If several items are repeatedly or obsessively joined in metaphor, unconscious factors may be at work, but there is no need to insist on this. It is enough, whatever the reasons, that diversity is coupled in metaphor, such as blood and moral qualities, gods and noblemen, trees and social hierarchy, formal gardens and society, kings and the sun, gold and the sun, shepherds and courtiers, the stage and the world, and so on. Nothing essential to the social reading of poetry depends upon the question of conscious or unconscious factors in the shaping of metaphor. Rather than trying to look into the inner psyche of the poet through the curved, colored, and polymorphic windows of his figurative language, we look through these the other way, out to his world and society. Clearly, therefore, social analysis must take in as many other poets and windows as proper study will allow, in order not to confuse the idiosyncratic with the common or typical; but when finding idiosyncrasy, as occasionally in Donne, we will try to grasp this too in the context of time and place.

In social literary analysis, the bridge between biography and history need not be encumbered with psychoanalysis. When I say that metaphor couples dissimilar things in the poet's experience, I also mean in the experience of the age, which usually — if we exclude crowd behavior — we can only get at through the actions and testimony of individuals. Accordingly, when I allege (Proposition 3, p. 2) that 'poetry enlists the whole of the poet's experience because of its linguistic and associative resources', I also mean that of all people the poet is — at least in theory — the one most likely to be capable of showing us the diversity of his world's experience. If this is so, can historians afford to neglect poetry?

STYLE, TONE, VIEWPOINT

Style issues from a social vision: from the poet's sense of who he is, of where he stands in his society and what he desires from it, as shadowed in his aspirations and anxieties. This claim sounds simple because it is cast in a theoretical and summary mold. The complexities belong entirely to the particulars of analysis, to the fine movements of scrutiny and minute synthesis, as the historian or critic picks his way through obscurities and puzzles to a convincing description of the poem's social vision.

The term 'style' usually means something like the combined effects of diction, syntax, figurative language, rhetorical features, numbers smooth or rough, and some quality of the poet's mind or imagination: all of which, working together, make for a style. When associated with a school or movement, it is likely to denote a whole way of apprehension and thinking, characteristic as much of a period, say the early eighteenth century, as of the individual writers working within the period's general idiom. Style thus is at once historicized.

Classical rhetoric discerned ties between society and literature, life and literary style.[32] This is apparent in its ideas of decorum (propriety) and of the high, middle, and low styles, which prescribed that style fit the specific occasion, subject-matter, and audience: 'trivial matters in a plain style, matters of moderate significance in the tempered style, and weighty affairs in the grand manner'. Cicero's recipe has an obvious connection with the modern linguistic notion of 'register', which refers simply to 'the fact that the language we speak or write varies according to the type of situation'.[33]

Steeped in classical rhetoric and born into a society in which rank and status had a surpassing importance, Elizabethan theorists looked for connections between style on the one side and place, occasion, or social rank on the other. The attendant poetic practice is not hard to find.

Elizabethan drama betrays 'class distinctions in style', a point fully evident 'in the early Shakespeare, and in *A Midsummer Night's Dream* there are even further refinements. The heads of state speak a dignified blank verse; the well-born lovers blank verse and couplets; the rude mechanicals speak rudely in prose.'[34] The rules of decorum required that fools and madmen, in comedy as in tragedy, also speak in prose.[35] And down to about 1800, 'There survived, in fact, though mostly unacknowledged, Puttenham's rule that the model for the high style was the speech of courtiers and governors; for the mean style, the speech of merchants and yeomen; for the base style, the speech of peasants and menial trades.'[36]

Scholarship on Renaissance poetry often distinguishes three general styles — the high, the middle, and the low — but more readily sorts out the extremes in the distinction between the grand and the plain styles.[37] One is embellished, sweet, copious, elevated, and fluent; the other is the style of plain or direct discourse. The grand style was originally associated with the Court, the plain one with popular taste. But whatever its original social identity, by the 1530s the plain style was 'no longer exclusively identified with the popular classes'.[38]

Between the 1560s and 1590s much highbrow lyric poetry was cast in the 'golden', sweet, eloquent, or modified grand style.[39] Citing abundant evidence, one scholar has argued that this style served — despite its courtly affiliations — the needs of ostentation and upstarts: essential features of the Court and upper-class life of England in the second half of the sixteenth century.[40] The style was glitter, surface, opulence, and show, as understood even in Puttenham's *The Arte of English Poesie* (1589); it was 'adornment', 'the expression of a lifestyle governed by the mystique of conspicuous wealth'.[41] It is clearly seen, for example, in Sidney's 'Queene Vertue's court, which some call Stella's face' (*Astrophel and Stella,* 9) and Spenser's *Epithalamion.*

The essential strategy for relating style to the world depends upon the recognition that style is not a mere choice, order, and flow of words; nor is it merely a sensibility or an arbitrary way of presenting themes: it is also an attitude, an allegiance to a core of values, and thus a mode of rejection or disapproval too. Once we see this, entry into the social world by way of style becomes less mystifying; and if we can recognize style's responsiveness to historical change, we can also begin to estimate its real value for social analysis. Beyond these generalities, however, how is it exactly that a whole way of composing and presenting poetry is also a way of looking at the world? A way that fixes a poet to a milieu, so that the world seen in his verse turns out to be a complex image of the seeing world, of the society *in* the poet?

The long answer winds its way through my propositions (pp. 1–4), emphasizing the presence and the effects of society in consciousness. The short answer, specifically with regard to Renaissance poetry, is that poets (a) knew their audiences, (b) were committed to a doctrine of communication — namely to move, delight, and teach, (c) therefore kept to pertinent themes or to received values, and accordingly (d) chose the most appropriate and effective forms of articulation. There was an intimate and vital rapport between poets and their readers; and those readers, coming mainly from the upper classes, were the avenue of exchange between poets and the dominant circles of authority and influence in the society. But in addition, items (c) and (d) also tell us that when selecting and putting words together in a poem, poets worked in accordance with the message borne, indeed made form and style an organic part of the message.

The simplest way to see this is in sonnets of the early 1590s.

Summary analysis   Convention ordains that the sonnet form equal love in a courtly manner, whereupon we already have the glimmerings of a social identity. More particularly, the sonnet's select diction designates a certain control and polish; the flow of conventional conceits bespeaks a familiarity with the idiom and still more courtly control; overall manner and style show a delicacy of touch, a sensitivity to ambiguity, generosity of spirit, a graceful but conventional wit, and adulation for the idealized lady.

Now, to which societal identity or groups shall we assign this code? To country folk, cottagers, yeomen, sturdy beggars, urban craftsmen, shopkeepers, hard-headed merchants, or indeed to any part of England's population (fifty per cent) living permanently in or on the edges of hunger? The answer is obvious. As a social signature or as a special way of seeing the world — in this case love, self, and 'woman' — the sonnet belonged, as form and style, to the society's most exalted circles. The idiom, however, could be borrowed, imitated, and even altered by poets born outside these circles.

It is wrong to link form and style mechanistically to the individual background of the writer. Such a link there may be, but it is far from inevitable. The son of a merchant may write like an aristocrat and an aristocrat — though this is rarer[42] — may write like a merchant. This does not invalidate the claim that style betokens a social identity, for style belongs, as we have seen, to a milieu as well as to individuals. But let it be emphasized that like mode, genre, and literary convention, the general lineaments of style belong more to the milieu than to the individual pen. And this explains apparent contradictions: jumped-up yeomen (Spenser) who command the idiom of gentlemen.

Let us consider Donne's style, in his secular poetry, from three angles.[43]

(1) *Group and class* Often mingling commonplace diction with inflections of learned and technical words, Donne used the combination to present elaborate, playful, or conceited argument: qualities akin to the wit and high standard of learning among his male friends, who sometimes begged manuscript copies of his poems. In this company of professional men, courtiers, and ambitious gentlemen, most of whom had been at one of the Inns of Court, there was vivacity of spirit, a grounding in the Latin classics, and a keen alertness — their worldly bent — to events and people about town. These interests find their corresponding features in Donne's style: in its townish and worldly slant, erotic touches, blistering ironies, audacious conceits, colloquial veneer, and rejection of highminded (Petrarchan) posturing. His 'irregular and prosaic metre', as in the *Satyres,* enabled him to tilt his verse towards the realism of speech. And in refusing to flirt with the platitudes of allusion to classical mythology, his style edged readers towards more knowing attitudes.

To recapitulate and expand, the following observations apply chiefly to the *Songs and Sonnets,* the *Satyres, Elegies,* and verse letters. Simplicity of diction, learned words and metaphors, meters inclined towards speech rhythms, a natural enough syntax, a wealth of ironies, studied hyperbole, erudite glitter, and immediacy of tone: all these go to bear the accents and viewpoint of a mundane man, well educated, well connected, traveled, socially alert, disabused, and given to reflecting on amatory matters — a favorite gentlemanly pastime.[44]

(2) *The social—biographic angle*   The same style is used to impress, to amuse, to win favor, to personalize utterances (as in the verse letters), and to indulge a ruminating penchant. Furthermore, in its ironies, quibbles, obscurities, stance against 'the golden style', and pitting of love against 'the world', Donne's manner says something about his alienation from Court and even, as Catholic and apostate, from his milieu.[45]

(3) *Historical period and social change*   Considered in the light of readers, imitators, and other poets who shared some of its elements — so that we pass here beyond individuals to a group taste — the same style points to a general shift in mood and outlook among sophisticated Londoners and the educated elite who frequented the city: a sliding towards self-questioning, pessimism, suspicion of public life, disenchantment with the Court, and uneasiness about religion. All these are seen in the style's critical bent, abrupt turns, deeper inquiring, strained tropical turns (especially in hyperbole), dissatisfaction with received forms, revolt against poetic convention, and insistence — via a simplicity of diction and prosaic meter — on a more direct engagement with experience.

The three angles have a cardinal importance for the social analysis of style: they help us to find its underlying vitalities. But any one of the three may call for more emphasis, depending upon the poet, the style, or the milieu. The grand style in Spenser, fit to celebrate the great and to impress the middling sort, served the author too, who made a career of it. Ornate, mellifluous, exalted, and archaizing, the Spenserian style distanced verse from speech, elevated poetry's claims, and thus worked to enhance the dignity of the professional poet as laureate. The followers of Spenser — Drayton, Wither, Browne, the Fletchers — all made extravagant claims for poetry and poets. The elegance and urbanity of Ben Jonson's style were garnered in part from the Latin classics, but they were also fostered by his keeping company with gentlemen, great-house people, and men of the sort received at Court. In his stout adherence to the classics, Jonson made it clear that these endowed him with credentials and a standard to rival the power and lifestyle of his rich patrons. If the latter had the urbane ways, he had the grace to put those ways into verse. Later, his elegance and 'ineffable cadence' were taken over by the Cavaliers and adapted to go with the civil poise and 'gentle' ways of 'noble' readers. They shaped the Jonsonian style more strictly into an idiom of social class. In political turmoil and civil war, the style was also turned into an exquisite way of treating non-political themes. Waller's famous ease, grace, and decorous propriety were fashioned to pay compliments, to acknowledge elevated rank, to prettify and frame the casual social activities of an elite, and really to see and interpret the world from their viewpoint.

'Tone and viewpoint' belong to style but they are sorted out here because criticism and scholarship often give them separate treatment.

By 'viewpoint' I understand attitude and outlook, and there is plainly a shadow of content here, of theme or subject-matter. The word requires some elasticity of meaning, for some poems express not much more than a simple attitude, say towards love, whereas others move from an encompassing point of view, indeed a world view, as in Donne's *Anniversaries,* in many of Shakespeare's sonnets, or in Marvell's political verse. Evidently, too, viewpoint is likely to determine 'tone'. But when we read poetry, we encounter tone first and then, through it, come to know the viewpoint. Tone, in turn, may be defined as the aura of the author's presence in the poem, his voice, his attitude towards his subject-matter. And so we return, in tautological fashion, to our starting point: tone and viewpoint being two aspects of a single characteristic which, in its turn, belongs to style.

There is a striking critical consensus on the quality of tone in courtly, Metaphysical, and Cavalier poetry, as well as in the verse satire of the 1590s. And though inexperienced readers are inclined to be doubtful about tone, politics has no such doubts. In 1981, when the socialist government of François Mitterrand gave ministerial posts to communists, Washington immediately reacted by declaring that this could not fail to affect 'the tone' of Franco-American relations.

Emphasis on 'the intellectual tone' of the Metaphysical poets — e.g., Edward Herbert — has been strong in scholarship, with the effect of removing their verse from the 'common reader' of the age and binding it to a select reading public. With Donne and the Herberts, moreover, criticism moves easily beyond their reading audiences to the details of their education, gentle birth, and well connected friendships, to catch in the finished verse something of the language and granulation of their immediate society. But the transition from Donne to Carew and the Cavaliers, the passage from 1600 to the 1630s and 1640s, is a shift in style, tone, outlook, and themes.

It is a shift away from a probing, often stubborn, intellectuality to a line that is more elegant and polished, more readily accessible — in short, more in keeping with the society of its readers. And while it is true, in marking this, that the influence of Jonson's amazing metrical elegance must be borne in mind,[46] scholarship has also offered more comprehensive explanations.

The chief strategy here is to identify a tone of some sort in the poetic text, a tone which is then traced back, or converted over, to something in the social world around. One of the leading studies of this kind frankly sets out to plot 'the evolution of wit, especially as it manifests itself in the social tone of poets',[47] and finds that the seventeenth-century definition of wit gradually becomes more and more social, while also remaining bound to an upper-class social identity. The first great poet in this main current is Jonson, who expresses 'in his non-dramatic verse a uniquely polite and civilized social tone and seems inspired by the very spirit of urbanity'.[48] This voice derives 'mainly from his classical culture', but it is a culture shared with the educated men of the upper classes, just as Jonson himself shared 'in the social activities which produced the manners and tone of their world'.[49] In brief, drawing accent and attitude from his contact with classical Latin poetry and Jacobean great-house (in part courtly) society, Jonson was able to endow his verse with 'a superlatively civilized tone'. This tone echoes at once the worldliness of classical culture and the authentic voice of the Jacobean nobility at its most cultivated, which still retains something of 'the old ideal of courtesy'.

The next wave of poets — Carew, Lovelace, Suckling, Waller, Cowley, and others — cleave to the new urbanity, 'the tone of the gentleman in poetry'.[50] In the 1630s, being gentlemen first, they move the tone of their verse closer to the Caroline Court, or closer to their peers and readers. They heighten its social tone by adding more grace, detachment, and ease, while also reducing passion and intellectuality. But at the same time, the emotional and moral climate of the surrounding world is changing radically. The royalist and great-house parts of their society fall increasingly under the raging criticism of the Puritan and parliamentary movements, until the outbreak of revolution and civil war in 1642.

Critics now shift the emphases in the social analysis of tone. They point to the enhanced element of grace, almost of fragility or preciosity, in Caroline verse and discern a retreat from commitment, a gliding over into attitudes that look away from the great problems of the day. 'The poems of the Cavaliers express an intellectual quietism, a recurrent emphasis on retreat, on rejection, on limitation, on exclusion. They are constantly drawing magic circles that will shut the world out, seeking to find an autonomous realm of love and art, a court immune to change.'[51] The new ease and heightened urbanity of tone mark a critical change. And looming behind this change is the deepening political and ideological crisis, with its bearing upon the content of poetry. The harmonious contact between tone and a prestigious social identity continues and is, if anything, closer; but now the impending political crisis is drawn into the consciousness of the 'mob of gentlemen who wrote with ease' (Pope) and so also into the tone of their poetry. Thus 'Carew's whole volume of 1640 may be said to represent the ideals of the Cavalier world in a series of poetical miniatures, graceful, elegant, perfectly crafted. . . . It is a world of art-forms too fragile to sustain the violent pressures of the times'[52] In like fashion, Habington, Stanley, and other Cavaliers distil a highly refined love verse, 'determinedly filtering out the unassimilable or chaotic forces of life itself and only thus preserving its fine grace and order'.[53]

Politics, however, could also make for a different tone, as in poems written just before and during the Civil War by the brilliant royalist, John Cleveland. Loathing rebels, Presbyterians, Parliamentarians, and mob rule, he turned his political poems into 'fusillades of conceits' — sneering, savage, decked out with clever polysyllables, staccato effects, biting couplets, and lines held by 'clench and catachresis'.[54] They record his mounting fury, making for 'snarling' forays and avid readers, as the Cavalier cause went to the wall. Here, the fears and hatreds of the political world have quite simply invaded poetry. Invective and fleering political attack speak for themselves (leaving little for social analysis to do), as do Ben Jonson's epigrams against fops and fawning courtiers.

GENRE AND INDIRECT REFERENCE

When relating the poem to its worldly context, critics turn surprisingly often to considerations of genre, convention, and form. These were capital matters for English Renaissance poets, because they associated genre and conventional forms (1) with the literary tradition, (2) with the uses and prestigious place of poetry, (3) with the expectations of patronage, and (4) with the rank-conscious, hierarchical nature of society.

Down to the late eighteenth century, and especially before the rise of the novel, poetry commanded larger listening audiences, a wider readership, and the occasions for poetry — thus its *usefulness* — were many. Patrons expected verse for different occasions in the different kinds, in return for hospitality, monies, or other tangible favors. The strong consciousness of rank — in a society for which the true model was hierarchy — *imposed* a sense of occasions, hence of corresponding forms, conventions, and literary propriety. Poetry had to take social degree into account just because it was closely joined to life.

The whole question of genre, therefore, was a social one, for it was ultimately connected with the occasions for poetry and the occasions were social: thus the verse epistle, the sonnet, epithalamia, epitaphs, pastoral, and funeral elegies or obsequies. Satire addressed itself to social evils. The epigram — the occasion for the transmission of distilled observation — was an obvious social mode. All these, moreover, had certain forms and a range of conventions, including the convention of decorum or literary propriety. Again, the heroic or epic poem was meant both to provide pleasure and to be an education for 'gentlemen'. Even the amatory lyric aimed to flatter, to please, to curry favor, or to seduce, while also winning bays for the poet. In its strictest and most courtly form (the sonnet), the amatory lyric was also a mode of behavior, a part of the ritual of courtliness.

The question arises, how exactly do literary scholars adduce genre to get at the poem's ties with the world? Generally speaking, they find that the lines of connection run from genre out to a readership, to an occasion, to patronage, to the poet's social background, or to a specific milieu.

It has been rightly noted that 'Elizabethan poetry was a highly formal art. . . . it expressed its meaning through accepted conventions and formal poses. If a poet wrote about love, he did it in the Petrarchan or anti-Petrarchan modes; if he wished to describe a wooing or to attack the Court, he would do it through the mouths of shepherds and shepherdesses.'[55] This meant that readers knew what to expect and quickly noticed any departures from the conventions, a fact which sometimes spurred the poet (e.g., Shakespeare, Raleigh, Donne) to alter or manipulate his forms. In the case of the verse epistle, Horace and Ovid provided the models. Yet it was only in the 1590s that English poets began to work in this form, which was obviously fare for an educated elite — the likes of Donne, Lodge, Daniel, Jonson, and their friends and readers. As a genre, it could have only as much vitality as went out to it not from Horace but from the life and social needs of the authors and receivers of the epistles. And one of the needs touched patronage, for poets also utilized the form to address current or wished-for patrons. Later, 'During the Civil War and the Commonwealth, the Horatian ode and verse epistle were the chief vehicles for the expression of the philosophy of rural retirement.'[56] But this 'philosophy' was the fashion — peaking in the 1650s — chiefly for men of royalist sympathies. Reeling back from the melancholy of defeat in the Civil War, and seeing nothing but political vileness in 'the great town' (London), they repaired to their country estates to read Horace and to reflect on the serene joys of rural retirement and friendships. In this mood, as an exchange between learned friends, the verse epistle came fully into its own, along with the dignified and contemplative rural ode. Henry Vaughan, who supported the royalist cause, openly admitted 'that the idea of retirement came to him and his generation as a natural consequence of the turbulence of the period in which they lived'.[57]

So, moving from the world to the poem, the above progression was: military and political defeat, mood, retirement, some sustaining theme, epistle, and ode. This chain of feeling enables us to see the way in which two poetic genres were vitalized by a social group and a specific milieu.

When we bring to light the relations between a social group (or a specific setting) and a generic form, we begin to see that 'the conventions of poetry are largely dictated by the society for which the poetry is written.'[58] The appearance of mock – heroic as a genre, in the middle decades of the seventeenth century, attests to the impact of society on poetic form. Here was a marriage of two strains, epic and satire, one in the high style for praise, the other in the low style for blame and criticism. The trick was to fuse biting derision with the elevated language and tone of heroic verse; and this meant breaking with the stylistic legacy of antiquity, which separated the modes and styles for depicting people of noble rank from those meant for the humble. The political violence of the 1640s, which trammeled the entire nation; the bold, upper-class involvement in politics during the post-Restoration years; and the reading habits of the elite groups, with their schooling in poetry: these circumstances propelled poets — Cleveland, Butler, and especially Cowley, Marvell, and finally Dryden — to develop a genre fit for controversy, mockery, attack, and cutting statement. But mock-heroic was a genre which also recognized the high estate of the enemy by urbanely mixing lampoon with epic strain.

'Indirect reference' means any allusion in a poem to the surrounding historical world, whether by pun, metaphor, symbol, allegory, inversion, irony, or some such other disguise. The topic rightly comes toward the end of this chapter, for the detecting of indirect references may require all our strategies. Yet owing to the resources of poetry and language, there can be no reading system so thorough as to be able to catch and decipher all the indirect references in a complex poem. Even when reading the verse of a poet who has lived with us, we can have no knowledge sweeping enough to detect all his or her allusions.

We have always known of allegory, such as *The Faerie Queene* or Drayton's *The Owl*, that there are things in it (e.g., episodes and emblems) which are intended to refer to public matters in the surrounding world. Working to locate points of indirect reference, the scholar normally proceeds in a hit-and-miss fashion, looking for parallels, consistencies, echoes, or clues, and gathering these largely from the structure of the poem, while also keeping an eye cocked on the attendant historical circumstances. Yet allegory's essential characteristic — the deliberate veiling of higher meaning by means of *planned* indirection — calls for a method of analysis whose ends diverge from our purposes here. The entire burden of this study is, in one respect, to set forth a method for finding poetry's relation to the encircling social world *despite* the intentions of poets. Therefore, when a poet distributes a hundred or a thousand tropes of all sorts, from irony and riddles to emblematic episodes and pointers, but so arranged in the poem as to add up to a given chain of meaning for the initiate, all we need for breaking his code is his word — a statement, his notes, or an autographed table of correspondences. Whereupon most of the challenge to analysis suddenly vanishes, the key verging on something mechanical. As it happens, much of the exegetical work which has been done on *The Faerie Queene* belongs to this type of inquiry, centering on the search for Spenser's premeditated correspondences. And while it is true that the quest for such correspondences may depend upon some of the strategies outlined in this study, yet the two inquiries seek different ends. The hunt for the poet's premeditated links between the poem and its social world serves the objectives of this book only insofar as such links, or the attendant analytical strategies, help us to get *beyond* what is premeditated to other forms of contact between poem and world.

Unless we have an externally validating document, most of the ways of discovering indirect reference depend upon establishing correspondences — points of contact between the poem and its surrounding historical reality

— by means of close textual readings; and the strategies of analysis, as we have seen, vary remarkably. Meanwhile, as the social critic works, we can observe him keeping an ever-ready eye on the impinging historical world: on major events, on broad institutional or social changes, on specific milieux, on commonplace symbols (e.g., rose, lamb, oak, sun, light, lion, eagle, ant, garden, wolf), on bestiaries and popular flower books, on social classes, or on the basic political and social assumptions of the day.

Scholarship has an indispensable route to the frontier area of poem—world correspondences in the study of diction, for words in poetry draw in their wake the range of meanings generally assigned them in the world. Use a feudal, legal, or financial term in a love lyric and straightway you import the ghostly presence of social, contractual, or commercial relations. Poetry relies upon just such transactions. Again, on a different plane and owing to their chronic conventional use, certain images had such standard nimbi of meanings that the moment they appear in poems critics must bear their semiotic legacies in mind. The poetic context is, however, decisive. In love lyrics, 'gold' and 'sun' were inevitably associated with the desired lady — gold with her hair, the sun with her face or eyes, and of course 'light' with all of her. But in political verse, or in some of the poems of the Cavaliers, such as Lovelace's 'The Grasshopper', the same images have a 'Royalist potential'[59] — that is, they are more nearly associated with the royalist cause. The sense behind this is that 'gold', 'sun', and 'light' also had traditional associations with kingship. Milton, perfectly aware of this, refers contemptuously to royal 'grooms besmeared with gold'.[60]

In oblique references to contemporary people and events, the main disguise — but also the chief betrayer — depended upon some form of parallelism or analogy. A fox was like a crafty privy councillor, a wolf like a royal favorite who piled up ecclesiastical properties, a vulture like an enclosing landlord, a jay like a prostitute, and kites or other carrion birds like loan sharks. Jonson's play *Sejanus,* set in imperial Rome, glitters with parallels to the English political situation, enough to have had him summoned before the privy council. On the advice of friends the poet—courtier, Fulke Greville, destroyed his closet drama on Antony and Cleopatra from fear that parallels with Elizabeth and Essex might be seen in it. He knew his contemporaries; he knew that as playgoers they tried constantly to identify the real people allegedly satirized in much of the comedy of the period.[61]

For all the bias against biography in contemporary critical theory — and it is no better than bias — the more such information we have, the more likely we are to be able to throw light on the vast stretches of allusiveness in sixteenth- and seventeenth-century poetry. If we did not know that Michael Drayton fell into some disfavor with the Countess of Bedford after about 1600, we could not know that a scathing allusion in his 8th Eclogue of 1606 (then expunged in the 1619 edition) issues from his embittered disappointment in patronage and certainly refers to her:

> Let age sit soone and ugly on her brow,
> No sheepheardes praises living let her have
> To her last end noe creature pay one vow
> Nor flower be strew'd on her forgotten grave,
> And to the last of all devouring tyme
> Nere be her name remembred more in rime.[62]

With regard again to the value of biographical findings, unless we know something about Marvell's religious and even political views, we are unlikely to read 'To his Coy Mistress' ironically. If such a reading is valid, the ironic tone of the poem is the trope which, when detected, turns the surface meaning upside down and makes it a mocking indictment of the Cavalier theme of erotic love. Given the partisanship of the 1640s and 1650s, this turns 'To his Coy Mistress' into a statement of anti-Cavalier faith and puts it on the brink of politics.

Scholars often associate poetic parodies of courtly love with the smart temper of the Inns of Court in the 1590s. Tone and content in certain of Sir John Davies's *Gulling Sonnets* are taken to be paradigmatic:

> What Eagle can behold her sunbright eye, (iii, 1)

or

> Into the middle Temple of my heart
> the wanton Cupid did himself admit (vii, 1—2).

Now in crossing over from a poetic parody to the Inns-of-Court setting, the critic is tracing lines of connection in the poet's consciousness, the connecting chain being rather like the following: (1) the poem's theme is love, really a type of anti-love; (2) the words and tropes violate a received set of conventions, are mocking, exaggerated, or inverted; (3) this stance is anti-courtly, critical, humorous, detached, knowing, and self-consciously superior; (4) the poet is an Inns-of-Court man with rooms in the Middle Temple during the mid- and later 1590s (this is in the poet's constitutive cosnciousness as a simple matter of identity); (5) the poet therefore partakes of that mentality, that society, that milieu, where the scoffing attack on the Petrarchan manner has become fashionable.

In one way or another, all five segments of this chain are seen through the critic's mind to have been in the poet's mind, presumably at the time of the poem's composition. And it is only after he has arrived at segment 5 — though there is an arrow out at 2, the break with convention — that he begins fully to leave the poet's mind, in a movement that carries him out into the Inns ambience of the 1590s. This is to say that having started with the poem, the critic moves out into the world only when he has done a convincing job of first negotiating his way, as it were, through parts of the poet's consciousness.

In this fleeting encounter with the poet's mind, social analysis makes contact with his way of seeing, thinking, and being. We do not thereby enter into his intimate life and biography. Rather, we approach the social man, the man caught up in a particular milieu, using speech in a certain way, drawing on certain literary conventions, favoring a given range of tropes, and giving a voice to viewpoints in the milieu. The connotative and tentacular possibilities of his poetic language tug at, and parade, aspects of his primary and secondary experience. If these matters are then related to the Renaissance poet's alertness to his audience and to his doctrine of communication, we see at once that the act of writing Renaissance verse was perfectly social. As social action, it was susceptible to forms of group consciousness, to general changes in mood and outlook, to sensed shifts in group and political balances, and to any decided strains in the society. There was nothing to keep poets from converting social change into literary change, as in the unquiet decade of the 1590s and during the Civil War period. The sonnet form was attacked or transformed; themes in other genres were first vastly enlarged, then much narrowed; the epigram scaled the heights of fashion; the search for metaphor turned daring and then cautious; diction was polished; the couplet was perfected as a medium for public statement; overt political poetry was born and so was mock-heroic.

When we reflect on these changes, we see that all are trends, all transcend individuals to become the common taste of groups and poets, and all constitute a mode of social criticism. All express the need for new forms or dissatisfaction with old ones, the desire to probe or the decision not to probe; all are literary responses to some important change in the range of consciousness, whether in mood, prospects, strains, or contemporary issues. In short, literary form is also social form. And what we see as a 'shadowy land' between literary change and social change (p. 31) is no more than a metaphor for a lack of discernment in us: for our inability to see that a literary response to social change is perfectly natural and also social.

The end of this chapter calls for a statement about social literary analysis as a 'system' at once open and closed.

Closed   Experience belongs to a time and place, and so is historical. Society *is* the historical universe; there is nothing in history that is beyond or outside society; and society takes in everything from language and institutions to personalities, ideas, and customs. We know one historical world — for instance, Periclean Athens — through another, our own. Therefore, being locked into our own socio-historical world is the condition of our being able to imagine or reconstruct another, Periclean Athens. But that other is not fixed because we are not fixed: *we* are the unsteady, unstable element. Being composed in time and place, a poem bears the voices of its social world, thus belonging to it. To try to relate the poem to God, or to hive it over to a transcendent world of art, may be possible as a mental exercise, but if we know how to read it, it will not lose the voices holding it to a time and place. Art may be entitled to a special sphere within the social world, just as are philosophy, politics, and religion; but none of these — and the claim is tautological — can be outside that world.

Open   The poem has a variety of parts: theme, diction, tropes, semiotic play, style, conventions. These make contact with different parts of the social world: reading public, the Court, the sense of hierarchy, the economy, the educational background of the poet, politics, social change, historical period, and so forth. We get at the connections between poem and world through the mind of the social critic, who in his turn, in grappling with the poem, is trying to reconstruct a set of 'motions' in the mind of the poet at the time of composition. How risky and provisional such an undertaking must be is obvious, particularly when we consider the poet's play of imagination and the resources of his medium. In fact, the variables in relations between imagination and reality (poem and world) are so many and subtle that we dare not dream that we can set up a heuristic framework so complete as to be able to detect all the contacts, for example, between diction and world, let alone between the world and all other parts of the poem. This means that social analysis must acknowledge 'open' areas in the field of relations between poem and world — areas where anything is possible theoretically. Moreover, because poetry's social circumstances change, such as with regard to patronage or reading publics, the strategies used in social literary analysis cannot be fixed or universal. Historical change dissolves all fixity of this order. Certain strategies may apply alike to Renaissance as to Romantic poetry, but the latter should not be bent into taking the same *combination* of analytical procedures as was developed for the former.

In thinking about what I have said regarding the risky and provisional nature of social literary analysis, as it moves over the terrain between poem and world, no historian who works on conventional subject-matter should suppose that his tasks are always safer and more 'scientific'. Such security may belong to historical work of the narrowest and most conventional sort. But any serious history should also take us into a general consciousness, a mental world — the necessary ground for relations between society and ideas, society and culture, or society and any scatter of attitudes. On this ground, the labor of the historian goes into reconstructing the motions in the thinking or 'mind' of the community, the village, the period, the populace, or the ruling groups. Can such *mentalités* be less complex — even if of a different order — than the individual consciousness of the poet? We should beware of lingering romanticism. There is no need to surround the poet with more mystery than we give to the workings of entire communities. To do so is to do poetry no favor.

3

Strategies: from world to poem

There are two movements in the social 'deciphering' of poetry: (1) movement *in* the analytical progression from the poetic text out into the world, and (2) the reverse. As a primary strategy, neither movement is superior to the other. The problem implied here, in any suspicion that there should be priorities, vanishes when we recall that the social analysis of poetry relies in fact on the two movements simultaneously. For even as the literary critic courses away from the poem, whether by a study of diction or metaphor, to make contact with the text's historical world, he is engaged in a procedure which makes no logical sense unless he is also tracking movement the other way. He cannot stretch a line from P to W without the line also stretching from W to P. To relate the poem to the world is to relate the world to the poem. And if it be objected, to be persnickety, that when the critic has the line only halfway across from P to W, we cannot talk as yet of there being a simultaneous operation the other way, the reply is that the critic had already done some scouting of W, or he could not know that stretching a line from P to W was even feasible.

Generally speaking, I began in the preceding chapter with different parts of the poem (e.g., imagery, style) and moved out into the world (patronage, political strains, etc.). Here I reverse the motion and will move from the world to the poem.

PATRONAGE, OCCASIONS, READERS

Since patronage is a social transaction, it transforms poetry into action and has it enter the world in a modality akin to that of visiting friends, proffering an invitation, or making a gift to someone. In this prospect, the economic view of the patron—client relation becomes radically short-sighted if it sees no further than economics, as we gather from the rich and resonant detail which flecks the lives of Spenser, Shakespeare, Donne, Jonson, Drayton, and others. For that detail reveals that the economic bond was combined with personal ties to patrons and with the vital status of poetry in the sixteenth and seventeenth centuries. The give-and-take in patronage pivoted as well on values as on material favors; and the moment we touch values we enter fully into consciousness, where the thoughts and feelings that go with patronage implicate other matters as well, such as themes, tone, and viewpoints.

Shakespeare's sonnets to the young man, some of Donne's verse epistles, Drayton's *Ideas Mirrour,* and Jonson's 'To Penshurst' are famous examples of a literature of patronage. When the patron—client bond is emphasized in the study of these poets, critics often find major signs of strain, self-abasement, and exaggeration (Donne); ambiguity, heightening, social rank, and social self-doubt (Shakespeare); a calculated idealization which underscores rank (Drayton); and a nostalgic, quasi-feudal view of society (Jonson). Moreover, all the indicated poems turn — some more and some less — on the keystone of flattery, the daily tribute paid to social rank in Renaissance Europe. But flattery was not necessarily crude; better perhaps, at least with some patrons, if it refrained from this. The call to avoid crude flattery was a call to vary, vitalize, or embellish the tribute. This made for heightening, for amplification, for idealization, for the right degree of generalization,[1] for a respectful or worshipping tone, and so for a grander or, if plain (Jonson), a more supple language. In any case, decorum — another respecter of social degree — was observed.

Moving from an understanding of Elizabethan society, the critic who draws a bead on patronage in the decades around 1600 is likely to suppose that the marks of deference, dependence, or social rank must somehow surface in the poetry of patronage; and it would be a miracle if they did not, for wherever patronage and flattery hold a place, there too are power and its effects. But the critic should not worry this and he must be ready — given the predictability of deference and flattery — to accept that he may be dealing with the dullest aspect of the verse in question. Dullness is, however, avoidable if he recollects that patronage is not a cul-de-sac but an open way leading to other parts of the poem and world.

Scholars who have used patronage as a springboard for analysis know that it took different forms.[2] To write for the theater, for the Court, and for a great house (the Egertons, Dudleys, or Sidneys) were different activities, especially playwriting. And even in playwriting there was some little distinction between writing for the public and for the 'private' (roofed and more expensive) theaters.

Scholarship distinguishes between professional poets and 'amateurs' (gentlemen), but a recent study argues for a three-part division, including professionals, amateurs, and 'laureates' — those who aspired to poetry's highest office and bays, such as Spenser, Jonson, Chapman, Daniel, and Drayton.[3] In this view — Jonson apart — professionals were those poets who wrote mainly for the stage. Clearly, however, the laureates were also professionals, not only because they were poets professed but also because their careers depended upon what poetry could garner for them. Gifted, socially ambitious, and dedicated to poetic composition, they resented bitterly the claims of lesser talents ('poetasters'), all the more so in a social system where the rewards of patronage were limited and where the preoccupation with rank, amidst so many jumped-up 'gentlemen', filled men's minds with invidious comparisons.

The amateurs rarely 'descended' to print, and never with their own names, because this was demeaning. Here plainly was a late feudal hangover: to write for money or material favor was really the job of a 'clerk' and this was something done for, not by, gentlemen. As a result, the poetry of gentlemen did the rounds in manuscript. To write poetry was 'gentle' and a most gracious activity; but gentlemen did not produce it for money and their verse was not in any case for the eyes of the vulgar, which is where the printed book ended. This attitude toward print began to change after about 1630.[4]

These neat generalizations are partly subverted by the intriguing cases of John Donne and Sir Walter Raleigh. Others also fit the bill of exceptions — Sir John Harington and one or two of the Cavaliers. Counted among the first half dozen poets of their time, Raleigh and Donne avoided print for reasons of status, yet they used their poetry — and for sure their poetic talents — in the struggle to secure favor, place, and fortune. They also used their brilliant conversation, as they did their verse, in the pursuit of patronage. Donne's disgrace and economic plight — with the ensuing *Anniversaries* and verse letters to potential patrons — are too well known for rehearsal here. Raleigh produced much of his verse in emergencies — in exile, in the Tower, or when place at Court was threatened: verse in the face of changes of fortune.[5] His wooing poems to the Queen were grappling irons, intended to catch argosies. Studies therefore of both Raleigh and Donne show that strain, anguish, anxiety, nagging resentment, and the uncertainty of place all appear richly in their poetry. An obscure West Country gentleman, Raleigh had made it big at Court; but he could set no claim to even a dubious serenity. To lose place at Court was more than hurtful financially: it was loss of being, loss of identity.

In the matter of patronage, how closely did poets tailor their productions to the tastes of their patrons? There can be no simple answer to this question, not only because the demands of patrons, like the talents of poets, varied but also because the decisive evidence is hard to come by. Yet there is much reason to believe that poets and patrons were close enough in their literary tastes for differences to cause little trouble. The similarity of the educational curriculum in the better schools went far to diminish such differences. And it was not, in any case (poetic conventions aside), as if poets wrote to prescription by patrons, the way painters might execute portraits in accordance with models prescribed by their sitters. Still, what remains unclear is how far a poet might bend to a special taste. We know that in the 1590s some poets produced erotic verse to satisfy and titillate patrons. Verse epistles to patrons — Donne's, Jonson's, Daniel's — were often specifically directed to a taste, a moment, a mood; but Daniel was also perfectly capable of drafting a flattering verse epistle for one patron, then changing his mind and actually addressing it — with very few changes — to another.[6] Drayton, Jonson, and Carew composed verse for Court masques, keeping to a silken line of eulogy which raised the Stuarts to the heavens. But taste could be more personal than this. Writing 'Upon Appleton House' for a remarkably learned patron (Lord Fairfax), 'Marvell could safely include philosophical or theological allusions of such subtlety that they would be beyond the range of the uninitiated. In this circumstance lies perhaps his subtlest compliment to his noble employer.'[7]

The matter of writing poetry to the taste of patrons brings us to the occasions for poetry.

Even in our time occasions arise, such as presidential inaugurations and royal weddings, which seem to invite the composition of poetry. I say 'even' because the occasions are rare and not, in any case, generally believed to provide a true reason for poetry; which is only to say that poetry has lost place and use among us, lost it in our unspoken assumption that it is a personal or *private* art form. So far as we can see some reason for affixing poetry to a public occasion — say the visit of a Roman pope or the death of a much loved national leader — we know that it should be celebratory and so are put on our guard about its quality as verse.

Medieval society, patronage, and the power of 'great men' (princes, feudal magnates, and bishops) had greatly increased the occasions for the poetry of praise, and therefore poetry flourished on celebration, grandeur, power, social degree, and verbal tribute. The poetry of praise had its converse in the poetry of blame and complaint,[8] the occasions for which arose from the poet's dissatisfaction with patronage or with larger social questions. Something of 'the great man' phenomenon persisted in the early seventeenth century and the effects of this should not be overlooked in the study of occasional poetry. Henceforth, too, much poetry for particular occasions was to be a transaction between equals or near equals, as is clear, especially after 1630, in exchanges of verse letters and in the Cavalier 'poetry of address'. The latter was a poetry of friendship spanning three different times: 'before the wars, the Cavalier winter of oppression [defeat of the royalists], and rural friendship while awaiting the King's return'.[9] Here the bonds of friendship, the occasion for writing, the political climate, and the rural setting dictated the poetic themes and stances. Moreover, among the Cavaliers, as many critics have seen,[10] the occasions for verse were likely to be more group-oriented and more fully grounded in a milieu. Themes too had to be more acceptable socially.

In thinking about occasional verse, students have noted that such verse is essentially social and sometimes egregiously public, as in panegyric. It aims to convey a statement and mood. The viewpoint and expectations of auditors/readers thus take on a major importance. For this reason, however personal or idiosyncratic its turns, the occasional poem seeks to transcend its maker. But the maker has his reward, for he knows that in commemorating the occasion, he is performing a useful social role, defined 'by some concept of "the poet" as having a special task or tasks in the society to which he belongs. The task may be to expose folly and vice, to praise virtue or great achievements, to celebrate a birth, a death, a war, a marriage';[11] and in his more personal relations with others, it may be to fix and frame an occasion which joins all those concerned.

When combined with politics, the fashion for occasional verse goes to help explain the mid-seventeenth-century vogue for mocking answer poems, a genre that went back to the sixteenth century. 'Often caustic and intemperate, the "mock song" marks the decline of the [old type] "answer

poem". . . another delicate flower of insulated court coterie life.' After
1640, 'Even elegant poets adopted a simple, crude style to reach a wide
public. A ballad or parody was a relatively safe way to express Royalist
outrage in Commonwealth times.'[12] A surprising number of Waller's
poems, for example, 'called forth printed or unprinted answer poems', such
as Godolphin's refutation of his funeral poem on Cromwell. The repairing
of St Paul's Cathedral, initiated by Charles I and Archbishop Laud in the
1630s, was bitterly assailed by Puritans. In this light, Waller's 'Upon His
Majesty's Repairing of St Paul's' suddenly becomes 'a party piece, arguing
the Anglican and Royalist position, justifying and glorifying the King's
behavior'.[13] Though 'the tone of the poem is not in the least combative',
here was the very sort of performance to elicit mocking replies in verse.

Patronage worked a change in poetry, making it a form of true action.
And political poetry — by the Cavaliers, by Marvell, Milton, Dryden, and
others — was action *ipso facto.* It is important to see that in the context of
the times, the 'occasion' also transmuted poetry into action. This point
bears illustration. If I compose a birthday ode to a friend, it may count as
'occasional verse' or as 'symbolic action' (Kenneth Burke), but it cannot be
action in the world because neither our institutions nor the state of our
language will sanction this. In the sixteenth and seventeenth centuries, on
the contrary, the occasions for verse were more social, more turned out
towards the world, and more group-, family-, or community-oriented. The
dignity of poetry, in education as in life, was such that it could enhance or
heighten occasions, while also being colored by them, by their transpersonal
tinctures. In addition, the language then was more keyed to celebration,
more primed for the marking and praise of occasions. And just as there
were also more celebrants, so too were there keener audiences for such
celebrants. In effect, the occasion and the poem were so naturally linked
that each took something from the other. For an elite of readers — the
Cavaliers or smart Londoners of Dryden's times — 'occasions' must have
verged on oblivion unless they were recollected in poetry.

The evidence from dedications, prefaces, notes to readers, and private
correspondence indicates that poets knew for whom they were writing.
Theorists — Puttenham, William Webbe, and others — stressed the
importance of the poet's having a concrete sense of his audience. Since
poetry belonged to the art of moving people (rhetoric), how could the poet
afford to be in the dark about his prospective readers and auditors? The so-

called amateurs — Sidney, Greville, Dyer, Donne, Raleigh, the Herberts, Carew, and the like — wrote with specific readers in mind, so it may be fair to say that they knew their intended audience down to the last man and woman.[14] When copies of their poems passed beyond the charmed circle, we assume that these went out in the first instance to readers much like the intended. Professionals like Daniel, Drayton, and Jonson were also fully aware of their primary readers. Their patrons and others of the same sort figured large — aristocrats, courtiers, and members of the gentry, but also men from the Inns of Court, London literati, and a scatter of readers and auditors from the most educated levels of the yeomanry and merchant class.

The primary audience for amatory verse, as exemplified in Sidney's *Astrophel and Stella,* included the poet himself and his different personae (as he spoke out in different moods), the loved one, and a group of close friends and acquaintances. Identification of the poet's different moods is essential because it catches the play of ironies and attitudes, which in turn hark back to values and social viewpoints. Epigram and satire were mainly directed at, and particularly well loved by, alert young men from the universities and Inns of Court, with other well read gentlemen following a close second. Heroic verse was aimed firstly at aristocrats, courtiers, gentlemen, and upper-class women: the education and delectation of these are what epic poets claimed to have in mind. The Cavaliers wrote for other poets; for a circle of close friends made at school, at Court, in London, or in the country; and for a given class of women, seen clearly in 'the flourishing minor genre of complimentary epistles to ladies'.[15]

A dry listing of primary readers and auditors means nothing, however, unless we understand that there was a reciprocal flow of recognitions, an articulation of shared views, in the exchange between poet and audience. To put this another way: 'the total empathy between poet and audience . . . arises when the poet is not so much a teacher of his audience or a spokesman for them, as both at once.'[16] The flow of meanings between Renaissance poet and auditors moved both ways. It was not only the poet who gave but also the audience. This audience was the voice and ear of the community immediately around him; he addressed it daily; it had helped to fashion him; he took from and responded to it, whether he directed his verse at groups or at individuals. For even when he addressed individual patrons, since his 'message' was something knowable, it could not be the unique because 'the unique as such is unknowable', uniqueness being 'a quality of experience, not of knowledge'.[17] Consequently, the meanings conveyed by the poet went out already bearing the imprint of the listening and reading community.

When we see that for all its metabolisms the poem's contact with readers was also a traffic in established attitudes, meanings, and values — particularly so in the midst of 'a traditional society' — then we must look for the silent but demanding expectations with which readers confronted poets, that is, the flow of influences from world to poem.

In the post-Reformation climate of moral seriousness, the Elizabethan poet was greatly attracted to the sonnet of the Petrarchan type, with its oppositions or contrarieties, in part because 'he was constantly trying to give love poetry an intellectual and moral responsibility.' He recognized that his audience might look upon this kind of verse as 'a toy because of its subject matter', and so he sought 'to make love seem an almost heroic subject, and to do so by the insistence upon the consuming nature of experience'.[18] Yet another feature of the post-Reformation period lay in England's astonishing energies and expanding nationalism, which had a profound effect on Marlowe, Spenser, Shakespeare, Drayton, Wither, and others. Scholarship has seen 'some historical connection between heroic writing and periods of national growth and vigour', but the surest connection is contained in the view that 'the best audience for epic is one that knows enough of actual greatness to be stirred by its actions and aware of its ironies.'[19]

We cut through the preceding examples by simply noting that all hinge on the silent solicitations of a *knowing* audience. Some additional variations show this in sharper relief.

The satires appended to John Marston's *The Metamorphosis of Pigmalions Image* 'require a comprehension of personal references, and the controversy with [Joseph] Hall in the third and fourth satires and the dark hints of scandal in the fifth presume a knowing audience'.[20] To understand him fully, Marston's readers had to be privy to some special information; but at the same time he was also invited, by his awareness of *their* knowledge, to wink an eye, to throw in further innuendoes, and to play up to them by buzzing round the coterie information.

The Donne file also provides instructive examples of the silent solicitations of a *knowing* readership. It is common knowledge that he 'used verse' not only to advance his career but also 'to compliment, or amuse, or rival his friends'.[21] His friends were steeped in the more conventional verse of the age and this fact had a direct bearing on him as poet. 'For the evaporations of so learned a wit could be caught only by those who were well read in the poetry of Spenser and Sidney, of Marlowe and Shakespeare, of Jonson and Daniel and Drayton, and therefore so well trained to the standards of decorum, that they could enjoy Donne's reversals of it.'[22] Thus, banking on the literary culture of his friends, Donne's novelties immediately hit the mark. In similar fashion, 'The Horatian echoes [in his Satire 4] are signs from Donne to his readers which acknowledge his original [Horace, *Satires,* I, ix] as a text to be remembered.'[23] Here, again, Donne's demands on his elite audience were a function in part of what they knew or, more accurately, of what he rightly supposed them to know. His readers worked on him, down even to certain fine details, although such influence was naturally spread out across the years of his many meetings, meals, and conversations with them.

BIOGRAPHY, CLASS, MILIEU

The concern with patronage is likely to involve the biographies and social backgrounds of poets, but we distinguish them here because literary scholarship often cites individual social backgrounds in the course of analysis, without making any mention of patronage. In picking out ties between the world and the poem, critics take biographical backgrounds to be a part of the world, just as they take occasions, patronage, readerships, politics and economic trends to be other parts.

Evidently, too, patronage and biographical backgrounds introduce considerations of social class. Here again, however, class is entitled to a separate listing because literary analysis is likely to emphasize the *individual* patron or the *individual* circumstances of a given poet. In emphasis of this sort, so far as the individual is held up high enough to hide representative matters, both patronage and background are wrenched away from their community framework and from established social practices.

A line in scholarship holds the view that the social origins of Elizabethan poets had a major influence on their attitudes and writings. One of the more comprehensive interpretations notes that just as the nobility and gentry began to send their sons to university after about 1550, so too did certain non-gentle families. Higher education brought snobbery, touchiness, and confused values for some of the students of humble origins. 'A Marlowe or a Greene is a young man uprooted. He is detached from his class but without the means of becoming fully accredited in any higher class, yet with heightened aspirations; discontent and disillusion stalk him from the moment he steps out into the world.'[24] This description of 'the university wits' also fits Harvey, Peele, Nashe, and Lodge. Later — though only by 'assimilation' — it will apply in part to Chapman, Middleton, and Jonson. Touchily proud, they felt that their studies and talents endowed them somehow with virtue and even a certain nobility. 'Their learning is not simply learning, but a gulf between them and their social origins.'[25]

This account is backed up by parallel observations concerning the satirists of the 1590s.[26] Though born into 'better' families and circumstances than any of the poets named above, Harington, Davies, Donne, Marston, Hall, and Guilpin knew that they must eventually find preferment at Court, in the Church, or in the legal profession. Some of them in particular hit on satire and the writing of epigrams as the highway to drawing attention to themselves, but the effects of such aspiring bob up in their verse — in its insolence, strain, self-promotion, *odi profanos* touches, and moments of fear or nausea.[27]

The yeoman, Spenser, took a different approach. He had so clear a view of poetry as a means of social climbing that in exalting its office he seemed to put himself 'on the same plane with his protectors and patrons'. All his poetry 'moves along two lines, one aimed at asserting his cultural superiority over the very world he wishes to enter, the other at modifying the poetic models proposed by that world so as to affirm his individuality within his own immediate circles'.[28] For the true courtier and nobleman born, Sir Philip Sidney, 'poetry was truth, whereas for Spenser it was prestige'.[29] Speaking of the *Amoretti* sonnets and starting off with these perceptions — thus initial movement from world to poem — one leading student has traced Spenser's instrumental view of poetry in his use of pronouns, which show him turning the woman loved and celebrated into an object of 'contemplation and meditation', but in such a way as also 'to raise high the intellectual qualities of the poet. Hence poetry as prestige.'[30]

For all its mobility, Elizabethan and Jacobean society was so conscious of rank and social degree that the use of biographical backgrounds in the social analysis of its verse carries us directly over to questions of group, class, and values. We must also take account of the psychology of social mobility, with its attendant velleities, envies, and constraints.

The most ambitious attempt to study poetry in relation to social place and hierarchy situates poets along the 'social slope' of the 'Hill of Fortune' — namely, the pyramid of material advantages and distinction (or obscurity) of birth. Here the poet of aristocratic birth (Sidney, preeminently) stands near the top and below him come all those who regard poetry as prestige, as a way of winning preferment, as their chief source of income, or as an idiom for the theater looked upon as livelihood.[31] Different positions on the hill involve different views because placement along the social slope 'is seen to imply a whole ethos, intellectual, temperamental and spiritual'.[32] In this arrangement, the psycho-social effects of class are diffused and mediated — Sidney and Shakespeare 'are somehow members of the same moral community' — but the hierarchy of attitudes towards poetry remains. The farther down we go on the social slope, the more urgent the economic pressures and the greater the need to turn poetry into paid employment. The glimmerings of patronage here are everywhere, and it is clear that social position — place relative to class and income — is bound to have some effect on 'the content, tone, and form' of poetry.[33]

Many subtleties follow from the preceding scheme, such as Sidney's view of poetry as truth, play, and private devotion; or Spenser's view of poetry as prestige — whence his professional earnestness, his need of public ('external') occasions, and his 'loading' of story in *The Faerie Queene* 'with allegory, and allegory with morality, and morality with platonism, to form a massive assembly of all the by-products of Renaissance learning and art'.[34] Donne's ambiguous position on Fortune's Hill went to help make for the satirist, for the blasphemous adulator who needed 'the metaphysics' as justification, and for the chancer who played down his poetic talents so as not to seem a professional.

To make the transition from social class to poetry the critic must pass through consciousness. Class as something *in* society is meaningless unless it is also in consciousness. It is here that class is a *sense* of class, something felt or dimly perceived, a sense of social identity. But to see or to reconstitute class *as a sense of social identity* is, in effect, to crystalize ideals and values. Almost instantaneously, therefore, the critic's initial perception — a rather crude one — regarding class is rendered useless in that form. To proceed with the job of social analysis, he must slip over into the realm of ideals and attitudes, fear and desires, and begin to track these out, in all their obliquitous forms, in the poetry, where they may affect anything from themes and diction to tone and style. Class, then, gives a direction and a general orientation to the social critic, but it is also the perception of something intricately and stubbornly complex.

There is something to be said for the view which accounts for the rich diversity and energy of Elizabethan literature and drama by hearkening to 'the greater social variety evidenced in its writers', which was indeed remarkable, but so too was the flux of movement in the society as a whole. The view collects more strength if tested against what happened in the Restoration and Augustan periods, when poets 'came more generally from upper-class backgrounds'.[35] Literary form and content necessarily changed. The Restoration theaters, for instance, were largely 'under court patronage' and 'the audiences were virtually limited to courtiers and their adherents.' Tragedy was turned into 'an elaborate mannerism', giving way to the increasing formalization of the conventions of honor and innocence, and poets 'reduced' the earlier blank verse, 'with its closeness to forms of ordinary speech, either into the heroic couplet, or into the stilted Restoration blank verse'.[36] These observations lock poet, audience, themes, and treatment into a social, moral, and artistic communion; but the shadow of class is all around.

Poets and readers after about 1630 — above all in the Cavalier phenomenon — led the way to Restoration attitudes and taste. In observing this transition, if we take class as our point of departure, we are struck by the fact that all the leading poets sprang from the gentry or, like Waller, from the affluent middle class. We also come directly up against political strains and a definite order of values. The 'self-confident mockery of a conservative class consciousness' is one of the attitudes that comes through Cavalier verse.[37] In the words of another critic, the Cavaliers expressed 'a conservative outlook', a vision of 'the good life', 'classical recollections, love of a very English way of life', the ideals of cherished 'friendship', and love of 'small groups': concerns or accents which *together* could only belong to the life of an upper class.[38] The values of love and honor also had a place in the same spectrum, and Lovelace's 'To Althea, going to the Wars' is 'the supreme document of the Cavalier spirit in its presentation of the aristocratic dilemma between love and honor'.[39]

It is seldom we get a short poem, like Shakespeare's sonnet 94 ('They that have pow'r to hurt'), which packs so much allusiveness into a few lines as to allow for an outright class interpretation. Empson's discussion of the sonnet manages just this, while certainly not shutting out other possibilities. There is about the young man, the poem's addressee, the aura of the aristocrat or brilliant *arriviste,* who disposes both of the power of beauty and of something (political?) more devastating. Oddly and sugestively the sonnet involves Elizabethan 'feelings about the Machiavellian, the wicked plotter who is exciting and civilized and in some way right about life'.[40] Words such as 'graces', 'riches', 'lords and owners', and 'flower' all go to help make for the 'class-centered praise' in the sonnet, only to be foiled by the last four lines, which are all shadow and warning ('But if that flower with base infection meet'). So it is fair to conclude that the sonnet's 'clash of admiration and contempt seems dependent on a clash of feeling about the classes'.[41]

The word 'milieu' in critical usage may be general or specific. Elizabethan London was a place and a milieu but it was also divisible into a variety of milieux: for example, the Elizabethan underworld; the world of the London money market, made up of big money-lending combines, lesser lenders, and loan sharks;[42] Cheapside and its more specialized areas, such as Goldsmith's Row lying on the south side between Bread and Friday streets; the great-house locality along the Strand; the Inns of Court or even, more specifically, the milieu of the most fashionable of the Inns, Gray's Inn, which attracted the largest number of young aristocrats and men from the richest of the gentry. Again, regional and generational considerations encourage us to distinguish still other milieux within the Inns, for members here tended, as at university colleges, 'to cluster at one Inn or another on the basis of geographical region'.[43] And it is clear that the old Benchers, Readers, and barristers of the Inns had interests and ties of friendship different from those of the many rich, first-year members who had no serious intention of ever studying law. For the latter the Inns were little more than social clubs and the best place in London for rooms, meals, and contacts. Of course they shared certain social, moral, and political attitudes with the older and more earnest professionals, so that in this respect all belonged to the same milieu. But young 'gallants' — e.g., Davies's audience for his *Gulling Sonnets* — were also the makers of another milieu within the larger ambit of the Inns.

The specific distinctions made above do not invalidate the more general uses of the word 'milieu'. Some lines of inquiry require a specific grasp of milieux, while others call for something less focused. To each question or relationship is due its own degree of generality or specificity.

The more we study references to 'milieu' in literary scholarship, the more we see that education, mode of income, and the ideals or attitudes of group or class are likely to be implied. In themselves these are often too blunt or unprocessed for the elucidation of certain insights, and therefore the notion of a more homogenized milieu is likely to be preferred. Homogenization turns milieux into *forms of consciousness* — dissolves them into values, interests, and attitudes.

Fashion may be as much the property of a period, of a more circumscribing mood (though this too must have its hidden causes), as of a place and group. Among the literati of the Inns in the 1570s, 'one had to pretend to be lovesick.' Peers egged one on. By the 1590s, however, 'not only had styles changed but the prevailing attitude at the Inns, among the wits at least, was one of ridicule toward those who made love by "force of teares and seeming languishment".'[44] A taste for erotic verse has also been associated with the Inns — and with a certain aristocratic milieu — in the 1590s. 'Here, as in the Universities, the informal activities of clever young men in an extremely orthodox setting led to an exploration of Ovidian eroticism and wit which must have had an aura of piquant anti-authoritarianism about it.'[45] John Hoskins, a true Inns man and friend to Donne, openly declared that even rhetorical conceits and verbal felicities went by fashion. He had groups and milieux clearly in mind, while at the same time recognizing the leading influence of the Court and of the 'great personage' type.[46] The allusion to the anti-authoritarianism of the young men of the Inns strikes an even more convincing chord when we see such 'piquancy' in the context of the escalating political corruption of the 1590s, the frenzied building of 'prodigy houses', and the awareness that the old Queen's coming dotage or death would soon turn the Court into a fierce scramble for power. Essex and Raleigh were to be only the most sensational victims. So why should not young men thumb their noses and boldly flirt with erotic fare? No doubt the Court itself had lovers of erotic verse.

Apart from the Inns, three other milieux, seen as shapers of literary activity, have drawn much attention from scholars: the Court, London, and the town—country circuit of the Cavaliers. Only occasionally, as in the glancing reference above, is the university setting looked upon as a milieu for poetry.

The leading Cavaliers — Carew, Lovelace, Suckling — had close contacts with the Caroline Court and with the big country-house circuit. Attempts to approach their verse by way of these milieux usually depend upon a tacit concern with coterie readers or addressees, as well as suppositions about the needs and fashions of the Caroline Court. Other contemporaries, like the poets Waller, Cotton, King, Cartwright, and Randolph orbited around the edges of the Court and were on close terms with a variety of great noblemen. In the 1640s Cotton and some lesser literati seem occasionally to have met in the Fleece Tavern, beside Covent Garden. And there are hints in the literary scholarship suggesting that these differences of milieux went to make for differences in the verse product, but the details have yet to be worked out. When verse was composed for or near the Court, the lines of influence were likely to be more exposed, as in this observation: 'Remote from the people and from political realities, the court [of Charles I] fostered a coterie atmosphere, a certain frivolity; as political disaster approached, the poets spent their time imploring Amarantha to unravel her hair.'[47] The analysis here turns entirely upon the idea of escapism, but we have seen (p. 32) that in some of her incarnations Amarantha could also provide a cohesive group ideal.

Using the larger London scene as a framework for understanding poetry has been done most often in connection with verse satire and 'city comedy'. Why this should be so speaks for itself. City comedy deals with urban character types and urban wiles in the language of the city; and formal verse satire is an educated taste, the polished aspects of which had been taken largely from Juvenal, Persius, and Horace. Moreover, like comedy, satiric poetry lives off the congress of vice, cozenage, and folly in the city, while also addressing itself mainly to urban readers and auditors.[48]

Milieu's effects on the literary imagination may also be ascertained in the ties between worldly ambitions at Court and the poetic theme of retirement, retreat, or *otium*. Like pastoral, this theme must be taken first as courtly just because the Court, as the very ground of worldliness, makes its worldlings long for the opposite, for some kind of rest or respite.[49] This longing is then idealized or mythified in poetry.

Certain aspects of the Cavalier phenomenon reveal that critics sometimes unite milieu and reading audience. Thus, the amatory verse of the Cavaliers occasionally expresses 'the courtly and "platonic" sentiments fashionable among the French-born Queen Henrietta Maria and her ladies'.[50] Here audience and milieu seem to be one. Some of their love verse, however, also gives voice to 'the earthy and ribald outlook of the young courtier, university wit, and man of the world'.[51] With this voice they are manifestly in different company, amongst close companions but different readers.

Stepping back to the 1590s, I find another clear example of the merging of milieu and reading audience. A student of Elizabethan professional writers has noted that there was a foppish, fashionable, fickle reading type, like the Earl of Southampton, who made 'a mockery of Castiglione's manual' (*The Courtier*) and thirsted for novelty, such as 'the decadent eroticism of *Venus and Adonis* and *Lucrece*'.[52] At least as to literary matters, the Earl frequented a certain milieu; or, more likely, the Earl was himself frequented, hereby being the center of a certain milieu, which at the same time included the readers in it. Richard Niccols, a contemporary, said of the Earl's type of reader that they disdained the 'verses upon which the vulgar in a Stationers shop hath once breathed as a peece of infection', for in their 'fine fingers no papers are holesome, but such, as passe by private manuscription'.[53]

The uses of 'milieu' in scholarship show a tendency for the meaning of the word to include reading audiences, group values, class attitudes, the immediate pressures of the setting, or other distinguishable elements.

POLITICS, PERIOD, HISTORICAL CHANGE

If politics touches poetry in 'political poetry' alone, the relationship is not worth examining here because it raises no difficult questions of method. In the political analysis of political verse, poem and world are set face to face, slotted into the same order of reality, and the job of the historian turns into little more than providing some factual information and a straight gloss on matters lying strictly within the stipulated political perimeters. There will naturally be questions of tone and irony, of intention and obscurity, but the answers will not depend upon the devious, allusive, or social mode of the analysis. For the political poem belongs, by definition, to the political arena and therefore reading it will be like reading a political document, even if one unusual in its composition and subtlety.

A well known study of Marvell has been carried out in accordance with this nose-to-nose view of politics and poetry.[54] 'An Horatian Ode upon Cromwell's Return from Ireland' is taken to be a complex political document and is read as prose. But the politics of Marvell's 'Upon Appleton House' goes entirely unacknowledged because this is not explicitly a political poem. It is a peculiar view of politics which finds the political dimensions of social life only in whatever is declaredly political.

Generally speaking, literary scholarship recognizes the wider scope of politics and is not timid about picking up political echoes in non-political poetry. Readers and poets in Tudor and Stuart England were sensitive to the political strain in literature: to the fact that influences radiated out of the great focus of power, the Court, to bear upon the entire human landscape.[55] They also knew that political power, religion, and society were so closely bound that to touch one was at the same time to touch the others. The period offers enough examples of poets who ran into trouble with the authorities, or who suppressed work, because allegorical readings — i.e., modes of devious social analysis — seemed to uncover political maskings. If we regard verse in the light of these considerations, then much praise by poets was indisputably political. In the social structure of Elizabethan and Jacobean England, any manner of flattering verse addressed to a nobleman was also — whatever the tradition of poetry — a statement of political faith, because it was tribute paid to (hence acceptance of) his place by birth in the political hierarchy. All the great eulogists — Spenser, Donne, Jonson, Dryden — were profoundly conservative in their politics.

If approached purely as political documentation, candid political verse cannot make for interpretative problems of the sort which lie at the heart of this study. Such problems must be for the politics of non-political poetry, whatever its subject-matter, even amatory and religious.

The political worries of the 1590s and early years of the seventeenth century, and the great crisis of the 1640s, were such as to affect even those aspects of life that are apparently non-political. The bright, observant, tattling Inns of Court — drawing heavily from among the best-educated, richest, and most esteemed families in the land — constituted the milieu most sensitive to the political humors of the 1590s and following. This sensitivity, we have seen, bequeathed a partial record of itself in the angry, biting, clever, or rambunctious verse satire of those years, nearly all of it penned by Inns men. It is a voice sprung from a new spirit, a new viewpoint. The same viewpoint — critical and scoffing — animates the new, anti-courtly love verse (including parodies) seen in Shakespeare, Donne, Raleigh, Davies, Jonson, and others. But though we are referring to a line of amatory verse, its shaping vision — since our progression in this chapter is from world to poem — did not begin in and with love. It came from the world around. If in the 1570s all Inns poets were love-sick, or affected to be so, and if twenty years later most of them were able to deride the conventions of courtly, Petrarchan love, then the change was a change in fashion and attitude, the causes of which had nothing at all to do with love *per se*. This shift to a critical mood drew indirect nourishment from the 1590s change in the temper at Court and in government, where the new scale of bribery and corruption went to provoke gossip, resentment, sneers, and anxiety.

Much of the strategy in one of the more sustained of recent studies, E. Miner's *The Metaphysical Mode from Donne to Cowley,* is in casting the passionate private voice of Donne's amatory and other verse against the unprincipled worldliness of the gaudy Court. Private love is a reaction against, a foil for, the Court — which is public, political, and corrupt: 'the private poetry of the Metaphysicals . . . is an alternative to public lives and represents a recoiling from public concerns either in revulsion or in times of failure in the world.'[56]

The psychological bent of these remarks is obvious. As the troubles of the political or public world expand, pushing in against more and more of life, the individual withdraws, to find some compensating standard, a sustaining alternative, in inner resources. Here is ample leeway for individual variation. All the same, an oscillating process is taken for granted: tensions rise and fall, troubles expand and contract, and those who are most in touch with public matters (the upper-class groups and especially their readers and writers) respond accordingly. The ups and downs make contact with life in all its moral essentials, including attitudes towards love, religion, and self-identities.

'The temper of Milton's time [the Civil War period] was attuned to politics; and politics, moreover, spelt out loudly.'[57] In this climate certain religious poets, unlike Milton, withdrew: thus 'Vaughan's retreat into the childhood garden and away from the world of miser, spendthrift, courtier, and statesman. There is [also] the golden garden of Traherne with its visionary fulfillment of promises lost to time.' The two 'in their retreat have in mind the victory of the Cromwellian revolution'.[58] A similar movement of feeling takes hold of Marvell. Some of his poems, and best of all his 'Horatian Ode', achieve a certain balance, but 'many of his other poems . . . have a strong tinge of escape; they seem the poetry of a man deeply disturbed by the chaos and horrors around him, who has managed, for a time, to construct a world of the imagination to keep out the conflict.'[59]

The brevity of these pages on politics is accounted for by the fact that most readings of political verse tend to turn the poetic text into a prose document. Where this is so, poetry is brushed aside and the critic eludes all true problems of method. It is the search for politics in non-political verse that poses the great challenge, and this hurdle requires all our analytical strategies.

So far as criticism and scholarship acknowledge historical periods and periodization, something of the general aims of social analysis appears in all approaches to the study of literature. If undertaken seriously, to trace major shifts in literary style, outlook, output, or content cannot be done by keeping strictly to literature or to the literary tradition, as then it becomes impossible to account convincingly for the breaks and changes that set one period off from another. History holds nothing in airtight compartments. To produce an adequate description of significant literary change, the student must allude to causes, however fleetingly, and here at once he is forced to look outside literature — to reading publics, changing tastes, politics, social and economic transformations, or something else.

Much of the admired tension in the best (troubled?) Elizabethan and Jacobean poetry may in fact express the 'highly precarious' settlement between two great upheavals — before, the Reformation and its consequences; after, the Civil War. In the interim, drawn by Puritan fanatics on the one side and fanatical Roman Catholics on the other, English society was harried by tensions which 'only just held. And this is exactly the quality of the age's poetry. . . . Chaos is very near; its nearness, but its avoidance, gives the poetry its force.'[60] A long-term religious and political struggle worked its way through the moral life of the society and poetry was far from remaining immune to the ensuing effects. This view of the period is not so narrow as to exclude other approaches, such as giving a primary stress to the vitality of the age, to commercial and colonial expansion, to the transition from feudalism to a new society, or to London as the heart of England's dynamic forces.

In Marlowe's verse drama, critics have found all the contours of 'unrestrained individualism', 'rapacity', and 'ruthless self-seeking' — namely, the psychology alleged to characterize a certain stage in England's economic development, the Age of 'Primary [Capital] Accumulation'.[61] Marlowe and other Elizabethans may also be seen in terms of the bounding energies of an age of expansion, though without any claim that this was part of a developmental stage in the economy.[62] The 'new economy' seems to have called for poetry to 'pay its way'. Poets hold increasingly that 'poetry is useful, that it is a vocation', and hence 'Sonnet after sonnet declares that in exchange for his bounty the patron stands to gain something of more value and permanence than an elaborate tomb.'[63] Here both poetic content and a vision of poetry are linked to the economic character of the age.

The most respected but questionable line of historical argument picks out the decline of medieval thought and the rise of 'the new empirical philosophy' — modern science: 'This flux of values is invoked to explain the quality of the [Metaphysical] verse, its uncertainty of tone and direction, its habitual juxtaposition of old and new, its restlessness, its propensity to fierce and almost outlandish argument.'[64] The attempt to angle explanations of literary change toward a pure history-of-ideas approach is deficient if it stops there, for we are asked to believe that Elizabethan and Jacobean poets experienced abstract methods and findings more pointedly than immediate, worldly matters. Donne was perfectly aware of the new cosmology and while he invoked it to sharpen and heighten his verse, he had no sympathy for it. His poetry was animated by love profane and divine, as well as by the needs and fears connected with his career, not by Copernicus or Galileo.

A well defined period is unlikely to be static, save in the mind of the historian. To renew itself, to retain its distinctive characteristics, a period must generate these more or less continuously; and while this may entail no obvious change, neither can it move from anything lifeless. This is to say that the characteristics of a period are made and maintained by its vitality. When we relate a period to its poetry, we look for the characteristics of the period in the poetry, however reconstituted or turned-about these may be. Literary scholarship often observes this procedure when dealing, for example, with the Restoration and its literature, as in the structure of the following argument:

The Crown returns in triumph, bringing moderation and civil order; the nation can relax; dissenting, unruly religion is disgraced and persecuted; all the ruling groups will soon be constitutionally involved in the political process; sustained political debate surfaces; articulate London and the Court itself desire spirited public entertainment; literature, therefore, unfolds in a public forum; and poets — most of whom are staunch royalists — now openly enter the political lists. The Cavalier poetry of retirement is rendered *passé*, 'as poets came alive to their more active role in national life'.[65] Great poetry becomes public poetry by definition, the 'poetry of public themes', and is meant for the stage, for male gatherings, for the Court, and for fashionable circles. It is John Dryden's poetry: engaged, superior, elegantly easy, rational, and brilliantly mocking, with the heroic couplet as the urbane instrument of its asseverating or punishing wit. Period, milieu, and reading public are here joined; the different parts of the social world are sewn together.

4

Reconsiderations

I propose to reconsider certain claims and strategies, in order further to clarify the procedures of social literary analysis.

We have seen that Renaissance poetry was often a form of true action, belonging to the world fully as much, say, as did Sir Walter Raleigh's political views or the way in which London financiers cast their accounts. Shakespeare's *Sonnets* are a poetry of patronage and love, the chronicle of a passionate human triangle, and a remarkable self-inquiry by a man who was ready at times to stack his 'art' up against anything in the world. He had come to know his value through patronage, through the reception given his poems and plays, and through the labor of self-examination inscribed in the sonnets. Seen in this light, the sonnets become a mode of analysis, of communication, and of inducement to action: acts enveloped by social realities, and difficult to sort out from them.

Being actions, poems could point *naturally* to other matters in the Tudor and Stuart worlds, and no texts do this more openly than political or 'locodescriptive' poems. The latter were much favored in the seventeenth century, making for a list headed by Jonson's 'To Penshurst', Carew's 'To Saxham', Denham's 'Coopers Hill', and Marvell's 'Upon Appleton House'. On the surface or literal level — though one strain of current theory, 'deconstruction', questions the whole notion of literalness — a poem of this sort is almost wholly one of direct reference; it purports to be a trustworthy description of a house, a scene, or a particular view. But this is at once denied by the poem's innuendoes, allusions, fleeting observations, and parade of rhetorical devices. The true aim, apart from pleasing, is to convey social, moral, or political ideas and feelings.

Verse satire is another form which grasps directly at the world by relying on direct reference, occasionally even in the midst of obliquity, as when satire is poured into the pastoral mode. The epigrams and satires of the years around 1600 provide pejorative descriptions of courtiers, monopolists, fops, Puritans, moneylenders, and love poets. Michael Drayton's sonnet,

> How many paltry, foolish, painted things
> That now in coaches trouble every street,

makes an angry stab at London fashion and ostentation. And his long satire, *The Owl* (1604), is 'an assessment of things as they stood in the last year of Elizabeth's and the first of James' reign. . . . The immense popularity of this poem in the early seventeenth century is owing to its reception as a *roman à clef,* by which news-hungry Englishmen might read gossip about the great.'[1]

Verse exchanges or replies made for an unexpected form of direct reference. The reply constituted a contemporary gloss on the principal poem, though the gloss in verse might end in a refutation of the original argument. Marlowe's 'Come live with me and be my love' drew a cold-eyed riposte from Sir Walter Raleigh, 'If all the world and love were young', which rejects Marlowe's posturing, pastoral innocence. The late 1590s saw the circulation of satiric verse epigrams, many of which elicited replies, particularly the sort aimed against prominent personalities, such as Robert Cecil and Raleigh.[2] Towards the end of the Civil War, Richard Lovelace's royalist 'To Althea, From Prison', which includes the well known lines, 'Stone Walls doe not a Prison make, / Nor I'ron bars a Cage', provoked an anonymous verse reply. The rivalry in this exchange was nakedly political: the reply was an anti-royalist parody of the original.

Reliance upon direct reference can only take us so far, for puzzles spring forth as soon as the poem employs any type of indirect reference or obscure liaison. Yet much of the territory of the poem in late Tudor and Stuart England is just here, in a landscape of obliquity. So must it also be for the historians of this poetry. And though large stretches of timely allusion are doubtless lost to us forever, we need not recover all covert or slanting references to be able to read history with the help of poems. Hidden references constitute only one of poetry's many ties with its historical world.

To leave the order of direct reference, because it offers us no help or is missing in a poem, and to glide over to the play of ideas is simple enough when the poem's ideas broach social phenomena. If a poem praises kingship, aristocracy, gentlemanly rural retirement, the rule of the few over the many, the bonds between old wealth and good custom, or the links between civil and heavenly hierarchies; or if it heaps scorn on upstarts, outspoken women, and the vulgar multitude, then the text proper makes a declaration of its ties with the world. But many ideas cannot serve as bridges from poem to world; they show no manifest ties with the impinging society. So far as certain topics, such as love and mortality, have a universal appeal, they cut across time and place. But insofar as they are strongly characteristic of an age, we must be on the lookout for the particulars that made them attractive then. This means — the point cannot be enough emphasized — that we should focus on matters of treatment: on the ways in which ideas and themes are handled in poems.

The eternizing topos enters naturally into the world of the aristocrat and political magnate, where the theme of you-shall-live-in-my-verse-forever belongs distinctly to the patron—client relationship. Such promises of glory are payment *in spirit* for material favors received. The theme issues from a deferential stance proper to an aristocratic society, with its compelling emphasis on the values of personal service. But in the conventions of those times, to confer immortality through art — adulation aside — was a poet's greatest service. Therefore, in love poetry, where the language and imagery of service was already rife, the poet easily and naturally transferred the promise of eternity to his beloved. Drayton, Raleigh, Daniel, and other poets went further: they used the themes of love, as well as those of service and immortality, to exalt their aristocratic patronesses and to elicit still more favors from them.

In the late sixteenth century — love of God apart — the theme of love in poetry is most likely to be courtly love or its parody; and it has been established, by the conclusive testimony of poets and their contemporaries, that it was closely associated with upper-class groups and people at Court.[3] Parodies of the courtly or Petrarchan idiom were also fare for a cultivated taste, since all the parodic meaning was lost to anyone unfamiliar with the conventions of courtly love.[4] The idiom reached England through the Continent's courtly milieux and was heavily marked by decorum, conventions, and aureation: qualities that made for delicacy and elevated feeling, while also answering to the expectations of a ceremonial, courtly society, where 'the code of love actually existed as a code of manners.'[5]

I have had to go around the love theme, to its treatment and background, to find a strategy which would enable me to relate it to its social circumstances. Much the same would be true of any effort to provide a social context for the poetic themes of lust, religious ardor, destructive time, the Golden Age, longing for England's past, and the theme of upstart versus ancient house. This sequence, indeed, already suggests possible links among the last four items, for in the late sixteenth and early seventeenth centuries, the speed of social change in England touched off a distinct nostalgia in poets and readers. In this scatter of feeling, I suspect that the Golden Age, England's past, and the theme of the illustrious old house served as fantasized foils for the effects of unnerving social change and for the image of the despised parvenu. The larger thematic ground was nicely provided by 'destructive time', the poetic apparition (arguably) of profound historical change.

DICTION AND IMAGERY

To study diction as a way of getting at the society of the poem requires that we bear in mind the history of the language, especially in a time — as in the Tudor and early Stuart periods — of its tremendous expansion. Astonishing energy seemed the order of the day: great social mobility; a dizzy velocity of land transfer, involving the vast quondam estates of the old Church; the swift rise of an aggressive clerical elite, dedicated to win the nation over to Calvinism; the rise of many new schools, making for unprecedented levels of literacy by the 1590s; overseas expansion keyed to the building up of a bigger fleet; and revolutionary changes in agriculture that would go to make the land more productive, farming more efficient, and agrarian social relations more exploitative. England gave rise to a more probing mentality, a more combative strain, a new political consciousness at the Inns of Court; while London topped all other English towns as the uncontested center of trade, shipping, finance, government, litigation, the book industry, and poetry.

   A surge of energies was one of the necessary conditions for the linguistic exuberance of the age. The widening scope of experience required new words, new rhythms, new phrases, new coinings of image and metaphor. This bond between language and historical change catches our attention, as we look for the ways in which scholarship relates the words of poetry to its social universe. For critical practice shows that by drawing on associations and ambiguities, the language of poetry reaches out to engage the world outside the poem.

Touching on the linguistic character of the age, M. C. Bradbrook notes that 'many words which to us are quite familiar would have jumped out at an Elizabethan as new and startling. The whole language was expanding at a prodigious rate and Shakespeare not only coined, but borrowed, adapted and wrested words to suit his own masterful will.'[6] Period and poet are here joined together in the vitality of the language, but convergence also follows from the pervasive effects of the overseas discoveries and the commercial revolution. In 'the sudden expansion given to imagination by the increased material wealth and the physical discoveries of the age, they [poets] shower on their kings barbaric pearl and gold or exploit for them the new resources of European luxury. . . . all names of far-off places imply mystery and therefore an attractive quality, and may be used to convey an idea of great but indefinable physical beauty or of invincible strength.' Having Christopher Marlowe in mind, Elizabeth Holmes focuses her analysis and provides particulars: 'though Marlowe disdains from the first the "lily", "rose", and "coral" of conventional metaphor, yet "gold", "silver", "ivory", "crystal", "amber", and "spices" are terms of wealth and splendour which have a more adventurous appeal.'[7] The penumbra of power and vast spaces in Marlowe's plays arises from the quality of his language.

The first seventeen of Shakespeare's *Sonnets* urge the young nobleman of the series to marry. On the basis of a lexical analysis, Giorgio Melchiori shows that these sonnets feature a vocabulary of economic pursuit, in such words — or their derivations — as contract, usury, lend, use, profit, thrift, sum, and spend. They transfer over to the economic realm the biblical call to procreate and multiply in marriage. Shakespeare's language thus betrays 'a precise awareness of the new economic mechanisms associated with the birth of modern capitalism'. Seeing marriage in economic terms, his call-to-marry sonnets accord with the views of the utilitarian 'bourgeoisie, which raises the values of industry and productive work against those of the hereditary nobility'.[8] But Shakespeare's lexical bent here need not be seen as unique or surprising, for in responding to the economic strains and changes of the sixteenth century, the nobility also increasingly turned marriage into an economic transaction.

Raymond Southall has observed that the socio-economic changes of the early sixteenth century strained the courtly—chivalrous diction and affected love poetry.[9] The strain is apparent first in Thomas Wyatt, who sensed 'the decay of habitual modes of life' and whose verse is 'pervaded by feelings of nostalgia at the sacrifice of old conventions'. In his time, 'capitalism had not yet transubstantiated the language of human relations', but the old feudal norms of service and duty, undermined by 'the increasing omnipotence of money', gradually came to be replaced by 'new norms and new idioms', particularly 'those of buying and selling'.[10] Feudal and economic terms — fee, in fee, a purchase, mortgage, price — all changed, or were changing, in meaning. Elizabethan poets continue to 'cast their lovers variously in the roles of servant, vassal and thrall, roles common amongst the lovers of Elizabethan anthologies. But these are already poetic extravagancies and old-world gallantries.' From about mid century onwards, but especially so in Sir Philip Sidney (1580s), beauty and worth are more and more related to riches, treasures, precious stones, and the like, evidently because for him, as for other poets, 'love gave rise to dreams of unaccountable riches. . . . The establishment of the lady as an expensive luxury is the effect of a large body of Elizabethan poetry.'[11] Caught up in the genre 'most intimately concerned with the relation of person to person', the imagination of the love poet, in its quest for an appropriate vocabulary, drew sustenance from the excitements and stresses of the time: the lure of distant riches, privateering, ostentation, menacing inflation, and the power of upstart money. In evidence Southall cites Lyly, Drummond, Lodge, Greene, Spenser, Dyer, Marston, and Donne. Most suggestive is the example from Dyer's 'Coridon to his Phyllis', where Coridon refers to his lady as 'the golden fetter of my mind'. She is turned into gold but the lover's mind itself borders on the alchemical change.

A. C. Partridge calls attention to a cluster of verbs in Spenser's *Epithalamion,* where birds '*caroll, sing, reply, descant, shrill, warble,* and *agree with sweet consent*'. These terms were 'taken from part-song, madrigal and psalmody, in which the educated Elizabethan gentry excelled'.[12] And the connecting social line here is: diction➝ musical training➝ gentry. Again, in the language of Jacobean and Caroline masques, we find that all the nomenclature of the heavens — firmament, stars, sun, moon, heavenly light — is conventionally applied to the king, queen, courtiers, and court ladies.[13] Such usage pins the texts to a milieu and a specific audience, whose members in part were also actors in the masques.

The astounding degree of wordplay in English Renaissance poetry, chiefly in the form of punning and near punning, is another sign of the age's linguistic vivacity. Wordplay was, however, considered townish, urban — a mark of the quickness and acerbity of the city, hence unfit for pastoral poetry. Here was the world imposing its social demands. In and around London, as in the university towns, the love of punning among the literate was widespread and often bookish, as is clear from the Latinate quibbles in Francis Thynne's epigram, 'A Puritane' (1600):

> Dame Lais is a puritan by religion
> Impure in her deedes, though puer in her talk,
> And therefore a puritane by condition,
> or pluritane, which after manie doth walke;
> for pruritie of wemenn, by lecherous direction,
> seeks pluritie of men to work satisfaction.[14]

Shakespeare also indulged in Latinate punning. In *As You Like It* (III, iii, 7—9), Touchstone says to the goatherd, Audrey: 'I am here with thee and thy goats as the most *capricious* poet, honest Ovid, was among the Goths.' Goats and Goths are playfully likened by their sound.

Puns may both reveal and conceal their duplicity. Those who have reason to know — whether by education, familiarity, or quickness — understand the quibble; the others cannot, though the wordplay may be at their expense. Because puns are aimed at particular audiences, a poetry rich in puns necessarily tells us something about the poet's intended readers. The Latinate pun — *puer, puritane (putane), capricious* — could only appeal to an educated audience: the men who had been trained in Latin at the better schools, not generally their wives or sisters. Thus the educational background of the poet, an aspect of his diction (wordplay), and the taste or skills of a reading audience are all strung together here: poem and world are joined.

One of the richest men in London, Shakespeare's patron, the Earl of Southampton, considered *Love's Labour's Lost* 'their' play, as if it had been intended for the Earl's coterie. True or not, the play is a bravura commentary on linguistic fashions in the 1590s and 'has enough private jests to show that it was aimed at a small circle'.[15] Not surprisingly, of all the plays in the Shakespearean canon, this one has the largest number of puns — over two hundred, whereas the average for Shakespeare is 78 per play.[16] *Love's Labour's Lost* singles out intelligence and social rank by the power of a character's control over words. It distinguishes the 'simpletons' from the 'sophisticated wits' by their wordplay, 'the clowns from the courtiers by one group's linguistic abuses and the punning virtuosity of the other'.[17]

Knowing that there were different audiences and levels of wordplay, we
can more readily follow the scholarship which tells us that Shakespeare
used a different, more private and secret language in his sonnets from that
used in his plays. For some critics, the sonnets are pervaded by 'a certain
deliberately chosen hermeticism or hieroglyphicalness', as though
Shakespeare 'were trying to ensure that no reader should be able to discover
from them the identity of the person addressed'.[18] And confirmation of this
may be inferred from the ingenuity which has been spent in deciphering
them.[19] Circulating privately for years before their publication, they were
meant for few eyes, even if they went beyond and got into copybooks. As in
verse letters, poets wrote at times with only a single reader in mind —
never, however, with so much personal idiosyncrasy as to make for a
mysterious language, although Thomas Nashe wrote 'for the Earl of
Southampton a poem of such erotic crudity that it had to be copied out in
cypher (*The Choice of Valentine's or Nashe's Dildo*)'.[20]

Looking back after the Restoration to the Elizabethan and Jacobean verse
dramatists, Dryden observed:

> They, who have best succeeded on the Stage,
> Have still conform'd their Genius to their Age.
> Thus Jonson did Mechanique humour show,
> When men were dull, and conversation low.

And again:

> Our Ladies and our men now speak mor wit
> In conversation, than those poets writ.[21]

He is talking mainly about their language, attitudes, and obscure social
backgrounds, as we know well from his many statements on the subject. He
and 'Congreve . . . modelled their writing on the conversation of Lord
Rochester',[22] the most worldly spirit of the post-Restoration period. In
F. W. Bateson's description, theirs was 'A new language . . . in process of
creation, and this language, as we can now see, was the mouthpiece of the
"squirearchy", the new dominant group that achieved its maximum
consciousness, its ideal self-projection, in the poetry of Dryden, Swift and
Pope.'[23]

Background and education entered (and enter) into poets' ways with
words. J. R. Mulder has underlined the grammatical and rhetorical content
of education for boys between the ages of eight and fifteen,[24] education for

those born into the gentry and aspiring middle-class groups. Schooled in Latin, in the tracking of word derivations and the fine distinctions among synonyms, Renaissance poets and their readers developed a taste for etymological quibbles. Since the program of classical education took for granted that poetry belonged to the art of rhetoric, so to public discourse of some kind, 'It followed that in his choice of diction he [the poet] put the emphasis on the conceptual core of the word, that is, on the known meaning(s) that he could share with his audience.'[25] Consequently, the more cryptic idiom of Shakespeare's *Sonnets* is a relative matter — an idiom achieved by means of studied ambiguities, anagrams, obscure quibbles, and higher levels of generality. When we compare his sonnets with Michael Drayton's, we find that Shakespeare's descriptive language omits all the particularities for catching the ordinary sights and sounds of the streets, whereas Drayton's language has more simplicity and tilts closer to a workaday realism. This is not to say that Drayton holds more substance for the historian. Rather, it is to say that the social analysis of Shakespeare's sonnets requires more strategies and more negotiation. But in comparing Shakespeare with Drayton, I do not mean to suggest that all Renaissance poets lend themselves equally well to the analysis of diction. Some prior discrimination is called for. Donne, for instance, is better studied from this standpoint than Samuel Daniel, whose diction tends to be bland and generalized.

Since the abrupt shift from literal designation to metaphor is chronic in poetic diction, as when the words for heavenly bodies are applied to princes or to the beloved of lyric verse, we now turn to this aspect of verbal play.

   The bookish quality of Elizabethan and seventeenth-century conceit has often been noted.[26] Donne's friend, John Hoskins, alleged a tie between changing fashions in London and the use of metaphor among the educated. The ties among metaphor, reading public, taste, and different social groups have also attracted attention. It is not only, for example, that the 'scientific image' appealed most to the educated men of the upper classes,[27] that Inns-of-Court men might be more titillated by a sonnet built on legal conceits, or that the erotic imagery of Ovidian narrative verse was thought especially right for the palates of jaded aristocrats, but also that certain classes of metaphor might have more appeal for some groups than for others. In drawing distinctions between 'sunken' and 'violent' metaphor, the one subtle (e.g., 'Ripeness is all') and the other sensational, H. W. Wells observed that the first would appeal to more sophisticated minds, the other to a more popular taste. He also considered the 'radical' or Metaphysical image 'too intricate to be popular'. In effect, he was sorting out an elite of readers, and at moments even 'a handful of aristocratic Elizabethans', from the larger body of untutored readers and playgoers.[28]

Scholars have looked for links between the nature of a poet's images and his social background or life experience. This strategy sees poetry's contact with the world as an aspect of biography or even of 'psycho-history'. Having done a study of Shakespeare's sea images, Caroline Spurgeon concluded 'that he had little, if any, direct experience of being on the sea, and that his knowledge of the sea and ships might well have been gained from books (Hakluyt, Strachey, and others), from talk and from living in a great seaport'.[29] In a more psychological vein, she surmised that the frequency of the images of 'purchase' and 'value' in *Cymbeline* may reveal a personal preoccupation at the time of writing, just as the images of building, construction, and planning in *Henry IV,* Part II, are perhaps 'connected with some personal experience, when we remember that Shakespeare was occupied in buying New Place in 1597, the same year in which he probably wrote' this play.[30] E. A. Armstrong found that the image of the kite in Shakespeare is associated with death and with sheets, most likely because of the poet's having been witness to a deathbed scene.[31] London in Shakespeare's day had many kites, a scavenger bird presumably often seen by the poet and associated in his mind with cowardice, meanness, and cruelty. But the biographical route to imagery's contact with the world usually associates a poet's images with more obvious things in his experience: with Marlowe's bookishness, George Chapman's war experiences, Dekker's 'first-hand knowledge of the daily work in a shoemaker's shop',[32] or — as in his specialized imagery of building — with Ben Jonson's 'apprenticeship to his stepfather's trade of bricklaying'.[33]

Studies occasionally pick out particular images as cyphers for upper-class birth: for instance, the image of the hunter (i.e., courtier, seducer), as in Wyatt's 'Who so list to hount'. In much love verse, 'however wounded and prostrate the lover pretends to be, the imagery of his poems is commonly drawn from upper-class habits of the chase: from hunting ... privateering ... hawking, archery, and birdcatching.'[34] In sonnet 94, 'They that have pow'r to hurt', Shakespeare's 'model [for metaphor] is the garden, which in turn gives an image of aristocracy in the independence and lordliness of the flower'.[35] Here are all images whose associations evoke the specter of social class.

Taken in the context of its times (1620s to 1640s), Herrick's fetishistic dress imagery — where the woman *is* her silks — has been seen as anti-Puritan in stance and tone.[36] This accords fully with Herrick's love of ceremony and rural festivals, also odious to Puritans. In the seventeenth century, 'images of ritual passed all too quickly from the pages of English poetry. . . . Puritanism was a hostile force. The imagery of poetry suffered with that of the churches.'[37] In effect, social groups, like currents of taste, had their preferred range or clusters of images. The Elizabethan sonnet's 'alphabet of love', as contained in its stock of conventional conceits, and especially antitheses and oxymora,[38] should be linked mainly with people in and around the Court, where the ambiguities of the idiom, looping from loftiness to lubricity, were most in touch with real life. Thus Sidney in *Astrophel and Stella* (lii, 13—14):

> Let Vertue have that Stella's selfe; yet thus,
> That Vertue but that body graunt to us.

Mythological imagery, as in John Lyly's plays, was certainly appropriated by the Court whenever Queen Elizabeth was called Diana, Cynthia, Zeus, or Apollo, and her ladies-in-waiting were called nymphs, goddesses, Graces, or Muses. Myth 'had the glamour of the antique, and so complimented the court by putting it in the line of the greatest of great traditions'.[39] Succinctly put, noblemen were gods.[40] But the world of the Court could also be summoned in concrete images — e.g., 'buckles of the purest gold' (Marlowe, 'The Passionate Shepherd', line 16). Harry Levin calls this a 'courtly refinement', evidently because Elizabethan standards of dress would have made this the automatic association in the eyes of the age. Other images again, in presupposing a hierarchical classification of plants and animals, answered to society's vertical organization in matters of status. Thus in Caroline verse the falcon may be princely, bees and ants are 'political', cows may be 'yeomanry', and there is the sovereign oak, the proud cedar, the lowly shrub.[41]

Intensity and intellectuality of figurative language in English poetry peaked during the late sixteenth and early seventeenth centuries, to be succeeded by a line of figured wit that was more lucid, moderate, and controlled: the difference *grosso modo* between Metaphysical and Cavalier, or (more so) between the Metaphysical and Restoration 'modes'. When our distinctions go no further than this in analysis, we are speaking about nothing more than two different periods, two different *literary* mentalities lying along a temporal continuum. But scholars have sought deeper explanations. Just as Donne's imagery betrays an interest in the new world and the new science, so Marlowe's interest in cartography and in vast spaces is unfurled in his grandiose imagery.[42] These are not facts about mere literary mentalities. They touch the excitement of the new discoveries, a vision of distant places and barbaric gold, and the inklings of an acquisitive psychology. Here was an outlook to go with England's leading energies: the push of English Calvinism, a booming population despite plague and famine, remarkable overseas exploits, and the soaring ambitions — 'the aspiring mind' — of the new gentry. In a noun of the time, this was the age of the 'overreacher'. For Marlowe the mainspring of human action was the greed for power, wealth, and knowledge. And again — pursuing our task of relating metaphor to historical period — in an age of discovery, death became 'the undiscovered country', while the art of a rival poet—lover became 'the proud full sail of his great verse / Bound for the prize of all too precious you'.[43]

In this arc of perceptions we discern the traces of a period and an outlook. Scholars tend to concur on the *quality* of the figurative language in the better Elizabethan poets — a quality marked by energy, boldness, expanding terms, hyperbole, and exotic evocations.[44] Having a 'gigantic conception of life', Shakespeare's 'tragic heroes in their imagery repeatedly express the presumptuous desire for the destruction of the whole world'.[45] They are always 'over-staters', much given to hyperbole.[46] Marlowe's characteristic form of hyperbole 'presupposes a state of mind to which all things are possible, for which limitations exist to be overcome'.[47]

If we draw these gleanings into a larger framework, it seems clear that much of the quality of Elizabethan and Jacobean imagery springs from the most vital ground of the age: the speed of change and the experience of transition — that is, experience of the strain imposed by the conflict between traditional but dying values on the one side and triumphing new ones on the other. For one critic, 'the rich procession' of Elizabethan imagery proceeds from 'the sudden expansion given to imagination by the increased wealth and the physical discoveries of the age'.[48] For another, Barabas 'adumbrates the capitalist . . . Marlowe has grasped what is truly imaginative, what in his time was almost heroic, about business enterprise.'

And 'while science, capitalism, imperialism [Faustus, Barabas, Tamburlaine] were at the beginning of their modern development, Marlovian tragedy was able to project the inordinate courses they would pursue, through Marlowe's insight into the wayward individualist and into the life that is lived . . . "without control".'[49] Other students relate the verbal exuberance of the Elizabethans, particularly as seen in metaphor and wordplay, to the magnitude of Elizabethan social mobility and to the fact that a large body of 'traditional thought and imagery still enjoyed the public status of a moral and philosophical language' but was on the brink of collapse.[50] 'English society [*c.* 1600] stood just on the edge of that long slow shift by which monarchical, Catholic, and aristocratic were to yield dominance to parliamentary, Puritan and bourgeois.'[51] More broadly, it was the shift from a rural—feudal society, where service and personal ties still counted, to a possessive market (or early capitalist) society, where worth and even personal identity came more and more to be seen in terms of use, gain, and marketable ends. The shift worked basic changes in the vocabulary and imagery of Elizabethan love poetry.[52] Thus Romeo to Juliet (II, ii, 82—4):

> I am no pilot; yet wert thou as far
> As that vast shore wash't with the farthest sea
> I should adventure for such merchandise.

Here the traditional language of courtly love, shaped by feudal relations (viz., his vassalage to her), is no more, and she is changed into exotic merchandise native to some vastly distant shore. Her worth is slyly converted into a market value, made all the dearer by the hint of the supreme dangers and trials involved in the getting of it.

Strains in the experience of the most articulate classes in English society gave rise to the ferment in Elizabethan figurative language. This squares perfectly with a body of observation on vitality in metaphor and hyperbole, where the suggestion is that metaphorical coinings are a primary vehicle for the expression of tension, anxiety, and a fumbling for new perceptions or new meanings.[53] In this light, a vast landscape of new metaphor, as appears in Elizabethan and Jacobean literature, is likely to signify a profound dissatisfaction with received perceptions.

STYLE

We have noted that 'style' issues from, and goes to make up, a view of the world, an allegiance to a core of values (pp. 37ff.) Let us track this further in the details of illustration.

The 1590s chronicle a break in the development of lyric style and so also, most likely, a shift in its social affiliations. Briefly stated, scholarship holds that the golden style of the English lyric is successfully challenged by a plainer, 'anti-courtly' style, seen in Donne, Raleigh, Jonson. This style has the biting edge and critical eye of the new satire of Marston, Hall, Davies, and Guilpin. It is more colloquial, townish, intellectual, and searching than the golden style; also rougher in its numbers (though regular in Jonson), and so is a better vehicle for the expression of everyday experience.

Critics find two mentalities here, or a transition from one to the other, but their emphases vary. The 'chief exponents [of the plainer style] belonged to the practical world, being soldiers, priests, and men of affairs' — e.g., Sidney (who wrote in both styles), Dyer, Southwell, Davies, and Raleigh. Again, 'The transition in the poetic style of the Elizabethans to that of the Jacobeans and Carolines corresponds to a change in the national spirit and temper.'[54] Often 'sceptical, tentative, self-conscious in its exploration of hidden motives', this period required 'a style that could express the mind . . . in movement' and hence 'a loosening of rhythm, a closer approximation to the diction of common life'.[55] For 'a new mentality was emerging, critical, dramatic, satirical, complex, and uncertain: with it, and part of it, came a new style in poetry to give it expression. This is the true style of the Shakespearean moment.'[56] In other views, the new style is directly connected with the irresistible rise of more austere ideals 'bourgeois' and Puritan.[57] It has vital ties with the Inns of Court and is the voice of dissatisfaction 'with the general decadence (or what was presumed to be decadence) of a court society'.[58] It is the style of honesty, 'the moral style' which stands as a foil to the golden style of the Court, where voices are moved by flattery, deception, and pretense.[59] After 1600, Fulke Greville rejected the golden or rhetorical style as 'harlot's weeds and flowers' and came to hold that 'the plain statement of general truths' is 'the only valid style for poetry in a decadent age'.[60]

Despite their differing emphases, these views have a great deal in common. None sees style as a property sealed off in literature; all, indeed, look through style itself to the world around — to changes in mood, outlook, and the environment for poetry. As J. V. Cunningham asserts a priori, 'a new style, a new meter, is a new attitude, a new form, new subject matter.'[61] One of the best ways to ascertain this is to look for the ties between style and reading audience.

'When Greene, for instance, began to grind out threepenny fare for "Al Yoong Gentlemen, Marchants, citizens, aprentices, yeomen, and plaine cuntrey farmers", he stripped his prose of euphuistic mannerisms, excessive alliteration, rhetorical figures, and allusions to fashionable animal lore.'[62] Jonson and especially Donne have often been considered 'coterie-poets' because they appealed in particular to an elite of connoisseurs. The two wrote 'emphatically for those who knew what was what'. Their 'strong-lined' poetry was 'close-packed and strenuous, requiring some effort and connoisseurship to appreciate it'.[63] Similarly, the 'pared down, plain style and the heavily intellectual, reasoned arguments' of Davies's *Nosce Teipsum* 'could only have been conceived with a scholastically trained audience in mind'.[64]

Public poets — e.g., Waller, Denham, Cowley, Dryden — have a close and special relation to their reading audience because of their function as critics and celebrants; and the link 'leads naturally to a style which will reach the audience in a way with which they will readily identify'. In Cowley's case, this made for 'Clarity, ease, neatness, and plainness' of style, 'characteristics which suit the national or public poet'.[65] Much the same point has been made of Dryden's verse prologues and epilogues: these 'would be impossible without . . . some sort of acceptance [by the audience] of the assumption that the author is an authoritative spokesman for values'. Relatively short, usually meant to stand alone, and spoken on stage by an actor, these poems had to be 'emphatic' and 'obvious' so as to make immediate contact with the audience. 'Dryden's poetic style is basically well equipped to meet these requirements becasue it is characterized by clarity of syntax and because its major rhetorical device is overt analogy or simile.'[66]

The link between style and reading audience is far from simple, for as it involves a core of values shared by poet and audience, the same core is likely to engage other matters as well, such as the poet's social background, particular milieux (city, Court, or university), and his very social identity.

In his book on Donne, Alvarez offers a detailed sketch of the poet's circle of close friends and acquaintances, profiling them in their education and careers. 'Donne's first and most formative audience was made up of the young, literary, [upper] middle-class intellectual elite who, like Donne himself, were to become the leading professional men of the time.'[67] Consequently, his 'style was based on the interests of the most intelligent professional men . . . instead of on the more technical interests of the professional poets'. Donne enables us to see that 'The purest Metaphysical style is the intimate voice of and formulation of the most intelligent class [mostly Inns-of-Court men] at the moment in English literature when even the professional class was creative.'[68] In effect, Alvarez relates the style, tone, and argumentativeness of Donne's verse to the outlook of those who went to school with him, remained his lifelong friends, held most of his values, and had special access to his poems in manuscript. Negotiating the connections between style and social group by accenting the group's intellectuality, he also presents their poetic 'formula': which was 'to begin with a question, usually personal, complex and concerning the emotions, and then to answer it with a considerable show of logic, bolstering the argument with occasional conceits'.[69] Pressing further, we may extend these observations by adding that Donne, Jonson, and the Herberts also had a wider range of vital contacts, for 'the social milieu of the Metaphysical poets was aristocratic in tone, connecting in one direction . . . with the inner circles of the Court, in another with the universities and with the middle and upper ranks of the ecclesiastical, administrative, and legal hierarchies, and in yet another with the prosperous merchant class.'[70] Appropriately, Donne's experience of love took place in 'a setting of cultivated, sophisticated people'. His love poems are as if 'spoken', and the man speaking 'is well-born, highly educated, able (and very ready) to refer casually to a wide range of reading and general intellectual knowledge, including theology, law and science'.[71]

The anti-courtly stance of the plainer style was also projected in the virulent satiric style of the late 1590s. Satire, its authors believed, 'ought to be rough and harsh. Just as its attitudes were the reverse of courtly "seeming", so its versification ought to be the reverse of smooth and elegant. The "satyre" thus personified not only an attitude but also a style.'[72] There was nothing humble or simple, however, in this style, nor was there anything in it for the populace. Satirists cultivated 'obscurity' and disdained 'the profane multitude'. 'Suppressed transitions, intense brevity, rapidly shifting dialogue with undesignated speakers and veiled ambiguous expressions were to become the regular characteristics of Elizabethan verse satire.'[73]

The grand style had its social ground in the supremacy of ceremony, ritual, affectation, and favoritism at Court, where power inflated language as well as interpersonal relations. When combined with the egregious political corruption of the 1590s and Jacobean years, this style — somehow felt to be right in the context of power — set off a reaction in literary circles, leading some men toward a sparer tongue. However, to be historical, to be more than a private gesture, this reaction had to find endorsement in a larger, discontented, nay-saying community: the Inns of Court, the gentry and educated yeomanry, or the most articulate urban groups.

This is the place to sort out an apparent puzzle. If the plain style of around 1600 is anti-courtly, but not anti-royalist, how does it happen that its later manifestation, the elegant Cavalier style, will be associated with the Court and pass over into the conservative style of the Restoration? The answer lies with the radical political shifts and changing social mood of the upper classes in the years between the 1620s and 1640s. The rhetorical virulence of politics and religion, particularly from the late 1620s, repelled literary men in and around the Court. Well-born and fully at home only in fashionable society, Lovelace, Suckling, Carew, Waller, and others pulled away from the intellectualism and learned language of the Metaphysical poets, so as to edge their verse closer to the 'ease' of their more refined reading audiences, which now included larger numbers of women. But in the 1630s and 1640s, the ease and grace of the Cavalier style also made for a retreat from the world of thundering political and social problems — a retreat in manner, mood, and subject-matter. And here all at once, as we have already observed (p. 32), the Cavalier treatment of love may be seen as a toy (frivolous by comparison with the realities of civil tumult) *or* as an affirmative mode, a self-protective posture 'in the face of a lowering night'.[74] The contradiction was in the Cavalier outlook, which could not avoid the crisis of politics, while yet seeking to rise above it.

Edmund Waller, who 'brought poetry into the salon to be guided by rules of etiquette',[75] figures as a key voice in the emergence of the Cavalier style. He worked a change in manner by his use of the 'French closed and rounded couplet', by his 'loftiness' and 'softness' as he sought more harmonies and fewer conflicts of consonants, by having fewer breaks in his lines, and by the repetition of key words:[76] all in all, the achievement of a more 'ceremonial' manner, based also in part on a more Latinate diction. The effects of Waller's 'reform' were twofold in the light of social analysis. First, his loftier language and more formal tone, as in his poems of courtship to Sacharissa (Lady Dorothy Sidney), show a marked awareness of social rank, just as in his poems of praise to 'the Queen and other ladies of high position . . . he is always conscious of court decorum and speaks as a distant admirer of clearly inferior rank'.[77] Secondly, his style deals with the realities of experience in a rounded, measured, distancing way, and hence is unfit for practical, workaday matters: in a word, it removes the Cavalier farther away from anything popular or colloquial.

The method of the foregoing paragraphs is simply that of pursuing tone out to its connecting ground in society. It reveals that style in Waller is an indicator of rank, an idiom for dealing with upper-class realities, and a means of ennobling the mundane activities of the well-born and well connected.

According to a recent study, 'common to all Metaphysical poets is a private speaker conscious of, often explicit about, his alienation from what is repeatedly termed the "world".' In Donne's verse, 'The private speaker is the norm of consciousness, of integrity in a world lacking in clear-sightedness, a world corrupt.'[78] Here, apparently, one of the fundamental characteristics of Metaphysical verse — the particular voice or tone — is instantly perceived as a stance *vis-à-vis* 'the world'. 'The values of love are set over against the values of the court and the world',[79] but this is done by flagging the imagery of the rejected public world. And in a wider context, 'The individualistic soul-searching and suspicion of conventionality which we meet in Bacon, Greville, Jonson, Donne, and in Shakespeare's tragedies is the mirror of a general loss of faith in society.'[80] With this implied criticism of the world, whose most menacing features are symbolized by the Court, there goes the rejection of 'eloquence' in favor of a plainer style, a more natural language.

Compared to its 'golden' contemporary, the plain style of the 1590s and following was a superior instrument for dealing with circumstance and the exactitude of everyday experience.[81] Well connected, well-off financially, and steeped in the Latin classics, Donne, Davies, Guilpin, Marston, Weever, and others of their ilk arrived at the Inns of Court as often as not to make further contacts, rather than to plunge seriously into the study of law. But the 1590s — in London dramatically so — were a decade of famine, war, plague, wild ostentation, flaring corruption in government, rising anxiety over the succession, ill concealed cynicism at Court, and narrowing opportunity. In this setting ambitious young men developed cynical, scoffing, angry, troubled, disenchanted views. Two voices rhyme perfectly with this psychology: the strident, critical voice of late Elizabethan and Jacobean satire; and the private, pithy, complex, dramatic, often tortured, and insecure or domineering voice of 'the poetry of the Shakespearean moment'.[82]

In steering the analysis from tone and viewpoint to a particular social milieu, I have touched on one of the ways in which social experience may be metabolized into 'literature'. The procedure helps to account for similarities in poets but cannot explain their differences, except insofar as it allows us, by its setting of perimeters, to see why some men, in the climate of the 1590s, retreated and went melancholy, while others went plangent and satiric. In the case of the ex-Catholic, Donne, we have reason to suspect that his 'apostasy' troubled him for years. If so, then here was something — though we are still locked into a social universe — that went to distinguish him from most of his friends and acquaintances.[83]

Because tone is always in the process of fading into viewpoint, it may tell us something about the poet's place in the social order, the pressures of his reliance on patronage, the changing political climate, or the moral and social profile of his intended audience.

To begin with the example of Ben Jonson: 'At court he was silken, bland; in the theatre he mercilessly satirized upstart courtiers.'[84] And if we ask why, one answer is that 'King James and his court *expected* a certain tone in poems, plays and masques, reflecting not their aspirations to greatness but the glory they felt manifest every day.'[85] Jonson suited his productions to his audience. Similarly, the poet who courted a lady of superior social rank had a fitting idiom in the Petrarchan mode (in its elevations and flatteries) or in 'a mild neo-Platonism. . . . Drayton's *Idea* suggested the method [in its very title]: if one woos the Idea of beauty, one's aims are wholly innocent.'[86] Tone and viewpoint acknowledged rank, simultaneously pointing to the poet's social position. Similarly, in Shakespeare's sonnets to the young man, by observing decorum, by keeping physicality out of the cycle (punning aside), and by the selective use of a generalized diction, the poet achieves a tone which makes us conscious of his being 'patronized' and 'of the friend's superior rank'.[87] On the other hand, the prose of Sidney's *Arcadia*, penned at the top of the social hierarchy, 'has the range, lucidity and assuredness, the independence and lofty sobriety of the Great House'.[88] His sonnet sequence, *Astrophel and Stella*, has the same tone.

Scholarship has not neglected the connections between tone and the educational background of readers and poets. The main points of agreement concern the high degree of argument and erudition — the clerical tone — in much Elizabethan and Jacobean verse, notably in the metaphysical and religious lines. Behind this taste lay school and university curricula, with their emphasis on Latin grammar, rhetoric, and logic. Herrick's 'cult of the curious in diction is stamped with the pedantry of the age when he addresses his conscience as his *protonotary* or calls the fancy-forming cells of the brain *fantastic pannicles*'.[89] Donne is in full harmony with the 'erudite temper of the Jacobeans', with their interest in 'the new science' and 'quaint learning'.[90]

Tone and style also sought adjustments with politics. It has been noted, for example, that in its obscurity and mere scurrility, Cleveland's 'The Hue and Cry after Sir John Presbyter' (1645) 'hovers uncertainly between burlesque and diatribe. It is probably a fair index to the uncertainty of attack in royalist ranks at that date.'[91] John Phillips's 'Satyr Against Hypocrites' (1655) also shows him tilting between Juvenalian grace and low ridicule or mere vilification. These poets 'had received the stylistic inheritance of the ancient world which strictly separated the modes and tones suitable for portraying noble and menial ranks in society'. But as the parliamentary assault on the monarchy put them on the political defensive, rendering them ever more incapable 'of any patrician coolness in the treatment of low comic material, the more emotionally vituperative [they] became . . . and consequently the more [their] verse became assimilated to the lampoon level of tone and matter of the street ballad.'[92] Here, clearly, political reality had made a direct hit on tone and style: the charged atmosphere of political defeat entered into the poet's satiric vision and treatment.

Marvell's greatly admired 'Horatian Ode' (1650) raises a different sort of problem. It has been read as having a royalist bias, a Puritan and pro-Cromwellian bias, and even as 'the quintessence of trimming'. The problem arises from the poem's balanced ambiguity of tone. It somehow corrals the conflicting positions; hence it is 'a poem that feels difficult and even unstable rather than secure and contemplative'.[93] Scholarship now largely agrees that the poem's centrally ambiguous tone, whether or not deliberate, echoes the deep ambiguity of public feeling connected with Cromwell's standing in 1650. Battered by the Civil War and fearful of mob rule, many royalists had passed over to Cromwell in temporary sympathy.

GENRE

Learned observation on the connections between genre and its worldly context has focused mainly on the courtly forms, on panegyric, on the taste of particular audiences, and on the mixing of kinds. A useful social distinction may also be drawn between the personal and public forms of occasional poetry. Thus great occasions, such as royal births and deaths, called for 'a poetry of ceremony . . . to compliment and to commemorate'.[94] But there was also verse of the sort intended for the friends, relatives, and acquaintances of the poet. It highlights graceful compliment, 'gratitude for small favors', and praise for the circle's way of life. 'Such poetry makes from the conventions of social life a subject for art. It can be written only by an insider who has the breeding and intimate acquaintance with the standards of decorous conduct . . . who has control, ease, elegance, delicacy, and lack of pedantry.'[95] Lovelace, Carew and Suckling were such poets.

The sonnet belongs to the world of the Court and to those who aspired to it. Meant to exhibit grace, dignity, restraint, and good taste, it spun these qualities around the theme of love.[96] And this theme sprang from the actual life of the Tudor Court, where leisure, music, games, and displaying one's finery took up the days, and where love was turned into a mode of play. In fitting into the Court (the fount of power and so of flattery), the game elicited a parallel mimesis (obeisance, adulation, etc.) from the supplicant lover, as he confronted the fictive power of the beloved. But this game had dangers, for upper-class marriage was still usually arranged and therefore sexual desire out of wedlock was all the more likely. The restraining conventions of courtly love — and the conventions of the courtly lyric — thus became exceedingly important because they were the means to keep danger at bay; and so it has been keenly observed that these conventions were 'so rooted in their society that their survival [in the sonnet and courtly lyric] is incomplete'[97] — incomplete because they come to us stripped of the concrete circumstances for which they were evolved.

When the Elizabethan sonnet is considered in this light, we see why departures from its form, and parodies in particular, get at a way of life. Shakespeare, Donne, Davies, Drayton, and others all at some point twist or parody the Petrarchan conventions with the aim of puncturing fashion, asserting the authenticity of their feelings, or deriding courtly pretense.

Something about courtly ways is now boldly seen to be false; and poets use the devices of the genre itself to make social observations, to attack it, or to establish an anti-genre. Yet there were also fans for this verse in the Court circle itself, a fact hedged by complexity and contradiction, especially because the height of the sonnet craze, in the mid-1590s, coincided with the beginnings of the sustained onslaught on the genre.

Recognizing the sonnet as one of the most courtly and prestigious of all poetic forms, men of humble origins — Spenser, Shakespeare, Daniel, Drayton[98] — often turned to it to display their mastery of the idiom and therewith their right to be accepted among the well-born. Most of them could claim the education to go with such aspirations; poetry commanded esteem; and Elizabethan London was, in any case, the setting for fierce social climbing. In addition, as we have seen, the courtly idiom enabled poets to woo patronesses in the safe language of unreciprocated, idealized love.

The convention of pastoral — to consider yet another form — was so dependent on the world of the Court as to be 'parasitic upon it. It only acquires force as a complementary image to the treadmill of care that a court imposes upon those privileged enough to be its victims; it is only in this context that the courtier finds virtue in the image of himself as a shepherd.'[99] For Empson pastoral has its 'essential trick' in the fusing of rich and poor, achieved by putting 'learned and fashionable' speech into the mouths of poor shepherds.[100] Poor and simple versus rich and courtly, or poor *united* with rich and courtly: either will do, depending upon the text and the specific tasks of analysis, provided we do not omit the looming presence of the Court. For as the pinnacle of power, the Court — more than the city — was the contrasting twin to the idealized life of the shepherd. But the life of the shepherd had to be idealized if pastoral was to serve as a meaningful foil for the Court and courtly audiences; so that when pastoral borrowed the fashionable amatory theme, while also turning the speech of rural folk into a courtly tongue, it became little more than a rusticized image of Court life.

Serious study has long recognized that far from withdrawing into escapist fantasies, pastoral often engaged current social matters. It was an art 'deeply involved in the central issues of life and society'.[101] If nothing else, 'The naturalness, freedom, and delightfulness of the pastoral ethos often criticized, overtly or by implication, the self-seeking, self-aggrandizing materialistic artificiality of any court.'[102] More comprehensively, 'The central meaning of pastoral is the rejection of the aspiring mind.'[103]

In pinning pastoral to the Court, these observations draw upon thematic concerns, imagery, language, and readerships. They also raise a major question: if pastoral was a courtly mode, then, in being critical of the Court ambience, could it also be anti-courtly? Quite simply yes, and this tergiversation illumines an area of contradictory experience; for as courtiers like Sidney, Dyer, Raleigh, Essex, and Greville well knew, none could seem to be more weary of the Court, nor more disgusted with it, than the ambitious men who most frequented it.[104] Pastoral, in short, was a posture; but it was also an ironic mode, a way of self-mockery and self-congratulation, a way of taking stock, of sorting out values, or of temporarily draining the wells of resentment built up against the Court.

Like the sonnet form, when parodied or deflected (as in its religious incarnation) from its original ends, the conventions of pastoral could also be routed away from courtly concerns to other social demands. We see this among the so-called 'Spenserian poets' — Drayton, Browne, Wither, and the Fletchers.[105] This professional clique saw poetry as a sublime calling, indulged in the 'dream of poetic fame and glory', and used the commonplaces of pastoral to comment on the social position of the poet. Their shepherd-persona usually symbolizes the poet: a fiction employed to snipe at the 'new' poetry of Donne and others, to speak out against the changed literary environment and patronage of the Jacobean era, to represent 'the economic situation of writers', and even to 'convey a considerable amount of economic *angst*'.[106] In the seventeenth century, as already in Spenser, the voice of pastoral was often to be the voice of the poet obliquely describing his loves, his circumstances, and his engagements with society.

Panegyric flourished under the Stuarts more than it ever had under the Tudors: a shift which indicates something about the changed times, perhaps the rise in literacy rates and the darkening horizons for James I as for Charles I, who came to need more and more cultural and ideological support.[107] We may define panegyric as 'a public, serious, ethical, external, historical, supposedly factual genre', whose job is to rehearse the praiseworthy deeds and virtues of illustrious men or women.[108] But the social ground of such praise is a society where deference and hierarchy are omnipresent; where literature, having an acknowledged utility, is spun into the social fabric; and where education may be correspondingly literary.

Scholars often assign the Elizabethan taste for Ovidian erotic verse to aristocrats and smart young men schooled in the classics.[109] Complex social needs buttressed this genre: (1) the nagging need of poets to find favor — thus Marlowe and Shakespeare, for example, writing for patrons in their erotic poetry; (2) the push on the part of modish Inns-of-Court men to prove themselves and of aristocrats to stand up to the constricting religious values of a mercantile oligarchy which — but for the Court — would have clapped locks on all of London's public and private playhouses, 'immoral' by definition; and finally (3) the growing penchant for tantalizing subject-matter, already hinted at in the Elizabethan educational curriculum, in a time of copious display and sybaritic proclivity among many of the rich and well-born.[110] We catch a fleeting image of the like in Mercutio's jibe: those 'antic, lisping, affecting fantasticoes . . . new tuners of accents', 'strange flies' and 'fashion-mongers' (*Romeo and Juliet*, II, iv, 29—34). In these enclaves of English society, Christianity was momentarily challenged in the taste for 'pagan' eroticism.

The search for the ties between genre and world is the search for how literary forms and their conventions come forth not only to satisfy social needs but also to help articulate them by working to clarify and sharpen consciousness.

5

A new discourse: needs and prospects

Since this book recognizes no professional boundaries between the disciplines of history and literature, the question of proof — of how claims are proved — becomes a problem. In crossing back and forth between poem and world, how do we *prove* the validity of the alleged points of contact? How do we press beyond provisional observation or intelligent conjecture?

We cannot, if we insist on holding exclusively to the thinking of the established disciplines, for these have conventions about how argument is constructed and proof adduced. Typically in literary scholarship, the critic keeps largely to his text and calls upon the evidence of theme, rhetorical movement, imagery, diction, or style. These establish the poem's intention, meaning, and effects. Typically in historical scholarship, the historian introduces event, explicit ideas or statements (as in a prose text), and quantities (as in economic or demographic history); and these are his way of building an argument or establishing an interpretation. Owing to the force of conventional routine and procedure, the literary scholar need not declare that there can be no 'hard proof' for much of what he says. He has the validation of his discipline. So also the historian, who takes *unacknowledged* realities constantly for granted and moves freely back and forth between events and minds — values and attitudes being in minds.

The traditional disciplines rely heavily on the power of consensus. There is no such automatic endorsement for the socio-historical analysis of verse. And therefore the question of how claims can be proven will persist as a problem, until its solution is worked out in a new body of scholarship.

As we have seen, Renaissance poetry teems with direct references to affairs and people in the world, and the references appear not only in satire and political poetry, but also in panegyric, *vers de société*, and even religious and amatory verse. Direct references are undeniable points of contact with the world — 'facts' in scholarly terms — though they are different, to be sure, from the ascertainable lines of connection that go out from diction, punning, and wordplay, where the poet is addressing a certain kind of public or coterie. This too is contact with the world, contact assessable as 'fact'. We may of course pass on to examples of more dubious or contestable fact, but conventional literary and historical scholarship is itself rife with problematic fact.

The more serious problem centers on the question of interpretation, on how we choose to regard and evaluate evidence, for this often touches the very way in which things perceived, or thought to be perceived, attain the status of fact.

Viewed as texts, Shakespeare's *Sonnets* are just as factual, just as 'hard', as Martin Luther's tract on *The Babylonian Captivity of the Church* (1520). But while *The Babylonian Captivity* deals polemically with the Church's sacraments, the *Sonnets* plot the movements of a love affair; and while the one looks *out* to the world of the institutional Church, the other looks *in* to the passions and to personal experience, to relations between the 'I' and the 'thou'. *The Babylonian Captivity* thus is 'public' and the *Sonnets* 'private'. Therefore, is Luther's tract historical and are the *Sonnets* non-historical, and does the difference between historical and non-historical turn simply on the public—private distinction? Surely not, as this would be to erect a curious and arbitrary wall between biography and history. Ah, but the *Sonnets* are not biography; they belong to art. And *The Babylonian Captivity* is religious politics, historical 'stuff' by the force of conventional definition. Yet the tract is also a brilliant polemic, artful and wonderfully rhetorical, whereas the *Sonnets* use art to talk about 'the world' — about time and death, youth and beauty, pride, humility, longing, the seasons, aging, frustration, disgrace, moral injury, and so on. Late Elizabethan and Jacobean, the voice in the *Sonnets* often converts love into a metaphor and art into the occasion for reflecting on the rich variety of strains, hopes, fears, joys, wonders, and melancholies that might be felt by a successful man in his thirties — actor, playwright, businessman, and poet — living in London in the 1590s and first years of the seventeenth century.

These general points about the *Sonnets* have a factual value and would count as facts of some kind, I believe, for the community of literary scholars in the Renaissance field. Their potential relevance for historians, however, does not end here. For Shakespeare's language in the *Sonnets* — and the language generally of the leading poets of the age — continually calls in a whole field of associations. And those associations — their codes, quality, and sources of energy — give the historian a new entry into the study of history, while also providing the social critic with the stuff for widening his literary investigations.

If now we turn to reconsider questions of proof and interpretation, it becomes clear that we are talking about a new kind of discourse: a new way of seeing things, of selecting 'facts', of setting up problems, and of introducing evidence. This means that we must claim the right to develop new modes of argument and different ways of organizing interpretation. Unite historical and literary analysis and the result is bound to be a new vision, something that neither of the parent disciplines will at first recognize in institutional terms.

We have noticed that convention in poetry is freighted with social meaning, that style and social identity are linked, and that literary change is a natural response to social change. Accordingly, we may suppose that when change occurs in one area, the other too will see change. More precisely, there may be significant social change without literary change (though I would think this improbable); but there can be no general literary change — in style, modes, or content — without some prior or contemporaneous social change, and in social here I also include the political, economic, and religious dimensions of experience. This premise is so basic that it sustains — or its dubiety wrecks — the whole edifice of social literary analysis.

Changes in lyric style about 1600 have drawn much commentary in this study. This is because, judging by the disquiet in the lyric then, we are driven to suspect that there were things going on in the society which have yet to be rightly understood. But once we grant a connection between lyric style and social stress, we still confront the problem of proof: the question of how exactly we find and demonstrate the particulars of the connection. Some things will be clear enough at the outset. (1) Our concern is with consciousness, with aspects of the consciousness of poets and readers, and this entails a search for resemblances and nimbleness, not fixity. (2) Since our subject is poetry of the sort which presupposes education, leisure, patronage, and a cultivated taste, we are dealing with upper-class groups. (3) Consequently we are seeing the world from the standpoint of these groups and taking hold of it, as it were, with their language. (4) This means that general shifts in power, status, outlook, or temper are likely to have a bearing on 'their' poetry because their circles are alertly sensitive to these matters and have the biggest stake in the status quo. (5) The preceding point gains additional credit when we recall the importance and vitality of poetry for many people from the professional and upper classes. (6) Finally, we must be on the lookout for the impact of the Court and of London, the great binary star of politics and commerce.

This framework narrows our focus but is still broad, and a variety of interpretations may go into it.

An attempt has been made to explain the sonnet form in terms of marriage and sexual tensions among the well-born.[1] The attempt begins with the sonnet's 'fixity of form', its conventional antitheses and dichotomies, its play of contradictory sub-themes and even rhymes, its 'strained idealism', the 'characteristic see-saw motion' of its syntax, and its high fashionability. The analysis is then carried over to the society, to the strains and energies that fostered and enlivened the genre. Since the sonnet form centered on the theme of love, while also variously swinging from Petrarchan idealization to overt sexuality, the vitalizing sources lay apparently in the patterns of sex, courtship, and marriage among the primary reading audience for sonnets. Now as is widely known, marriage for the Tudor nobility and the rich gentry was 'an act of economic diplomacy'. It was arranged with social and economic ends strictly in mind, the larger material good of the family preceding any private desire on the part of the individual. The result was that sexual satisfaction was sometimes found outside of marriage, above all wherever the sexes customarily mixed freely. Men philandered and their wives followed them into adultery. The excitement of love was found illicitly, and therefore 'the personal emotion of love and the public institution of marriage were dissociated: *individual love* was habitually opposed to the *social structure*.'[2]

Nourished in this milieu, the sonnet form seems to have done an uncanny job of catching the contradictions in the conflict between erotic love and marriage, between private passion and public conscience. It incorporated the conflict but recast it as the compressed play of antitheses in some of the best sonnet sequences. Accordingly, when attitudes toward marriage among the well-born began to change about 1600, with the coming of 'a bourgeois sexual code' and a greater personal choice in marriage, the need and fashion for the sonnet passed away.

Although boldly suggestive, especially in implicating the structure of the sonnet, the foregoing analysis raises insuperable objections, the most serious being that the sonnet craze comes and goes too swiftly to be rhymed with gradual change in the institution of upper-class marriage. And just as the implied cause-and-effect link here is too closely drawn, so also are the relations between conflict in the would-be adulterer and the pattern of moving contrasts (antitheses) in the sonnet. The patriarchal 'fixing' of marriage went on in many quarters long after 1600. Other continental literary milieux, such as the French and Italian courts, also favored the sonnet form, hence the question of social comparisons necessarily arises. The mixing of sexes in a society of arranged marriages doubtless made for strains and ambivalences which fueled the courtly taste for sonnets, but such strains were a fixture of the early modern period as a whole and registered no marked changes in the 1590s. What is more, lyric forms other than the sonnet also carried adulterous and sexual tensions both before and after the height of the sonnet fashion.

Evidently, then, in addition to getting our history and literature right, we must get the hardest task of all right — the job of concatenation. The parts of our poetry—world construct should fit well and we should expect the whole to harmonize. In the case at hand, to get the desired consistencies and concinnity into our analysis, we would have to put the sonnet craze into the larger context of changes in lyric style during the 1590s and early years of the seventeenth century. If we take this route, we see at once that while the sonnet collected force from stresses originating both in and out of wedlock, its amazing rhetorical and semiotic repertory also allowed it to be brilliantly used, for example, to woo the Queen, to extract patronage from great ladies, and of course, as we have seen, to enact social climbing by an exhibition of control over the genre's courtly idiom. In the 1590s, however, following the publication and great success of Sidney's *Astrophel and Stella,* social imitation and the urgent hunt for publicity and patronage go far to explain the immediate promptings behind the sonnet rage.

No sooner does the fashion for the sonnet peak (1594—6) than it is parodied, its conventions altered or toyed with, and its themes extended. The very cycle that launched the fashion, *Astrophel and Stella,* called for a return to primary amatory experience and included an attack on the Petrarchan manner and conventions, while also in part observing them, so that in fact the sonnet streaks onto the literary scene bearing a message of discontent with lyric style. This is ground of the sort for touching on problems of proof and interpretation in the new discourse.

Scholarship on the period from about 1590 to 1610 sees it as a time of distressingly rapid change, involving shifts from optimism to pessimism, from belief to skepticism, from acceptance to inquiring criticism, from something chanting and 'bardic' to something tense and dramatic, and from group loyalty to personal doubt.[3] These at least are some of the shifts noted in lyric and dramatic literature. And scholars call on a variety of explanations in their accounts, ranging over much of the socio-historical world: such as the transition from feudalism to capitalism, the triumph of a world market economy, the decline of the nobility, the passage from Catholicism to a new Protestant order, the intellectual effects of 'the new science', the rising force of feeling against the Crown, and the abrupt appearance — in the 1580s and 1590s — of a wave of professional writers of humble birth, pressing forward in search of patronage or emolument. Of all these, only the last two are specific enough to serve in the job of concatenation (the linking of lyric change with social change), but there are additional suggestions and insights in the scholarship.

The highest degree of agreement gathers around the supposed link between the new element of critical realism in verse (seen most readily in satire) and the atmosphere of London and the Inns of Court. Linguistic, thematic, metaphorical, and tonal matters give the lines of connection. For one of the premier workers in the field, the masculine society of the Inns and universities made for a literary output which went to challenge the preeminence of the courtly manner, on which the influence of women had always been strong. Thus he juxtaposes not only two milieux but also two different reading audiences, male and female.[4] For another scholar, the decade of the 1590s brought the sorting out of 'two mentalities' in the verse, the old and the new: the one smooth, simple, lyrical, abstract, undramatic, and rather unreal; the other 'critical, dramatic, satirical, complex, and uncertain', often subtle and even obscure.[5] Coming midway between two historic upheavals, the Reformation and the Civil War, the 1590s marked the pivotal moment of change between medieval and early-modern, hierarchic and individualistic; and the change in literature was the transition from the sweet (golden) to the moral (drab) style.[6]

But can we draw the lines of literary—social connection more closely still? We can, and where this is possible we should. That there were contacts between the milieu of the Inns of Court and the new style is clear enough, particularly in the affinities between the irreverence, verbal play, wit, erotic interest, and readership of the Inns on one side and the new verse's outspoken, smart, critical, challenging accents on the other. To indicate the best route for argument on the matter in question, I offer a number of suggestions, putting them in the form of hypotheses.

(1)   Battening on the purchase and resale of the old monastic lands — once the fourth part (?) of England and Wales — a new class on the make, sprung from the upper-middle sectors of society, sent sons and grandsons to the universities and Inns of Court, directing them toward careers in law and government service, the surest ways of status and prestige. By 1590 the Inns and universities teemed with the likes of such men, but behind them loomed the economic destruction of the old Church, a feverishly active land market, and a major change in the aims and content of education.

(2)   The 1590s were a decade of narrowing opportunity for the educated, offering fewer places in Church and government, with the result that the hunt for preferment and patronage turned ever more intense.

(3)   Well educated, even when they had no better than schooling up to the ages of fourteen or fifteen, many young men in London turned to writing, attracted by the flourishing theater, the book market, and the hope of literary patronage, particularly as there was no sufficient increase in place and favor for intellectuals. Their uneasiness was no doubt enhanced by the dramatic incidence of plague and years of famine (1594—9).

(4)   The spectacle of unleashed ostentation in housing and dress struck young contemporaries in London, and if they thought at all about famine and plague, they must have been moved to questions or criticism, as appears in the sudden emergence of formal satire, a new genre for England.

(5)   The aging Queen, the sense of an impending change in the monarchy, the Crown's much resented sale of commercial monopolies, a costly war with Spain, and the flagrance of corruption in high place (a new phenomenon of the 1590s): these also affected consciousness among the 'better sort', darkening moods, stirring up questions, and provoking resentment.

(6)   Finally, and more tentatively, let us put the foregoing items into the world of a new market society (nascent capitalism), much commented on by a number of scholars.[7] Here again the 1580s and especially the 1590s may be decisive, as it is then perhaps that the full force of an expanding market economy — where 'Every ones price is written on his backe' *(The Jew of Malta,* II,iii,3) — is first both deeply felt and given an insistent voice: market relations now trammel not only interpersonal relations but also the

very way in which certain classes of aspiring men see and define themselves.[8] A sense of inner worth (traditional, static, hierarchical: the stamp of an earlier society) gives way to a sense of self in terms of use or market value, a notion fully articulated by Thomas Hobbes two generations later.

These six items and their parts make up the context for lyric and stylistic change in the 1590s and first years of the seventeenth century.

Into this world we have no trouble fitting a wide range of new and older poetic themes: such as turning people into objects of profit, greed for money, gulling in the big city, adulation in exchange for patronage, foppery, ostentation, every kind of pretension, as well as the image of the Machiavel, the overreacher, the 'vile' upstart, the evil prince, and the corrupt counsellor — some of the themes of Marlowe, Shakespeare, Chapman, Jonson, and the new satirists. The theme of sexual lust belongs to the same world — lust as a willful and destructive force, profoundly corrupt, individualistic, and anti-social. Like the gaudy upstart, lust becomes a metaphor for social disorder. The power of sex, viewed as something evil and primal, is obscurely used as a way of taking hold of the new forces, mobile and menacing, in market society.

In the world of my six items, we can also account fully for the anger and keening of the formal satirists; for Donne's repeated use of the amatory ideal as a foil for the corrupt Court and busy world; for the new personal voice in the lyric, impatient with poetic convention and resolved to hearken to private experience; for mocking dismissals of courtly posturing in love verse; for the epigram — another new fashion — with its sharp edges, humor, and cold-eyed social observations; and for the choice in verse of a simpler or plainer language, pitched closer to speech, in opposition to the copious and fluent eloquence of the golden style. A touch of obscurity in manner, as in Chapman and Donne, also fits into the pattern of lyric change, to be seen as a mark of the poet's alienation from a readership bred to a sweet and easy accessibility of texts. The arrogance of the poet as social climber is evident here, in his occasional insistence on obscurity against the sway of popular taste. This line makes contact with the fashion for epigram, a genre in which the poet — made proud by patronage but also striving to be above it — sees himself as a dispenser of wisdom and the lessons of experience.

Getting the social context right — that is, the historical and social world of the poem — is fundamental. Everything in a sense begins and ends here. But no sooner do we have the perimeters of our social world right, as in our model above of the six items, than we shall also know how to select the specific strategies to be used in the analysis and how to give them a precise focus and direction. For example, again apropos of lyric change in the 1590s: in studying a poem or a whole body of verse, we shall look (a) for the emergence of new themes and for the particulars of how these relate to the six items of our world; (b) for trends in syntax and diction, to see if these depart from received practice, and thus imply a critique; (c) for patterns in the use of pronouns, articles, and active versus passive constructions, to see what these reveal about relations between the self and the social world;[9] (d) for imagistic clusters or persistencies in metaphorical usage, to see what these introduce — and how the material is used — from the world of commerce, husbandry, the law, overseas venture, and traditional versus innovatory attitudes; (e) and we shall look for shifts in tone—voice—outlook, to see where and how these touch the six parts of our late Elizabethan world.

As we work our way through these strategies of analysis, our findings will result in an interlocking configuration (historical milieu plus poetry) of increasing complexity. This means — to modify a point made above — that getting the milieu right can never be something definitive, because historical interpretation goes on in our own historical flux, because the milieu under study was itself changing, and because our deepening analysis of the verse may lead us to alter our grasp of the surrounding social world. In other words, the point comes in our analysis where we shall find ourselves using poetry as historical documentation. In the beginning, in order to get our milieu right, we envisage a picture of broad outlines drawn both from historical scholarship and from conventional primary sources. In similar fashion, we take our picture of the lyric in the 1590s from the verse and from literary scholarship. But according as we splice poetry and world together at more and more points, something is gradually altered: our view of the verse and our view of the historical world. This again is why I refer to a new discourse: we end by seeing poetry as history and history as a process which goes on in poetry.

Once we *begin* to get our milieu right and therefore are able to see which strategies to use, the job of concatenation (world plus poem) has already started and the soundness of the argument will depend upon the degree of achieved concinnity: the fitting relationship of parts in the conjunction between poem and world. We shall have continuing problems or puzzles and these will be the front line of research, but we shall also wish to have simple guidelines in the developing architecture of interpretation and complexity, such as I have tried to draw in my social corralling of lyric change in the 1590s.

Since I am dealing with the problem of argument and interpretation in social literary analysis, I want to record a clear warning before concluding this section.

In the search for ways to relate poem and world, it is tempting but wrong to begin by looking for themes — ideas or topics in the verse — that *directly* engage the most urgent political and social questions of the day. Poetry *can* take things up this way; we often see the effects in satire. But it also favors the evasive mode, indeed often goes this way despite any intention of the poet. It takes the indirect, slanting, ruminating, ambiguous, or allegorical route, along the way of which the effects and variety of experience may be more fully sounded. And therefore, to cite a variety of examples, sexual lust may allegorize the social energies of the sensational upstart; the general attack on pretense and hypocrisy may add up to a reaction against the sensed malaise or corruption of the outstanding model for the world, the Court; love may be the still point, or point of dalliance, in a tormented political world or in a world of shrunken economic opportunity, but then the quiddity of such love is partly shaped by that world and should not be cut away from it. The chronic, imagistic linking of youth, beauty, and mutability may amount to a perception — by means of metaphor — of bewildering social change. Obsessive metaphors of size, energy, and expansion may arise from a new 'imperialist' or domineering mode of consciousness. And praise of the quiet countryside may be a censuring of the unruly, revolutionary city. We return, thus, to an earlier axiom: things in poetry are and are not what they seem. Though life and art are inseparable, art is no mirror, certainly no simple mirror. Even in the discovery of verse themes that seem to deal directly with pressing social or political issues, we have to be on our guard. Satire, one of the most realistic of literary modes, traffics in exaggeration.

There is a lesson to be drawn from an unfinished poem by Abraham Cowley. In the midst of the Civil War, he set out to write an epic poem about it but only completed three books and took the story up to the first battle of Newbury (1644). Although writing from a royalist point of view, he had somehow planned to rise above partisanship and to keep close to the actual record of events. In the third book, however, he reels between two styles — satire for the Parliamentarians and elegy for the Cavaliers. In effect, his vision or sense of two realities invades the very structure of the poem. 'Caught in a fierce oscillation between satire and elegy, a language for 'them' and a language for 'us', Cowley found the epic frame increasingly inhospitable. He abandoned the poem when the course of events turned against the King, but it was already a deeply flawed undertaking.'[10] Genre, language, and style — clearly all were affected by events, by his divided vision of events, until the undertaking itself was wrecked.

The example of Cowley's *Civil War* helps us to see that there are realities — in crisis above all — which poetry dare not look at too directly or it capsizes. This is less surprising than we may think. Ordinary historical documents, political and military, rarely look into the eye of catastrophic events or see them in their totality; they do not know how, and so they are always partial or fragmentary. But when a historical witness really does begin to see the fulness of events, his testament paradoxically is likely to turn into theory or even art, as in Machiavelli's *The Prince* or Koestler's *Darkness at Noon.* Cowley was foiled as much by commitment to the genre as by military and political realities.

NEEDS AND PROSPECTS

We turn to the prospects for social literary analysis. Where does it stand, what are its more urgent needs, where is it likely to go in the short run, and what are its new avenues?

The field of Renaissance poetry has scarcely been touched by any kind of sustained social analysis. This must be obvious to anyone who has worked along the boundaries between Renaissance history and literature. And the true field is *between,* or rather in their fusion, in their interminable interconnections, not in one as background for the other. In methodological matters, there is great need for new premises, strategies, and argument. In other areas, almost everything remains to be done: work on genre, satire, relations between lyric and dramatic verse, reading audiences, diction and syntax, London and country-house milieux, relations between major and minor poets, literary and social change in the 1580s and 1590s, fluctuations in patronage, religious lyric and milieu, the place of poetry in private life, the book trade between 1620 and 1660, and so on. I could go on reeling forth desiderata, to indicate the uncharted spaces for social analysis. The greatest need, however, is for the collaboration of historians. This is so crucial a matter that it calls for a chapter apart and so I conclude the book with it.

Nearly all social literary analysis in the Renaissance field has been done by literary scholars, for in the course of studying Renaissance literature, they feel the need to reach out to the life around, in the conviction that this helps them take better hold of their literary texts. Several things about this are immediately apparent. They pick up their historical knowledge in a haphazard fashion and usually have no disciplined historical training. When their reading has been more directed, the knowledge gained is often excessively focused, as in efforts to understand political events around Andrew Marvell or John Dryden, or to pin down laws relating to marriage, dower, and jointure as 'background' for Elizabethan and Jacobean drama. Such interest is apt to turn into a converging on fine points, and while this is often helpful in the elucidation of particular passages, as work it is closer to chronicle than to history; it centers on the gathering of select facts, not on analysis or on perceptions of process and interaction.

I seem to criticize the historical grasp of scholars in the literary field. More damaging things could be said about the literary preparation of historians. But the point here is not the need for historians to prepare themselves as literary scholars, nor for the latter to seek training as historians. This is taken so much for granted that it requires no discussion. The point is that we need to seek a mode of thinking so thoroughly grounded in the two fields that our way of looking at each will be decisively affected by the other. When this happens, we shall have ways of seeing and putting questions that would have been impossible for historians and scholars working within the conventional perimeters of the two disciplines. We might ask, for example — to take a purely hypothetical question — whether or not the political cataclysm of the 1640s is echoed in the fortunes of the religious lyric. For if it is, we have there a form of consciousness whose workings do not appear in ordinary historical documents.

Why historians of Renaissance England have not generally felt the urge to steep themselves in the poetry of the age,[11] in answer to the crossing over by literary scholars into history, would appear to be self-evident but is not, as I shall show in the concluding chapter.

Enough work has been done in recent times on the dynamics of language to allow for a near a priori acceptance of the socio-linguistic claim that 'writers express their attitudes towards inherited ideology in the minute particulars of language.'[12] If we keep to the language of traditional scholarship, how do we translate this claim into a more common idiom? What does it mean? Putting the claim into the orbit of my theoretical propositions (pp. 1—4), we can draw the meaning out at once. It means that we use language in accordance with a socially conditioned view of the world; hence our ways of speaking and writing, the particulars of those ways (as in language's breakdown and strict classification of reality), contain all the lineaments of a world view. To study poetry from this standpoint must be daunting, but neither art nor verbal genius puts Renaissance poets outside time and society.

Language and social identity, literary style and social view of the world, change in style and historical change: these make up the most fruitful new area of study for social analysis. The urgent research needs are here and so, too, the most promising avenues; but since practice is also thinnest here, the pertinent theory is apt to seem excessively general.[13]

In the suggested approach, scholars are likely to study the textual context and meaning of pronouns and articles, the active and passive voices, mood, grammar as classification of the world, and the syntactical distance between agent and action. These are studied with a view to establishing what they tacitly assume about the mainsprings of order and authority in the society, how the poem's speaking voice defines the self in society, and what the hidden, 'deep', or disguised social vision of the world is.

Giorgio Melchiori finds a pattern in Sidney's use of possessive pronouns in *Astrophel and Stella*: 'The social rank itself of the poet suggests to him to prefer the more detached plural form *your* over the singular *thy*.'[14] In Spenser's sonnet sequence, he discovers that '*thy* is virtually absent and is scarcely compensated by the 67 appearances of *your* in the *Amoretti*, which are directed to an anonymous addressee . . . as if to a being with a purely intellectual existence, who is thus celebrated in the third person. The poems speak *of* her not *to* her.' Here also, in contrast to the pronominal norms in four other contemporary collections of sonnets,[15] the dominant pronoun is no longer the first but the third person singular, accounting 'for nearly 50 per cent of the total of used pronominal forms'. Spenser's use of pronouns touches his preference in the *Amoretti* for the definite article over the indefinite *a,* for he 'prefers the absolute, the idea of the thing, to the thing itself in its everyday reality'.[16] In Melchiori's analysis, these findings (or 'deep structures') underline Spenser's stance as a professional Court poet, the man of middle-class origins in the act of pointing to the 'prestige' of poetry by exalting the intellectual qualities of the poet as he contemplates the object of celebration, not a woman but an 'essence'. Poetry, after all, had made Spenser.

Shakespeare's sonnets exhibit a different pronominal pattern. Here the 'I' does predominate and the incidence of *thou* and *thee* is much higher. Significantly, however, in the first seventeen sonnets (the call-to-marry series), first-person pronouns are outnumbered by second-person forms (thou, thee, thy) by a ratio of 16.3 to 83.7. This disparity helps to account for the tone of these sonnets, where the exalted social rank of the beautiful young man, the addressee, is conveyed by means of innuendo and glancing suggestion.[17] In an earlier study, Francis Berry had already observed that *thou* in the first twelve sonnets 'does indeed betoken a worshipping regard'. Their theme, moreover, the triumph of time over beauty (so hurry-and-marry), 'simply provides an opportunity for the "I" to write to "thou"'.[18] By comparison with the *thou* of the first twelve sonnets, the *you* and *yours* of 13 is paradoxically more intimate, more familiar. Depending upon its context, *thou* may also be a distancing form, and therefore the picking out of deferential attitudes by means of pronominal forms can only be done as part of a more exhaustive analysis. In many of John Donne's poems, 'the colloquial tendency . . . is aided by the *I-thou* relationship.' Revealingly, in his 'Letter to Sir Henry Wotton' ('Sir, more than kisses'), we find that '*thou* is used as the pronoun of address to a personal friend . . . but in the ending . . . *you* is employed because Donne's mood has changed from familiarity to deference, as shown by the courtesy word *Sir* with which the letter began.'[19]

Melchiori's lexical strategies and his use of Herbert Donow's concordance are supported by his thorough grasp of the relevant scholarship. He is more likely to move from established scholarly positions than from *aperçus* suggested by Donow's tallies; and even when he appears to take pronominal totals as his point of departure, he relies continually on the best scholarship and on his own intimate familiarity with Elizabethan sonnet sequences. Accordingly, his view of the sonnet as a genre for a social elite is based upon his knowledge of its history and his understanding of the audience for sonnets. With this knowledge, he is able to interpret the prevalence of the first-and third-person pronouns, in the five collections tabulated by Donow, as grammatical testimony of the poet's contemplative relation to the world (I → she, it, they). 'Rarely is the sonnet opened up to a direct relation, to a dialogue with one or more interlocuters.' And therefore 'this attitude qualifies the English sonnet as elitist verse linked to a strictly compartmentalized society, in which the Court poet exalts his own I and puts himself at the center of a well circumscribed world, in a position where he can contemplate from on high the rest of humanity — all those who do not share in the same culture.'[20]

In this purview, Shakespeare's 'They that have pow'r to hurt' is likely to seem his only political sonnet (94), in part because of its unusual pronominal *incipit* in the third person plural. The argument of the sonnet, 'in direct or metaphoric terms, is the conduct of the powerful'.[21] Obviously then, as we also know from the careers of Wyatt and Spenser, even poets who worked in a courtly vein could cast a cold eye on the center of the world, the Court.

The first and secondary meanings of words cannot alone disclose 'deep structures', although the study of verbal and syntactical ambiguity in verse already goes beyond the order of *prima facie* meanings. This observation tells us why Professor Miles's studies of the 'primary language of poetry' have had a limited impact, for all their interest and perspicacity.[22] Thanks to her word counts, we know English poetry's most common nouns, verbs, and adjectives throughout the Renaissance period and beyond. We also know that the 1540s shunned extremes and were 'less metaphysical', 'more humanistic', than the 1640s; and we have been told that although Carew, Shirley, Cleveland, Sandys, Cowley, Herrick, and Lovelace — poets of the Civil War period — were not friends and formed no school, yet they 'were of one poetic mind'.[23] The interest of these remarks rests in what the mere incidence of words can tell us; but the method also obscures things and therefore should not be used alone, for while the homogeneity of diction among the poets of the 1640s reveals a certain unity of temper, there were also major differences among them, such as between Cowley and Shirley, or Cleveland and Herrick. In simple word tallies, done to get at the incidence of words or to pick out the preferred words of substance in a body of verse, all neutral words have the same value as strongly affective ones; and what is more, all are wrenched out of context, all are seen as discrete units, so that nothing can be said about what happens to them as they truly appear in verse — in a syntax, in a semiotic system, in paronomasia, imagery, simile, or metaphor, let alone in rhyme or meter.[24] I am not suggesting that lexical tabulations have no value for social analysis. Melchiori has shown how useful they can be. They must be used, however, in conjunction with other strategies, as part of a more inclusive and more directed method of analysis. No expert will be surprised to learn that Donne used more verbs than any other contemporary poet except Jonson and that

Jonson's 'common active language' leaned neither toward 'appearances' nor 'speculations' but was 'rather one of event in thought or deed'.[25] That the mere counting and listing of words can suggest so much about the quality of verse is revealing; all the more reason to draw this device into a larger analytical framework.

Berry (1958), Melchiori (1973), Aers, Hodge and Kress (1981), as well as others more transiently, have made a start into what can be done with 'deep structures' once we pass beyond a primary concern with diction to basic questions of grammar, syntax, and ambiguity. The shifting, nuanced function of the personal pronoun — especially *I, thou,* and *we* — may signify social status, social aspiration, anxieties rooted in the social system, interpersonal distances or proximities, and conceptions of the self (self-definitions) either imposed by traditional societal gradations or extrapolated from a new and subversive notion of 'use' — use as market value or use as 'policy' (thus 'Machiavellian'). Melchiori picks out Spenser's preference in the *Amoretti* for the definite over the indefinite article, a grammatical choice which distances, formalizes and idealizes, all fully in accord with Spenser's glorification of poetry, of the poet's office, and of the objects of contemplation in poetry. This was the best way to conceive of poetry if, born a commoner, he was to win place and honor in a strutting, brazen, spendthrift, upper-class society which yet had serious pretensions to learning and culture.

Aers and Kress have observed that the characters in *King Lear* verge on the use of diverging syntaxes and modes of classification, and note that these indicate different ways of defining the self and differing social—moral positions *vis-à-vis* Lear, legitimacy of birth, and other matters.[26] But though a kindred form of analysis could be used in the study of lyric verse, their analytical particulars are too intricate for summary here and too closely tied to the text to allow for any ease of generalization. The procedures are still so novel or labored, and the theoretical parts so little tested on poetic texts and sometimes hazy, that there is a pressing need for a larger body of 'empirical' work in this vein. Somehow too, in work of this sort, at least in the beginning, there must be a readiness to do things by 'feel', to make mistakes, and to move daringly or intuitively, depending upon the text and problems. In time, the progress of such scholarship will draw out and correct the early mistakes. We cannot let the quaint old honor of positivism get in the way of our trying to answer certain major questions. Historical and literary scholarship are littered with the bones of bygone views — a history of trial and error.

More readily communicable is the notion of an 'anti-language', often seen in Donne's verse. The poet imagines an ideal — say love — and sets it up as an alternative reality, a rival to the world. The essential linguistic resource here is that of negation, but insistent contrast and opposition will also do. Everything that the busy world is the lovers are not, so that all the points along a broad front are taken from the world, but only to be opposed or denied. Here is a 'language' of flight, yet 'it reveals, through its evasions, what parts of reality are problematic' either for the writer or for the larger community. Any anti-language is largely shaped by the impinging social world.[27]

Since Empson we have known that the study of lexical ambiguity takes us into a vast underworld of entailed, stubborn meaning.[28] Like other people, poets often say more than they mean to or mean more than they say. The force of semantic association, as here implied, is likely to involve the whole question of figurative language, and so allows for a natural transition to one of the most suggestive areas of study for social literary analysis.

The famous opening hymn to gold in Johnson's *Volpone* necessarily introduces the image of the beloved mistress of amatory verse (though no woman is mentioned there) because, like the gold of Volpone's paean, she is conventionally and indeed obsessively associated with the sun, with light, and with saintly touches.[29] Often, too, she was equated with precious stones and treasure hoards. This means that for readers steeped in the idiom, as literate contemporaries were, the central human image of Renaissance love verse is somehow present in Volpone's opening lines and is, I believe, an ingredient in what is strong and disturbing about them.

Gold (power), the beloved (love), saint or relic (religion), sun (light, life): these would seem to be natural metaphorical equations — especially as all stand for a supremacy of some kind — but they are nothing of the sort. There is nothing *natural* in the linkage. Specific metaphorical possibilities are a product of culture and social experience. The discovery of the new world had opened the way to a vision of untold riches. Educated Elizabethans and Jacobeans were fully aware of overseas investment, hazardous naval exploits, international commercial rivalry, colonization and a raging inflation. Their history unfolded around a great turning point in the world and national economy, though few of them could see this. Yet the anxiety and excitement, the strain and audacity obscurely connected with the inflation and the quest for riches, all appear in poetry's figurative language.[30] Here — in Marlowe, Shakespeare, Chapman, Donne, Jonson and others — we find a straining for new expression and new figures, for the right ways of confronting new experience or new perceptions: matter which in many cases had not previously been handled or felt in literature. No wonder, then, that contemporaries were extraordinarily sensitive to change in literary fashion. They took change and fashion for granted in dress, fortunes, domestic architecture, and literary taste, even if Jonson looked to the classics as anchor and ideal. His learning lent him a sense of identity in a world riven by invidious status and made pettish by the feeling that 'base' parvenus were everywhere.

Modern scholarship offers many studies of imagery and metaphor in individual poets and works, especially in dramatic verse, and scholars occasionally trace a commanding image or a metaphorical cluster in the work of diverse poets.[31] But while doing different things, we should also strive to match the boldness and amplitude of vision of the field's early workers — for instance Wells, E. Holmes, and Spurgeon. Following are some questions and hypotheses for future work.

We may begin by asking why Renaissance poets make so much of the seasons and what they do with these in their figurative language. Has their concern to do with literary convention, with proximity to the land, the obvious importance of farming, discomfort in the wintertime, or the hope of plenty and fear of famine in pre-industrial societies? Has it to do with the best observable way of marking the regularity of natural change — a cycle of predictability? Or should we take notice first, where the case invites it, of the poet's preoccupation with *mutability,* and is it this that fixes his attention to the seasons? Therefore, are we dealing with the thematic convention of mutability, hence with a matter more social than private, or does the theme do double service? How routinely, and how slyly or openly, are the seasons converted into *the* order of nature and thus used to help describe youth, beauty, aging, worldly fortune, change in the social order, or social supremacies of some kind? In other words, how is 'nature' recruited to aid in the job of circumscribing 'culture' and validating judgements about society, authority, social groups, family organization, and 'natural' superiorities? If youth is held to be superior to age because of the latter's nearness to death or the former's vigor and beauty, and the seasons are continually used to underwrite this claim, may there not also be, in the general diffusion of such a feeling, some devious but telling statement about the stresses and fears of the particular society?

Kindred questions could be raised about all imagery relating to the sea, shipping, navigation, maritime enterprise, naval power, and overseas adventure. In the sixteenth and seventeenth centuries, in and around London especially, these made for a critical part of the English experience. As with the Genoese three centuries earlier,[32] all things connected with the sea and with ships came to provide the English with a vocabulary which was transferred over to other spheres of experience — to love, religion, trade, property transactions, and certainly to politics, war, personal feuds, and ways of self-definition. English attitudes toward the sea were transcoded into a language of contemporary experience. And I suspect that the social analysis of this entire imagistic range would tell us something about the emerging, domineering (?) psychology of England's upper-class groups. If so, any such finding would bear directly on our understanding of social and political values, social climbing, and even — looking to the longer term — southeast England's readiness to stand up to Charles I in the 1640s.

The whole register of words pertaining to profit and gain is so emphatic and colorful throughout the later sixteenth and seventeenth centuries, that there must be, in one of Kenneth Burke's locutions, a 'perturbation' here — more than meets the eye. What is going on at the psycho-social roots of such usage? Sustained study of this line of diction, particularly as observed in figurative combinations, would tell us more about Tudor and Stuart ways of thinking, feeling, and perceiving: steps on the way to a deeper understanding of the period's forms of consciousness.

An attentive reader, alleging bias in my picking out of the vocabulary of profit and gain, might ask, why not also choose figurative language built around verbs of donation, generosity, and charity? There would be nothing wrong with this in principle, but I fear that such study would turn out to be profitless (!) and enormously laborious for two reasons. First, it would center on the analysis of traditional (and Christian) themes, leading back to time immemorial, whereas the strategy I propose, in dealing with the poetry of a time of profound change, calls for a picking out of what is new, disturbing, and vital. Secondly, verbs of giving and generosity are too easily drawn into an idealizing mode,[33] as in courtly or eulogistic verse; but wherever 'idealization' is the problem for analysis, we must look for strategies to go around it, not to connive with it.

Elsewhere in this study I have noted that the theme of sexual lust in

Elizabethan and Jacobean poetry is often joined to a variety of supposed evils in the society.[34] The mechanics of conjoining in this case are simple enough. Having selected a fierce and insinuating passion, already condemned by the culture, the poet uses it as a metaphor for ambition, usury, pride, greed, or even political corruption. Lust can be pinned easily to a self-serving egotism (individualism) and this may be seen, in turn, as a menace to society and the moral order. I hypothesize that in the decades around 1600 London saw such a spectacle of new money, unprecedented display, and reckless speculation, that in the effort to understand and summarize this show of disturbing energy, poets hit on the imagery of sexuality as a catch-all metaphor. Indeed, imagination glided this way with so much ease that poets sometimes ended by taking the metaphor (lust, illicit sex) for the real thing (alleged corruption in society and the body politic) in believing that the suppression of lust would lead to the elimination of society's evils.

The image of the eyes, so pervasive in Renaissance love poetry, is a convention of course, above all when the eyes of the woman addressed are metaphorized, for example, as light, stars, the sun, or the power of sovereignty. This convention lost out in the course of the eighteenth century, when its social world passed away; but its vitality in Renaissance England (and on the Continent) serves, I believe, to help underwrite the claim concerning an 'Elizabethan world picture'. The picture centered on the notion of a 'hierarchy of being'. Eyes, light, the sun, stars, and sovereignty were all intuitively linked with 'higher' things: with sight (the most 'spiritual' of the senses), soul, mind, God, kings, power, nobility, and supreme values. The model was hierarchy with a mind—matter dualism. As a result, for all its conventionality, eye imagery in Tudor and Stuart love verse must have filched a good deal of its affective force from received social, political, and religious views — views, however, that tilted much closer to gut feeling than to intellectual constructs.

Wherever they have gone to work on legal and court records, historians have found that late medieval and Renaissance Europe was a litigious place, particularly in and around the cities and towns. Appropriately, a line of legal diction found its way into the verse of the period, introducing a variety of ideas that reveal the track of changing attitudes towards property, family arrangements, and trade. But more challenging for social analysis might be the stuff of the sky, storms, rivers, countryside, and wild animals. The imagery of these abounds in Renaissance verse, attached in simile, antithesis, or metaphor to concrete social and cultural observation. A remarkable study has singled out the ways in which the face of landscape in seventeenth-century verse teems with political, social, and ideological concerns.[35] Working its way into figurative language, the great political schism of the century tainted the most innocent-looking verse.

One scholar has noted that by the 1670s 'The main Tory model for society was that of the family, the Whig model that of the contract.'[36] In effect, the struggle for power was also a struggle for metaphor: the marketplace and the process of exchange came to be ranged on one side, while the other side sought its models in the imagery of the household, central authority, the king, cohesive love, and stability. If this was so, we have a clue here to the way in which clashing political and social ideals enlist the help of imagery which then, on being drawn into verse, is already tainted with ideology. In these matters, the informed poet — and the seventeenth-century poet was informed — cannot be innocent.

The preceding observations and suggestions may be converted into proposals for the social analysis of certain themes and accents in poetry's figurative language. All would have a common aim: to find the social vision in poetry, to situate vision and poems in time and place, and to use the spyglass of poetry to help us peer into the historical process — which is to say that the historical process is also a history of consciousness.

Having touched on questions of imagery, I should mention the sheer quantity and variety of metaphor in Elizabethan and Jacobean verse, especially in relation to a corresponding expansion or vitality in English experience. Although there are many hints of this relationship in the scholarship, it has not been truly studied.[37] Inventories of metaphorical usage may turn out to be helpful in this connection but do not in themselves broach the point.[38] The direction of inquiry would have to seek consciously to connect historical experience to the production of metaphor. If we grant this connection, where might the inquiry begin?

Since the search for metaphor is a search for new expression, I assume that a pullulation of metaphor is indicative of rapid social change and a widening of experience and consciousness. The bubbling up of new metaphor cannot be the mark alone of an ordinary quest or simple desire to talk about old things in new ways. We are trying to account for ferment. If we accept this line of reasoning, then we can project a number of starting points for our inquiry by moving from our understanding of the history of the period rather than from any particular text. I have already cited two matrices of experience that hold energy and novelty in this period — enterprising contact with the sea, and commercial—financial activity; hence the study of imagery and metaphor drawn from these might be a point of departure. Seven other new matrices for metaphor also occur to me: (1) the urban scene, (2) the new astronomy, (3) the ephemera of nascent skepticism, (4) the idea of fashion as vogue, fad, or latest usage, (5) ostentatious display (carried to astonishing levels in the late sixteenth and seventeenth centuries), (6) the decorative arts (also seen on a new scale), and (7) poverty as an ominous or wicked condition.[39] I am proposing that to do a social exegesis of metaphor gleaned from these matrices might issue in a major contribution to the tracking of change in the consciousness of the literate, upper-class groups. The study could be concentrated on a particular use of metaphor, on imagistic clusters, on individuals, or on a scatter of poets over time.[40]

A clutch of remarks on satire was inevitable.

Although satire has unsuspected pitfalls, it is an obvious subject for historians and social critics because it seems to deal directly with aspects of social reality, such as the vices and follies of people in society, usually in urban society. The importance of satire for social analysis is in its alerting us to central themes. It puts us before a lively dialectic of social attitudes, the attitudes both of those to be pilloried and those doing the pillorying; and it is likely to supply us with idioms, or even with speech rhythms, that are closer to ordinary usage than the like in other forms of 'privileged' — as opposed to 'popular' — verse. At the same time, however, the power of censorship must be borne permanently in mind. Satire had to sidestep all controversial matters pertaining to Church, state, and official doctrine. What hearing could early seventeenth-century 'atheism' get? How aim derisive or mocking attacks directly at the Church of England, at corruption in high place, at monarchy, the nobility, London's municipal and financial oligarchy, patents of monopoly, or the sale of baronetcies? Satire was hounded with restrictions, quite apart from the fact that publication of the formal genre — though it went on — was halted by episcopal order in 1599. Yet criticism of tabooed subjects did get into the mode, and this means that any effective social analysis of satire must know how to detect its devious strictures. Late in Elizabeth's reign and under James I, for example, the thrusts of wit against exhibitionism must on occasion have been directed at the very Court. When this happened, how was the attack both disguised and made known?

I mentioned pitfalls. We cannot take simply for granted that Elizabethan and early Stuart satire makes immediate contact with social realities.[41] This may be what satire is supposed to do and in the years around 1600 the illusion is certainly there, so far as satirists scoff at or censure upstarts, prodigals, usurers, fawning courtiers, lawyers, Puritans, painted women, Inns-of-Court dandies, and so on. But it is also true that satire selects, exaggerates, and caricatures — thus its *mediating* activity. It snatches men or situations from their norms and puffs them up or reduces them to bare essentials: the glutton ('essence') is made monstrous and the miser or usurer is reduced to wiles. Now the general presumption is that the social critic knows how to discount and adjust satire's distortions of reality. If so, then we can turn directly to the cardinal question, and that is, how can we draw social insight from satire's *ways of distortion?* Interestingly, once we qualify the notion that satire makes immediate contact with reality, then we are back to where we have to confront the devious, layered, or fictive core of Renaissance poetry — the true problem for social analysis.

The question of how to gain historical insight from satire's mode of distortion has no general answers because what we need is guidance in the many and fine particulars of the mode. Two examples must serve.

One striking feature of Marston's *The Scourge of Villanie* (1598) is the angry, bitter, exhibitionistic tone of the speaker, also typical of the other railing satires of the period. Tone and railer have been associated with the archetypal figure of the fool, who could be either scapegoat or central actor in a life-giving ritual 'wherein he was called upon as a magical protector against evil forces'.[42] The anthropology of this to one side, in London in 1598 Marston's tone belongs to the frustrated voice of young talent, to an ambitious Inns-of-Court man standing before the sight of narrowing career opportunities, rampant cynicism in high place, spectacular visual differences between rich and poor, and a taste for vigorous sermon. Here, in short, the social insight is likely to be taken from tone and theme in satire's distorting mode.

The second example looks to metaphor rather than to tone. We noted that the eponym of Jonson's *Volpone* (1605—6) opens the play with a hymn equating gold, the sun, saintliness, and light. The vision aims to evoke both sudden astonishment and laughter, for the traditional structure of Christian values has been abruptly turned upside down. To raise a mineral, the basest matter of received doctrine, to the heavens is so calculated, extreme, and jeering that explanation propels us to beware of some nagging disturbance in social consciousness. This is underlined by the play's great success at the time and by the wholesale removal of London doings to Venice — a ploy on Jonson's part to dodge criticism and defuse tension. We could then go through the text, picking out a mode of metaphorical organization, including the names of all the main characters, designed to carry the play's fleering indictment. And though set in Venice, *Volpone* undoubtedly touched an exposed nerve in London, where the money market, quickened by royal borrowing and the swift resale of former monastic lands, turned fiercely intense in the decades around 1600. This is chronicled in the scale of ostentation and bankruptcy among peers and rich gentlemen, and in the feverish activity of loan sharks, middlemen (brokers), influence peddlars, and lending combines.[43] There was little if any Christian *caritas* in this world and no quarter was offered.

In finding the link between Volpone's praise of gold and the hunger for cash and assets in London, I have moved as well from the text as from historical circumstance, with the positive response of playgoers supplying an essential contact. We can substitute poem and readers for play and playgoers. And in my movement both from text and world, we see something of the circular procedure in social analysis. The movement is paradigmatic. To the question, therefore, whether it is better to take poem or world as our point of departure, the answer is that we should move from both more or less simultaneously. The literary scholar or critic may favor the poem as starting point and the historian may favor the world. But if the gap between poem and world is to be bridged, soon enough the historian must look out for the poem and the literary scholar must look away from the poem to consider its impinging historical world. Indeed, the circular movement in the search for connections between poem and world will have started long before this, for whoever undertakes the social analysis of verse will already know something about the period and its poetry, and will therefore proceed with a sense of where he wants to look and the kinds of relations he is likely to find. This is to say — to go back to the beginning — that when the social critic picks up the text of a poem and begins to read it, his mind keeps darting back and forth between what the text seems to be saying and what he already knows about its historical world. It is also to say that as the historian thinks about the Renaissance period, reflecting on politics and social groups, on the economy and on the culture, he keeps wondering about how certain poems, poetic fashions, or schools fit or do not fit into the world he has envisaged.

I have said something apparently scandalous about method, in proposing that the social historian of poetry begin with a sense of what he is looking for. Am I saying that he should begin with a thesis and then go out to rustle up the evidence? Of course not, although some historians of the first rank — Gibbon, Burckhardt — seem to have worked in this manner. The fact is that when starting out to do a sustained piece of work in a richly documented field, any historian must journey with a sense of direction or expect never to return from that sea of particulars.

When the historian or critic confronts poems that do not fit into the social world he has envisaged, what then? The answer comes of itself: either there is something wrong with his social analysis of the verse, or he must be prepared to accept that he has the society and period wrong. If the latter, then he must alter his views. Hard as it may be for historians to swallow, this indicates that poetry has a potential input to make in our ways of reconstructing the past. To restate and amplify this, for we brush up here against the possibility of circular reasoning: if a set of poems does not fit into the historical world such as we have cast it, then we may have to shift both our grasp of the period and our mode of social analysis. So doing, we call on poetry to help us readjust our picture of the historical world and we allow that picture to guide us in deciding upon our strategies of social literary analysis. There is a circular give and take here, but not circular reasoning. That is, we do not use A to prove B, then call on B to establish A. However, if both A and B are unsteady but interdependent, then the firmer one is, say A, the more it may help us to give a place to the other, B; and when B is more clearly defined, it may then, in its turn, tell us something novel about A, owing to their interdependence. Historical reasoning is full of operations of this sort. Not, of course, that the historical world depends upon poetry. But when I suggest that world and poem (i.e., world and a sliver of consciousness) are interdependent, I do not mean as to existence; I mean, rather, with respect to the way in which we as historians and critics perceive them.

Since the efficacy of social analysis rests on movements of perception commencing from both poem and world, can there be any value, say, at some early stage in research, to giving more attention to one or the other? In theory no, in practice yes, above all when the student is working out of his particular preparation and talents.

Example   Literary scholars know that in the development of lyric style between about 1610 and 1670, Donne's passion and intellectuality cede to smoothness and to Jonson's mode of urbanity, although the Cavaliers convert this into a more social idiom — less elliptical, more restricted in its thematic range, and having at once more ease and more formality when needed. Moving from a view of this change, Walton, J. H. Summers, Chernaik, Weidhorn, Squier, and other scholars have referred fleetingly in their accounts to escalating political tensions and the stimulus of changing relations between poets and their reading public. This projection is perfectly sound from the standpoint of social analysis. But a student with a prior commitment to history, on turning his attention to the same question (change in lyric style, 1610—70), would most likely cast about first for a deeper and more comprehensive shift in social and political attitudes. Bringing a different cargo and viewpoint to the question, and called upon, in *his* terms, to explain a change in (literary) consciousness, he might turn to the deepening crisis in Church, state, and society, especially as attested from the late 1620s; to the expanding and provocative influence of Puritanism, the rising sense of beleaguerment at Court, the altering consciousness of men in high places, and the larger reading public of the 1640s and 1650s.

Putting all these together and steeping himself in the poetry of the Cavaliers, the historian would inevitably come up with additional reasons for poetry's direction in the time of Carew, Suckling, Cowley, Lovelace, Waller, Herrick, and Marvell, as well as lesser lights like Davenant, King, and Denham. He would have to get their verse right, to be sure — no easy task in itself. When he had it 'right', or right enough, having also familiarized himself with the best scholarship on Marvell and the Cavaliers, he might then find himself having to revise some part of his picture of the history of England in the seventeenth century, But in getting down to the question of change in lyric style, he would be forced to narrow and focus his analysis finely enough to enable him to deal with matters of language, theme, imagery, tone, syntax, and style. Here, finally, historian and literary scholar converge, as they seek explanations that bring them ever closer together.

A strategy untouched by the preceding projections is neither historical nor literary but a derivative of both. The fact that the rise of Cavalier verse coincides with the greatest period of English religious poetry (Herbert, Herrick, Vaughan, Crashaw, Milton, Traherne) is unlikely to be an accident. The levity, wordliness, and social face of one is rivaled or contradicted by the privacy and moving spirituality of the other, although Herrick often moved back and forth between the two. It is as if this opposition sums up the conflict between the nation's more austere and more sensual energies: private responsibility versus some kind of social 'recklessness', in a reckoning in which the latter is made to appear all the more reprehensible by the Puritan onslaught, so that even Herrick lands in the devil's party. But proof of the pertinence and vitality of this opposition, and its worth for our way of apprehending the entire historical scene, would require a close comparative analysis of the two poetries, especially with regard to language, style, and metaphorical usage.

I have often implied but at no point stated what may now be asserted outright. At its best, social literary analysis requires the skills of an ideal worker, one who moves the course of inquiry not only from poem to world and world to poem but also inclusively, taking in as much of the two as is relevant and possible. So far as the poem is concerned, this means that he is likely to touch upon themes, diction, figurative language, style, social viewpoint, tone, and all related matters of syntax and prosody. So far as the world is concerned, he must display the competence to speak in historical detail about society, politics, the economy, the principal institutions, the process of change, the religious and intellectual traditions, patronage, education, levels of literacy, elite groups, and the immediate context of poetry. Beyond these proficiencies, the ideal worker should have a sustaining interest in questions of methodology, for his distinguishing aims will depend upon procedures and strategies, hypotheses and solutions, that have no conventional rules or validation in any of the established disciplines; and this will also call for a readiness to familiarize himself with subject-matter in the fields of linguistics, semiotics, and anthropology.

As the substance of an intellectual preparation, these requisites seem, but are not, unreal. The conditioning pessimism lies in the specialization imposed by the structure of our universities. In turning ourselves into specialists, whether in history or literature, we spend much time on trivia and inessentials. Replace this with a more directed program of wider reading and research, and we could do far more to prepare ourselves and others for the tasks of social literary analysis.

Drawing fully on the resources of social analysis, say in the study of Donne, the ideal reader relates the different aspects of his verse to the London scene, the Inns-of-Court setting, the unsettled religious milieu, the pull of elite social circles, the fickleness of patronage, a rising mood of disillusionment with the Court, the swagger of wealth and rank, a certain stage in the development of English society, financial and career pressures, the use of the new and old astronomies in social statement, and a similar use of accents drawn from late medieval philosophy and science. To these, in variant ways, he relates Donne's imagery, the learned features of his diction, alleged colloquialisms, his shifting uses of the middle and low styles, certain dramatic stances, and metrical roughness; also his smart, wheedling, and *odi profanos* tones, as well as his satirical, amatory, and religious themes. Now, in splicing world and poetry thus, our reader also makes us aware of the lyric and short-poem traditions, as he underlines Donne's conformities with and departures from them. But in the process of drawing his findings into a coherent account, he works from a core of observations concerning Donne's ambitions, preparation, whereabouts in the social structure, and the way in which these relate to the course of English society around 1600. For it is likely that the unsteadiness of Donne's social identity will show up in all aspects of his verse.

Having said enough about the ties between language and society to raise possible questions about the traces of social content in the key words of this study, I dare not conclude without a comment on the language of social literary analysis.

The main assumptions of this book have been set forth in a series of propositions (pp. 1—4). These provide the reasons for the language of social analysis as understood here. But I also see that the shadow of the present age falls across the propositions. The wish to break through the surface of the language of poetry, to its underlying social and historical flux, belongs to the suspicions and disenchantments of the late twentieth century. We know that words may say one thing and signify something else. What is that something else, what is going on beneath the surface of discourse? The very form of this question is a roundabout statement of twentieth-century worries and assumptions. It is a response to fundamental controversy (the haven of rhetoric both as art and knavish instrument); it comes out of a time of wildly conflicting interests and world views, 'an age of ideology', where all the sides in conflict lay claim to truth, reality, nature, and humanity. In the sixteenth century, another age of total controversy for Europe, the spokesmen for a world picture, whether Catholic or Protestant, all believed in God, natural hierarchies, and the fixed order of nature. But in the twentieth-century clash this is gone; the conflicting claims are, for the most part, absolutely worldly; anything goes; and this makes for a disposition on the part of some observers to try to see through everything. In this mêlée we have part of the explanation for the rise of linguistics, semiotics, deconstruction, and certain sociologies; for the demotion of 'elite' history, the militant espousal of the study of 'popular culture', the campaigns to write 'history from below', 'women's history', and 'Third World History'. The same mêlée also helps to explain the rise of 'quantitative history' — an effort to escape ideology (though this is failing) and endorse 'science' by putting social history on a numerical basis, chiefly by means of demography.

All this I see and attest. Does it mean, therefore, that the call for the historical and social analysis of poetry is a late twentieth-century quirk?

That language is used not only to express and communicate matters but also to conceal them and control people was a fact well known to the rhetoricians and philosophers of the ancient world. Again, at different times during the many centuries between Aristotle's work on the Athenian constitution and Machiavelli's *The Prince,* men have known that the vital interests of people, social classes, and elites may be masked by claims that invoke nature, reality, the general good, God, or other 'sacred' values. What the twentieth century has done in these matters, apart indeed from using language to conceal and control affairs, is to search for ways of getting behind the face of all discourse, so as to identify its shaping forces and interests. Rightly considered, poetry may be thought the target *par excellence* of such a search, precisely because its language and themes are likely to be heightened or lapidary, figural, devious, or fictive. Its stock in trade is direction by indirection.

So much, then, for the why of social literary analysis and its moorings in the experience of the twentieth century. The underlying vision issues from a long-term crisis. This guarantees its living features but also reveals the vision's temporal character, the fact of its belonging to a time and place. Does this return us to the matter of a late twentieth-century quirk? No, instead it faces us with a paradox which turns in favor of social analysis. Once we accept that there is no exit from our times, we come to see that our involvement in the present, our own vitality, is alone what links us to what is vital in the past, vital also for us, for the past exists as a past and is meaningful only through us. If we do not care about the present, we cannot as historians care about the past, although we may look upon it as antiquarians and collectors of curios. We pick out the vitality of the past through the life we live, and it is this living interplay, a function of our very rootedness in time, which enables us to look at history with fresh eyes and to pose searching, new questions.

The notion of 'social identity' — a capital phrase in this book — is the key for bridging a pervasive dualism in Western thought: that between art and reality, consciousness and society, 'high' culture and social structure, imagination and power. These are variations all of the presumed cleavage between 'mind' and the social world ('reality') lying outside the mind. A social identity — a person's identification and placement within a social structure — is both in the mind and outside. We sense, think, and feel that we are what we are in a social milieu of some kind; and *others* also perceive us to be more or less that. Along with our sense of self-identity, when this is thought out, there also goes a sense of our society and indeed a whole social vision, a view of the world. This sense of self-identity, which is a social vision too, works its way into the language, style, paraphrasable content, and outlook of poetry, be it Renaissance or modern. The dualism is overcome.

I have sought to limit my usage to the language and idioms of scholarship of the past fifty or sixty years. Yet even so some of my words and epithets must occasionally seem difficult, particularly at the points where an attempt is being made to join poem and world. The trouble here rather speaks for itself. Most people believe that *society* is something 'out there', some force or near tangible in 'the real world'. They do not see that it is also in them, in their minds, in all the values and signifying codes, loyalties and censures, that go to make and maintain a society.

In keeping the language of this book to scholarly usage, I am conscious of having skirted a large body of contemporary literary and social theory, which is often charged with being a dark forest of jargons. This is the place, therefore, to comment on the matter of 'jargons' and new theory.[44]

Until history comes to an end, the rise or 'production' of *new* meaning must be an ongoing process. Plato cannot reach to the end of time. But the rise of new meaning — most apparent in periods of profound change — is likely to require neologisms and novel turns of phrase. This alone suffices to explain and vindicate much recent 'jargon'. New words help to sharpen new ways of seeing and thinking. For the science of signs — semiotics, semiology — this is no more than to say that we cannot have new 'signifieds' (concepts) without new 'signifiers' (words or acoustic images) or without new combinations of signifiers.

Semiotics and 'deconstruction' have three claims that bear importantly on social literary analysis.

1   We know reality through our systems of signification, language preeminently; and cognitively we cannot get outside these systems. More extremely put — though this claim is highly debatable —

there can be no experience, no meaningful experience, outside language. Again, our semiotic systems are not natural: they are culture-bound codes for breaking down and classifying reality. This means that their very structures are rife with social views of the world — ideology.

2 Meaning or signification may be transposed from one code to another, from one sign system to another, but something is always lost or distorted in the transfer, because every semiotic system comes to have a certain self-sufficiency, and consequently signifieds — meanings, concepts — may in some measure be a function ('product') of the system itself.

3 Language is fundamentally metaphorical, presumably in its design to refer to things that lie outside itself. For deconstruction, accordingly, even the plainest and most rigorous philosophical argument rests on a substratum of metaphor, so much so, indeed, that when we confront the argument with its figural substratum, we threaten it with a process of deconstruction.

Pushed to their limits, the foregoing claims bring up another, which I shall mention and remark on but not list, because it is excessively contentious: I refer to the radical deconstructionist claim that language is not referential, cannot really point to anything outside itself. In this view, literature turns into nothing more than the free play of signs; it is self-referential.

For historians, the most laconic response to this radical claim must be as follows. Either they reject the sealed-off autonomy of such a frank semiotic idealism, or they agree that historians normally turn historical events into signs, whereupon all written history becomes an account of the history of change *in* systems of signs. If, however, this be the case, then even the most complex of all games of signifiers, poetry, remains as close to history and social reality as it ever was.

As listed above, the third claim calls for a fleeting, but pointed, observation. By alerting us to the presence of basic, constitutive metaphor in all written discourse, including historical analysis, that claim raises questions about the way in which historians see and represent the events of past time. As a result, it puts them under the obligation to study the deposits of hidden metaphor in their writings; otherwise they run the danger of never recognizing that ideology *in* language works to help shape their historical interpretations.

6

Against specialization: history, poetry, milieu

The question of how academic subjects relate to our lives and present concerns — 'relevance' — was much raised by students in the late 1960s but was often so crudely put as to be easily scorned. So far as any plea for the relevance of study is a plea to turn *all* intellectual matter into an instrument for solving the problems of daily life, we are asked to do something mad. No present crisis, however catastrophic, could be so capacious as to receive the knowledge of all academic disciplines; nor could we take all studies and convert them into utilities, save by such a labor of surgery as to leave nothing but field of bones.

The real question of relevance is another one and is especially applicable to our two disciplines, history and literature. How these relate to life is a question which I have been asking throughout this study, though in another guise, because it is at the core of the problem of relations between history and literature. More precisely, this is the problem of how Tudor and Stuart society and politics, economics and institutions, affected people in their sensibilities and thinking: in their values and velleities, fears and attitudes, speech and imagination — the ground of literature. Evidently, history's relation to literature (and the converse) involves nothing less than the question of how each of these relates to life. We may say that the history of the seventeenth century *is* the life of the people of that century, and this is partly true but it also verges on metaphor. It would be truer to say that the history of the seventeenth century is whatever we, the living, salvage and make of it. No, not quite, for a great tradition of historical study comes down to us, determining our grasp of the seventeenth century. However, we validate the tradition, or not, and alter or pick at it continually; so that the way we view the past is an intellectual derivative of both past and present.

Our living preoccupation with contemporary economic and political problems, or at any rate our feeling about how these affect us, is the guarantee of our interest in seventeenth-century problems and in how these touched contemporaries. Here 'interest' has two senses that cannot be disentangled: the seventeenth century intrigues us in itself, but we also have an 'investment' of energies and personal predilections in it. One vitality (twentieth-century) is drawn to another (in the seventeenth century). This is why the student who asks that study have a relevance to his life is looking for something of the first importance. He is saying: 'Don't tell me how seventeenth-century politics affects me — it doesn't. Tell me, rather, how it affected the people of the seventeenth century, for in this "true" knowledge there may be something of value, something even of use, for me.' An element of self-interest underwrites the desired objectivity of study.

We read history and literature for pleasure. This is the ordinary way. But at the level of a discipline, in sustained study, we also read for some kind of knowledge and are supposed to have a sense of what we are doing. We want to know how a text works: how it is put together, what it seems to be saying, and these questions — as we have seen — are also historical in nature. Again, as historians we want to know how a society works, how it hangs together, and this requires the analysis — surely the literary analysis too — of a vast multiplicity of texts. But the question of how a text or a society works cannot be separated from acts of reading and the process of thinking. The observer is always present. In this engagement between past and present, between text and reader, we have the condition which imposes the existential relevance of study, though we shall not see this unless we know what we are about. Our being implicated, as observers, in the heart of literary and historical knowledge obligates us to raise questions about the ways we read and think — questions of method.

History is what historians tell us it is. They define it; they dress and present it. In an age of experts and specialists, we leave the defining tasks to them and perhaps rightly so, but let us also be aware of the consequences.

Since the early nineteenth century, when historical writing drifted away from its humanistic and literary origins to become a 'scientific' and academic discipline, its movement towards specialization has been continuous and unimpeded: from the history of politics, diplomacy, and war, to the history of law, economic history, the history of ideas, art history, the history of religion, the history of science, down to our own day, with urban history, agrarian history, parish history, quantitative history, women's history, psycho-history, the history of the family, of childhood, of climate, of popular culture, of human ecologies, and so forth. Specialization proliferates and academic careers are made on it. To bring history under scientific control, we turn its vast compass into a scatter of microscopic spots. Universities offer 'general surveys' and 'service' courses, as in the national histories, so as to 'introduce' students to the study of history, but the aim is, as students advance, to corral them in an ever narrowing field, culminating in the *specimen eruditionis,* the doctoral dissertation.

Specialization has made its point. History has had no greater array of choices, no more sophisticated techniques of research, than those before us at present. It is not true that we have come to know more and more about less and less — the eighteenth century went in for much airy generalization. Building on highly specialized competences, we have opened new fields and have come to know far more about the things that interest us; and while it is true that the microscopic image in historical study appears before us bearing the shadow and tremors of the observing specialist, yet the intensity of focus has allowed us to see things that no one had ever imagined were there.

But we have paid dearly for this intensity. We continually lose sight of historical wholes. The so-called 'cultural historian' — the type exists even in our day — is rarer and made to seem ever more 'subjective' in his studies, as monographs pour forth at a punishing rate.[1] Working perforce in a variety of staked-out fields, he cannot absorb all the specialized studies, and his wide sweep, as he moves from one field to another, from one order of problems to another, is bound to strike specialists as 'unscientific and careless', or even as 'frivolous and irresponsible'.

We know well what the advantages of specialization are. What are the consequences of losing sight of historical wholes?

As students of society past or present, if we ever take for granted — however fleetingly — that any society is likely to have some kind of functioning, organic, or vital unity, then we are also saying that its different parts are interrelated: its institutions, shaping values, practices, and variety of communities or classes. In fact, we do more than fleetingly take this for granted. At the university, this is what we suggest in general historical courses. This is what we feel or somehow know the moment we get away from the monograph, which after all is meant to fit into a larger whole. The most remote peasant village, whatever its autonomy, has beliefs, a dialect, folklore, tax burdens, methods of labor, and import needs (such as salt, iron, or textile goods), which graft it, as living tissue, onto the larger national world.

Where monographic work is concentrated on important parts of the large historical whole — 'important', an a priori value? — we may argue that the whole is being taken care of to the best of our human abilities, and hence the invaluable work of scientific specialization can go on.

Rather than seek an engagement here, in the specialist's mechanical use of the scientific model,[2] I shall take a more roundabout route.

Historical method, far more than scientific method, is subject to changing views and needs. The reason is that being *in* history and therefore in movement, we change the past in the very act of trying to see or interpret it. The more our society changes, the more likely we are to alter our vision of the historical past. In the past twenty years, we have seen the rise of a variety of 'new' histories, as noted above, centering on women, children, and family organization, as well as on urban life, village life, ecological balances, folk festivals, and folklore. The scale of change in current historical thinking is so remarkable as to suggest that we live in a time of extraordinary and distressing flux. The distress gets into the kind of history we write.

The use of computers and the quantification of historical fact is an attempt to make sense of the 'mess', to elude our entrenched values, to put things on a more scientific basis, and to resolve controversy. The attempt deserves our praise and close attention, because it has made exciting contributions and raised pivotal questions in the fields of demography, family reconstitution, the distribution of wealth, the incidence of poverty, and more recently in matters connected with the history of literacy and 'dechristianization' (the decline of piety in the eighteenth century). But working with computers also means 'preparing' evidence, so as to make it 'machine-readable', and this narrows or eliminates lanes of inquiry. Certain questions regarding consciousness and the fitting together of historical wholes are not readily quantifiable.

As if to compensate for, or even supplement, the insistence upon numbers in the quantitative approach, there is a new call for the historical study of popular culture, seen especially in studies of folk festivals, customs, religion, and folklore.[3] This trend aims to return 'folk mentalities' to history. It seeks all the elements of a practical and down-to-earth culture, but also the irrational, superstitious, mythic, and magical fictions that characterized the thinking and consciousness of most people for millennia. The quest is one, in Le Roy Ladurie's words, for a 'non-elitist mentality'.[4] And here suddenly, in the aims of work on the history of popular culture, we have all the validation needed to call for the restoration of literature to historical study. If it be important and urgent to study the fantastic and the imaginary in popular culture, why may the socio-historical study of highbrow literature not be countenanced? Is it because the culture of 'the people' has definite and obvious roots in society, whereas 'literature' does not? A few years ago, when there was a great deal of talk about writing history 'from below' — meaning the history of women, peasants, workers, the poor, and Third World people — the same speakers dismissed the historical study of 'elite culture' because it was 'privileged', detached from 'reality', and anyway 'has always been studied'. Nothing of the sort, as we shall see.

Meanwhile, something curious has happened. Le Roy Ladurie's *L'argent, l'amour et la mort en pays d'oc* (1980),[5] the most elaborate study ever done by an historian of a text rooted in the oral tradition of folk culture, has been hailed by one of the pundits of 'the semiotics of poetry', M. Riffaterre. To fit J.—B. Castor Fabre's thirty-page tale, *Jean-l'ont-pris* (1759) into its oral tradition and larger European background, Le Roy Ladurie was driven to seek help in the work of anthropologists, structuralists, linguists, semioticians, and folklorists. His analysis is checkered with words like code, encode, homology, structure, kinship, function, equivalent, decipher. He looks for homologous events, characters, and dramatic sequences in a whole cycle of tales; for linguistic affinities, puns, verbal parallels, and exact reversal in incidents of plot; and he also examines names, symbols, metaphors, and lexical ambiguities. The intent of his analysis is not only to delineate the folklore lying behind the story of *Jean-l'ont-pris* but also to separate fiction and fantasy from the social realities of southern France (Languedoc) in the eighteenth century, in order to establish more accurately the connections between tale and social world. Lesson: the images, tales, and dream-life of popular culture, while having much to tell us about the social life of a people, also slant away from 'reality'. Here too, therefore, in striving to hurdle the gap between social world and fantasy, the historian must turn for help to anthropology, folklore, and especially the strategies of modern literary criticism.

The more historians take up the study of popular culture, the greater will be their need to seek the aid of literary analysis, but not alone for the decoding of folk texts. As Le Roy Ladurie found in an earlier study, *Carnival in Romans* (1979), popular festivals in pre-industrial societies glittered with visual signs and symbols and these also must be 'read', their code cracked, if the historian is to reach around them to the strains, fears, and hopes of everyday life. The medieval 'Feast of Fools', popular in France, was a dramatic public orgy. Relying on carts, costumes, and jesting, and drawing these into symbolic action, the fête turned the ecclesiastical and social hierarchy upside down, involved the hurling of excrement through the streets of the town, and ended in church with a burlesque parody of the mass. Turning to speech proper, one scholar has observed that 'Peasant communication itself is often story-like in character, repetitive, and highly symbolic.' But by close study of 'the precise terms of the description of a conflict in value, illicit behaviour, or protest, the historian can often reconstruct the logic of peasant behaviour and the structure of his symbolic world'.[6]

The fantastic and symbolic world of folk culture brings a certain irony and justice into this discourse, touching all those who have supposed that 'the people' stand closer to life, closer to 'reality', than elites and that popular culture is, therefore, more practical, functional, and 'earthy'. There is doubtless some truth to this, provided we note that 'life' and 'reality' here are being defined chiefly as work, hardship, the quest for staples, and the rudimentary forms as well of social assembly as of recreation in town and country. Yet what about the fairies and goblins, the witches and devils, the Cinderellas and 'Godfathers Death' of folk culture? If the culture of the privileged, particularly as represented in literature, tends to idealize the life of society, making it seem larger or more noble than it is, then highbrow idealizing may be juxtaposed with the marvellous and the fantastic in popular culture. In this alignment, which of the two stands closer to social reality, idealization or fantasy?

Obviously the former. On pressing further, however, the answer might be fantasy, if we assume that topsy-turvy reversals make for a basic device of imagination. Thus, in a setting of grinding poverty, the most loved and delightful story becomes the one about the poor orphan who grows up and, after many strange adventures, finally marries the king's daughter. Here poverty and the wishful thinking of fable are drawn closely together; the tight relation between the two is in the principle of opposites. But fantasy is likely to be far more complicated than this and the intended point here, in any case, is another: namely, that if our aim is to conduct a social and historical analysis, fantasy as well as idealization — whether in popular fables, highbrow verse, or the symbolism of festivals — must be 'decoded' and interpreted. By the sixteenth century, privileged and popular culture had already divided at many points, above all in education, art, music, and literature (sustained thinking — philosophy — had never belonged to anyone but an elite); but both cultures present ticklish and stubborn problems for social analysis and we need superior methods of inquiry for both.

However we choose to delimit it, the historical study of folklore, fable, or the symbolism of popular festivities and rites of passage is a quest for popular consciousness: for the way in which community thinking and imagination — as condensed ('structured') in tales, symbols, symbolic action, and fanciful images — sum up experience, ricochet with life's urgencies, and offer us a unique commentary. It is a search for the vivifying relations between culture and society, mind and action, imagination and history, fantasy and social world. Label this binary interplay how we will, the focus is here:[7] in two different orders of being, yet joined indivisibly together because one could not possibly be as it is without the existing condition and input of the other. Pick up a painting by Vermeer, or a Jacobean poem which is not pure imitation,[8] and you also pick up some important aspects — not reflections — of its world. Yet the unity underlying this relationship, the unity between culture and society, is negated by the practice of extreme specialization in historical scholarship.

The claim that 'privileged culture has always been studied' is true and false. True of course in the sense that 'literature', 'art', and the history of thought are studied in our schools and universities; but false in a deeper sense, in that they are given no determined or probing examination as cultural phenomena which are also social phenomena in a concrete historical world. We study 'the humanities' under a system of higher education which does not know how to see the unity of culture and society;[9] and with its fundamental commitment to specialization, it is organized to deny that unity.

We have seen (pp. 6ff., 98—9) that historians will accept any piece of prose, however literary, as a specimen of historical documentation, in the trust that some scrap or more of social reality is likely to be found there. Poetry alone is denied a place in the canon and I have shown that this is indefensible. Now we see that any aspect of popular culture, however fantastic, is fit for historical study, the carefree assumption being that the analytical strategies for deciphering fantasy already exist — the strategies that enable historians of popular fantasy to return to their ground in social reality. It is amazing how flexible historical method can suddenly become, and how ample its resources, provided only that we exclude poetry from the canon, although popular ballads — more of the material of folk culture — are fully acceptable.

Poetry held a prominent place in the syllabus of education for boys and young men from the upper classes of Elizabethan and Stuart society. It was a fundamental part of their rhetorical training, in pursuit of which they translated and retranslated Latin — rarely Greek — poetry until they could reel forth endless passages from memory. They were also encouraged to write poetry in accordance with classical models. Any bright young man with 'small Latin and less Greek', in joy, stress, or on imagining himself in love, was likely to try his hand at verse, for it had long been pressed on him. And we can scarcely open a printed collection of seventeenth-century poems by one author, without first coming on a series of commendatory poems by friends and occasionally close kinsmen of the poet, attesting to his literary skills and talents. Leading poets were not more likely to receive a larger number of poetic accolades than poets of the second or third rank, like Richard Lovelace and James Shirley. The latter's 1646 collection opens with poems of praise by Thomas Stanley, Thomas May, George Bucke, Francis Tucker, Edward Powell, and George Hill. Who were Bucke, Tucker, Powell, and Hill? Thomas Stanley's *Poems and Translations* of 1647 — 'Printed for the Author and his Friends', says the title page — are preceded by complimentary poems from the pens of William Hammond, William Fairfax, Edward Sherburne, John Hall, and James Shirley; and while all have entries in the DNB, who has heard of the first four, apart from a tiny handful of experts?

Owing to the central place of rhetoric and poetry in the grammar schools, and the likely effects of this in the formative years of well placed young men, we may assume the poetry of the later sixteenth and seventeenth centuries to be an important source for the study of mentalities among the affluent middle classes, educated gentry, and aristocracy. Study of this sort, however, would have to spurn the conventional academic walls between history and English literature.

The question of mentalities is supremely important and may be treated here from a different angle, which also looks to the problem of 'milieux'.

With its emphasis on 'the poem as a work of art', the New Criticism often verged on suggesting that 'the work' could be turned into a metaphysical entity and sealed off from the social world of the poet. We may wrench the poetic text from its historical and social context, but we do not thereby snuff out the lights that show it in its world. These come on in any probing study of the text and in this sense, at least, poetry is not divorceable from its worldly context, though we may elect to ignore or deny the binding relations.

We have seen that poetry is linked to a time and place by its language. An interesting point emerges here. Since we cannot wrench poetry away from its historical context, how can we wrench the context away from its poetry, from the body of literature which properly belongs to it? That is to say, how fully can we understand educated, upper-class London in the Elizabethan and Stuart periods without a study of poetry? The logic of this question should haunt historians and specialists. Just as we cannot isolate consciousness from its social reality, so can we not strip social reality away from the consciousness that goes with it; and in the seventeenth century, poetry belongs intimately to the thinking, outlook, taste, and reading of too many of the educated to be ignored by historians.

Let us consider this matter from yet another viewpoint. Suppose a historian asks, 'But if my field of specialization is the politics of the Civil War period, why need I know anything at all about poetry?' He need never have read a poem, of course, and therefore he will write a certain kind of history. His question, however, does not afford him the kind of protection he imagines: his announced boundaries remain vague and he still faces a multiplicity of options. What kind of political history will he write? How narrow and focused will it be, how drily construed, how *purely* political, how far responsive to ideas or to the values and emotions that impinge upon political action? Is his story to be biography, prosopography, a study of institutions, a venture in county history, a linear narrative with not much analysis? Or is it to be a searching inquiry, cutting across questions of social structure, economic interest, group psychologies, or movements of feeling, mood, and outlook? Will it delve into pamphleteering and propaganda, the incandescence of religious controversy, or the frontier of relations between political ideas and religious attitudes?

Clearly, then, if the task is taken seriously, to say that 'my field of specialization is the politics of the Civil War period' is to say something ambitious and encompassing. On looking into it the specialization disappears. For commitment to the politics of the 1640s may reach out to take in such a wide radius of affairs, that we begin to see the potential importance of poetry — even excluding the body of outright political verse — for any political historian who aspires to say things about the sensibility, fears, or outlook of some of the period's leading groups.

Let the preceding comments be illustrative. In the program to deny poetry a place in the repertory of historical documentation (a program certified by scholarly practice), specialists seek to define their subject-matter — economic, demographic, political, religious, institutional, and so forth — in such a way as to make poetry seem irrelevant. Yet the moment we press and probe within the specialization, trying to discover what kind of history is truly intended, what its alleged borders are and how satisfactory are its aims or ways of analysis, all the boundaries between historical fields begin to crumble; the different histories (e.g., intellectual, political, economic, religious) break up; and we get an open, richer, far more complex prospect of historical experience. Reality resists being segmented and diced.

The question of *how* we write political history, or any history, is always in part a question of 'milieu', of how we perceive the world around the events that we propose to examine. What kind of world is it? What are the things that matter in it (significance)? How do they interact or interrelate? What are the major forces there? How large a world, how ample an explanation, do we seek? Are we asking very limited and pointed questions, or questions that are more comprehensive, devious, and difficult? Questions about personalities or about 'conditions' and 'forces', about change or about persisting tradition? In explaining a crisis or major development, how far back do we go in time? Lawrence Stone looks back 130 years in his analysis of the causes of the English Civil War, while other historians cast no further back than the late 1630s.

As every historian knows, there are no set answers to these questions, no binding rules or axioms at this conceptual level that we either learn or teach in the professional study of history. The reason is that we continually alter our causal and material stresses in recognition of the commonplace that every historical situation is different, yet not so different that we develop a new method of analysis for every situation. In writing history, the truth is that we learn from practice and go by feel. But unless we are shaken up by a shock of events or a social crisis, our learning from historical practice is conservative. This is because the method we learn comes to us with a professional stamp of approval and therefore goes largely unquestioned. We take what is handed down to us, but what we are handed is full of built-in, hidden lessons, and one of these is especially revealing.

The more conservative the method of the historian, the narrower his envisaging of historical milieux and of the way things happen there and why. His is a labor of reduction and control. The economic historian who works in this manner tries to exclude as much of the 'non-economic' as possible, although this operation thrusts him at once against the problem of definition, of how he segments historical experience, of what is 'economic' and what is not. His conception of milieu is in fact an encounter with historical reality: he grapples with it so as to pare it down and make it manageable for study and presentation. Who would deny that this is an honorable purpose? But the operation is far more complex than practice tells us. For in our work as historians, as we project the lineaments of a milieu (something we come to do by intuition and almost unthinkingly), we are making fundamental discriminations and tacitly declaring in our practice, 'This counts and that doesn't. This belongs in the picture and that doesn't.' Here we have the historian's way of putting together his working milieu, in the light of which he will render his entire account of events, personalities, and developments. In short, as reconstructed by historians, every milieu — setting, environment, context — is in fact an analytical milieu.

I linger over the problem of milieu because it is precisely there, in the process of its being cast, as the historian's *evaluation* of reality is taking place, that poetry is eliminated. Historical practice offers no choice here: generations of students are schooled in the ostracizing of poetry from the historical canon. And the occasional use of epics, such as *The Song of Roland* or *Paradise Lost,* in courses on 'Western Civilization' cannot be viewed as serious historical discussion.

Specialists in the history of thought often speak of 'the intellectual milieu'. They mean a context made up of ideas and viewpoints: it is a construct for the analysis of the rise, movement, and modification of an idea or an idea cluster in a framework of flanking, contingent ideas. If the purview is wider or three-dimensional, then aspects of the social world of the thinkers may be taken into account. But the notion of an 'intellectual milieu' is a composition abstracted from the larger historical world, presumably so as to preserve the 'true' ground of ideas and to enable historians to discuss them properly. In this usage, 'properly' must mean something like 'correctly' or 'according as the subject matter demands'. But does the subject matter impose such demands a priori? If, in addition, we insist upon the autonomy of ideas, then the abstraction or model — the milieu consisting purely of ideas — becomes all the more important, as it is only there, on that ideal ground beyond the reach of social structures, that ideas can have the imagined autonomy. Much the same sort of mental operation — abstracting and reconstructing — goes into elaborating the specialized milieux which provide the ground for the supposed autonomy of art and poetry.

The foregoing work of abstraction is fully endorsed by the aims of specialization. I offer two summary observations in response. First, ideas may appear 'pure' on the written page, but in addition to any genealogy of ideas, other matters also enter into their production, such as the historical moment (i.e., current urgencies), educational preparations, the state of the language, and the subtle glow of influences cast by the deepest values of thinkers. Consequently, to try to grasp an idea in its socio-moral context is not an exercise in 'reduction' — far from this; it is an attempt to press closer to the existential reality. The charge of 'reductionism' is often delightedly made by historians and reviewers who insist that ideas be immaculately treated and who lean toward a belief in their autonomy. Coming on an inquiry which links ideas and social interests, they pounce triumphantly on the analysis, alleging that it 'reduces' ideas to social quiddities of some kind. Is it not rather the other way around? Is it not the immaculate approach to ideas which reduces the three-dimensional wealth of milieux to elementary constructs, rendering them geometric, static, and more manageable?

My second response to the elaboration of specialized (thinned out or reduced) milieux is that wherever the history of art or literature is broken by emphatic new directions, by swift changes in style and content, there we shall find the impact of 'outside' forces. These may center on religious revolution, changes in patronage and audiences, rapid economic transformation, profound political dislocation, sustained war and invasion, or other matters of this magnitude. But once we find or admit the effects of non-artistic phenomena on art and poetry, the argument regarding autonomies becomes indefensible. To have to explain swift and decisive change in art and literature is what undoes all autonomist approaches.

I have introduced the subject of special milieux, as used by historians of ideas and in histories of art and literature, to indicate how simple it is for professionals to turn their fields of study into little worlds by abstracting them from the larger historical universe. The practice is universal, but it is an expedient convention, not a method imposed by the nature of the historical process.

To banish poetry from history is no innocent act. It is to say that poetry had no significant bearing in any milieu which might be of interest to the historian. Put thus, the claim suddenly seems absurd. In the hierarchy of 'things' that go into a milieu, if politics, economics, and social structures have a prime importance, do community values, religion, and ideas merit a secondary place? Obviously not, as these are likely to be inextricably joined to social organization, institutions, politics, and economics. Then is it only philosophy, the arts, and folklore that are secondary? Are these the artefacts that need no place in *significant* milieux? The governing class in Elizabethan and Jacobean England tended to attach emphatic importance to music, family portraits (obvious social emblems), dress, and the decorative arts. Do these, when studied, reveal nothing about consciousness or mentalities? The houses of the gentry were often decoratively painted with the armorial bearings of the leading local families. Social rank worked its way onto ceilings and wainscotting.

The argument may now be extended, in a series of questions, by a return to my political example.

What was the feeling, mood, or temper in and around the Court after 1638, when the political skies began to darken fast? What did courtiers and their close acquaintances talk about when they averted their eyes from politics? How did they carry the rising public strains over into their private lives and recreations? Did royalists turn to frivolous or carefree pastimes for distraction from the menace of political crisis? Since politics would soon menace their very existence, how irresponsible, self-deluding, or out of touch with 'reality' were the ardent followers of the king in the early 1640s? Is it not true that Cavaliers and Puritans looked differently upon love and marriage, and if so, *how* so, for we think we know why.

Every one of these questions could be discussed and partly answered on the basis of material drawn from the large body of late Metaphysical, Cavalier and affiliated verse. Evidently the questions are slanted toward verse, in procedures of the sort regularly observed by historians, who confront their streams of ordinary documentation with pertinent queries. But the questions also enlarge our analytical milieu. No doubt some historians will think them not worth asking. No doubt questions about poverty, incomes, productivities, birthrates, and local authority have more substance and a higher causal importance, particularly when seen in the light of twentieth-century problems. While readily granting this, I simply say that the urgency of topics such as poverty and productivity underwrites the importance of our learning how to decipher or demystify the proud 'documents' (the 'literature') of the privileged and powerful. Privilege is, after all, a function of its denial to the many. And the right study of society is a study of parts and wholes, not of some parts only. That something like fifty per cent of the English population lived chronically in or on the edges of poverty was not unrelated to the superabundance of goods, leisure, and the conduct of those at the top of society. The contrasting forms of consciousness were also necessarily related, though in ways as yet scarcely understood, because the matter involved contrasting social codes. As the satirist, John Weever, said in reply to one of Guilpin's satiric claims that England was given to gluttony,

> For each rich glutton that too much doth eate,
> There's ten poore beggers starve for want of meate.[10]

Yes, but what were the deep or structural effects of this in the contrasting mentalities?

We have seen that the historian shows his hand, reveals all his presuppositions concerning reality, in his way of delineating a milieu. Past and present come together in his twentieth-century eye, in what it sees and selects, as specialization takes over in him to arrange and determine the resulting picture. That poetry above all should be proscribed is nothing demanded by 'objective' Tudor and Stuart realities. The ostracism is imposed by our way of seeing and organizing milieux. We have trouble recognizing forms of consciousness *as social phenomena*, particularly the more elite forms, though these too are the stuff of history. We know well that there can be no human history without consciousness, but we fumble confusedly when called upon, in the study of any given society, to fit its different parts together, the most difficult task being to relate high culture to social structures.

Why this is so should by now be obvious. Our conditioned blind spots come from excessive specialization, from our abstracting and freezing of the different parts of culture and society, as we struggle to isolate, control, and clarify the parts that belong to our specialized competence. In the process, we lose our constructive sense of living wholes and end by assembling historical milieux that are skeletal matrices, within which poetry can only have a weird appearance.

With its work on peasants, village life, and popular culture, the French historical school has shattered the walls of specialization, in the determination to construct bigger, denser, and more complex milieux. Work of this kind, however, is far from having been fully extended. We need parallel, 'anthropological' studies of highly literate, upper-class groups. Then we should be better placed to put poetry and highbrow thought at the center of social analysis. But something else also holds us back from this.

Given to a life of study and cerebration, and working under the powerful influence of scientific models developed for the understanding of the physical universe, historians and scholars often lean towards the belief that some things 'after all' — e.g., historical method, abstract ideas, works of the highbrow imagination — may ride above the storm of change, may verge on breaking out of history into timelessness. This obscure faith is also fostered by the fact that we live in a time of persistent structural flux. In response, particularly when the rapidity of change takes on a menacing appearance, we want to believe that certain products of mind and imagination stand above change and have nothing to do with immediate fears and values, although we are profoundly subject to these. Insofar as this desire courses through us (the desire to rescue something of permanence, hence an impulse to rescue ourselves), we are constantly tempted to reify parts of culture, that is, to see certain parts in a transcendent light, and we are unable in our study of the past or present to subject those parts to a tenacious social analysis.

For most historians the primary historical realities cluster — rightly, I believe — around social structures, government and politics, institutions, economics, and community values, including religion and the prevailing ideas. The larger the numbers of people studied — thus the assumption — the better, although biography is entirely acceptable as a mode of interplay between society and the individual. In this prospect, the study of popular culture easily finds a place, partly at least because many of its features — little touched by the alchemical work of imagination — are rather directly keyed to a social structure. But the inherent bias against the social study of high culture is plain enough. Political theory is a notable exception to the bias, clearly because no elaborate negotiation or decoding is needed to relate its claims to existing political institutions.

If we construct a milieu which includes *all* the primary realities, thus breaking with specialization, the result is bound to be a broad and complex picture, despite the indicated bias. This, it seems to me, is an ideal to strive for, provided we also insist upon the centrality of consciousness. We may then close in on any part of a given analysis in order to examine particulars, while yet never allowing ourselves to lose sight of the whole. The poetry of the English Renaissance fits into such a milieu at the points where values, actions, and upper-class social identities interrelate, and this means along a stretch — which we must of course reconstitute — in the consciousness of Renaissance readers and poets. We may focus upon politics, or we may shift the lens over to the economy and to demographic statistics, but if poetry — or literature, really — is to surrender its argosies to historians, then the adhesive reality of consciousness must always have a central place in our milieu.

There remains another direction of study for our 'new discourse', but it must pass through the primary realities, as noted above, or run the risk of lapsing into antiquarianism. I shall get to it by noting recent trends in English historical writing.

The fortunes of traditional historical scholarship are in no danger in Great Britain, where most historical publication keeps to the established paradigms and the first year of university is already a venture in specialization. This leads to specialized studies of individuals (biography), politics, administration, war, diplomacy, government policy, the constitution, ideas, social groups, economic affairs, matters of religion, and — more recently — aspects of agrarian and urban history. Some of this scholarship — e.g., Conrad Russell's *Parliaments and English Politics, 1621–1629* (1979) — is work of the first order, solidly grounded in primary sources and often the result of arduous research in archives. Moreover, the strength of much historical writing lies in its very traditionality: the main lines of inquiry are instantly recognizable (and approvable); the current state of the matter in question is known to all the specialists; anything contentious is immediately apparent; and the new claims, if any, are unfolded along tried and tested paths. All the force of an established discipline — the intellectual skill of generations — is at once brought fully to bear.

Consequently, the emergence of wholly new trends in historical writing is unusual and problematic, and largely a function in the first place of socio-historical disturbances occurring outside the discipline. Yet we have seen something like this in the rise of a 'new' social history as practiced in Europe and North America during the past two decades. Its primary strategy is to demand a quantitative foundation for new findings and its principal subjects of study, we have noted, are populations, family structures, peasantries, groups (e.g., lawyers, servants, merchants), sexuality, wealth, poverty, crime, and social mobilities. The method has also been utilized in the study of literacy, the construction industry, and urbanization.[11] It takes no insight to see that these interests derive from urgencies in our own contemporary concerns.

Most of the best vanguard work on early-modern England has been concerned with questions of demography, group, and family history. And a fair part is regionally based, being devoted to particular counties such as Kent, Yorkshire, Sussex, Durham, Cheshire, Lancashire, and Northumberland.[12] Thanks to these and related studies, we now know that the gentry were an expanding class (though not in Lancashire), that they favored endogamous marriage (no surprising conclusion), that the rural poor were remarkably mobile in geographic terms, that infant and child mortalities were remarkably high, that local county interests had an enormous importance for local elites, and that the period saw 'revolutionary' improvements in agricultural techniques.[13]

To insert these and other such findings into a larger (more historical) picture, however, will require a sustained engagement with problems of group consciousness. The attempt has been made, in some of the same studies, to get at collective viewpoints or mentalities. In his study of the Durham region (1500—1640), Mervyn James found that thinking there in the early sixteenth century was rather strictly local and particular: a mode rooted in the solidarities of family lineage, neighborhood, and the old values of loyalty and service. By 1640, in keeping with the fleetness of social change and revolutionary reforms in religion and education, the old 'lineage' mentality had given way to a more mobile cast of mind, where a sense of market values, individual choice, private space, personal merit, and a feel for the national scene came to predominate. By contrast, in emphasizing the priority of local concerns right down to the Civil War, county-community historians (Alan Everitt, John Morrill) have highlighted the provincial outlook of the ruling groups and yeomanry in the different shires, an outlook rooted in emotional attachments to the parochial community. The partial character of this emphasis is immediately obvious when we see that it neglects religion, education, trans-county political concerns,[14] and a literature shared among the educated — namely, all the features that relate the local mind to the national community. In addition, the rich and pervasive culture studied by Keith Thomas, in his *Religion and the Decline of Magic,* shows that the dark superstitions of the many underpinned the more learned superstitions of the well educated few, who often put their trust in astrology, humoral medicine, Neoplatonist vitalism, and certain forms of white magic.

What we have then are group, class, local, and national concerns — divisible, if we wish, as values, preoccupations, and ways of thinking. The new social history, therefore, should aim to reconstitute a clustered and layered consciousness made up of the input of diverse groups, though a consciousness which was always in process of change, sometimes more so (as in the Elizabethan period) and sometimes less (the early eighteenth century). It was possible for one man to have much of the aggregate mentality in his head, amidst all his personal worries; but illiterate cottagers and their urban equivalents shared little, in intellectual terms, with learned clergymen, courtiers, poets, or government functionaries. Here — despite the supposed uniformity of religious doctrine — there must have been different ways of worshipping.

With notable exceptions,[15] the work of the scholarly vanguard has been least helpful in providing us with footholds for getting at the flux of values of the different social groups and so at the literature of the age. The many diaries and epistolary collections of the seventeenth century — rich memory banks of observation, idioms, everyday doings, and recorded custom — have yet to be given, as a body, any kind of a sustained analysis, and it has occurred to no one to study them in the light of the socio-literary strategies set forth in this book.[16]

In stark contrast to the historical profession's ostracism of verse, the field of literary studies teems with scholars who work, in part, in a socio-historical vein, though their chief commitment is to literature. All recent study of this interdisciplinary sort is the work of literary scholars.[17] Yet the historical world of the Renaissance, ruled over by proud elites, cannot be adequately understood without *their* literature. Moving, therefore, from the scholarship of men like Keith Thomas, Christopher Hill, and Lawrence Stone, and combining it with the pertinent studies of the quantitative school, we need as historians to provide the perspectives and put the questions that will coax literature into giving its historical secrets up to us. With this end in mind, I conclude with a program of study.

We seek the mental world — part of a larger consciousness — of the Tudor and Stuart upper classes, a world fused with their social order of reality. But if we are to enter and chart that world, we shall need a history — call it an anthropology — of the everyday life and rituals of the dominant social groups. I refer to the historical study of household space and interiors, furnishings, family relations, friendship, kinship, letter-writing, food, dress, paying visits, games, offering gifts, favorite eating and drinking places (taverns), dinner parties, personal chattels, habits of expenditure, fads and fashions, church-going, travel to and out of London, festivities, sexuality, relations between the sexes, reading habits, oral recitation, styles of address, rank and precedence, and relations with both superiors and underlings.[18] For all these bear the accents, organization, and signs which — when fitted together and explained — would go to constitute a model of upper-class society, centered on views concerning authority, status, property, self, God, and nature: in short, a mental world, a social world, and a shaping vision. Need it be observed that verse would be a prime source in the working up of any such construct?

Speaking of dress, for example, we know that high boots and swords were only for gentlemen and noblemen, that the law barred commoners from wearing cartwheel ruffs and silk, and that a red sash across the breast was the emblem of command in wartime. At Whitehall, in the Church, the university, the Inns of Court, and in assemblies of gildsmen and urban officials everywhere, rank and degree had their smart visual affirmation in dress. The like was also articulated in the order of seating at church, where a proprietary bent called for inscribing the names of the leading local families on the front pews (and there they sat), while the poorest parishioners stood at the back of the church. Place at table was exceedingly important — men at Court or in Government might refuse to sit with an upstart — and all processions were governed by strict precedence. Was there an obsessive (touchy?) preoccupation with rank, betokening social instability, or were its many signs merely a customary but needed endorsement of the civil order? A university degree conferred gentle status. Why exactly, what lay behind this perception of learning, rank, and social promotion?

Some whisper or hint of the rich punctilio and ceremony in Queen Elizabeth's public taking of meals must have carried over to the formal meals of the well-heeled and well-born, perhaps even in connection with the serving order of food and drink. And down to the end of the sixteenth century, generally speaking, only the master or lord of the house sat at table in a chair; the others sat on stools. Matters of this sort mean little in themselves, but they were not in themselves; they had their place and meaning in a whole social and moral circumscription, where they functioned as sign language.

Was the doffing of a hat not sign language? Did men not uncover before authority — God, king, nobility, bishops, gentry, justice of the peace, and lord of the manor? In many households apparently, down to the seventeenth century, women kissed the hands of their husbands to seal the end of a quarrel. The children of the upper classes often stood bareheaded before their parents, sat when they were told to, and kneeled to receive parental blessings. The not infrequent beating of apprentices, servants, pupils, children, and wives was in one sense pure action, but it was also sign language which pointed to the moral loftiness of authority and even to the necessity of beating underlings, minors, and 'the weaker sex'. Moral and social order were spun together.

I noted household furnishings and by implication the decorative arts. The houses of the rich saw significant changes during the Elizabethan and Jacobean periods, as in the promotion of private space by the increase of separate rooms. What were the causes and import of those changes? Why, for a time, was interior decoration so eclectic and swift to change, and so also styles of dress? As an item of decoration and furnishing, the so-called 'state portrait' — say of a Cecil, a Dudley, or a Russell — was noteworthy. Apart from any immediate pleasure given by it, was the commissioning of such a portrait, with its brazen vocabulary of power, a flashing of rank, a search for self-assurance, a form of propaganda and self-promotion, or a tinsel of fear in a world where epidemics were rife? And why were members of the gentry and peerage eager collectors of portraits of leading royal dignitaries? Some play of class, power, and self-identification was going on here.

The 'pagan' themes of much Elizabethan verse could be enlisted to help support the recent view that religious indifference then was more common than we have suspected,[19] but to draw verse and indifference into an unquestioned brace, we should have to know more about church-going customs. Lady Margaret Hoby's diary (1599—1605) shows a most religious woman, yet her pious movements could also be read as public show. The right understanding here would depend as well on a determined analysis of the diary as on our having a comprehensive view of the physiology of daily life.

There is a major need for studies on the place of poetry in the private, recreational, and social life of the English in the sixteenth and seventeenth centuries. Such inquiry would center on a variety of questions. How common, for example, was the practice of verse exchange among men, and between men and women? We know that there were circles of men who exchanged verse, but where and when and under what conditions? The Sidney, Donne, Jonson, Rochester, and Dryden circles, along with the Cavaliers, are among the most studied, but seldom with this question in mind; and there were other similar circles as well, such as that made up by Joan Grundy's 'Spenserian poets'. Again, how widespread was the oral recitation of poetry in group gatherings, both within the family and outside? Some families, such as the Sidneys, Astons, and Herberts, were well known for their love of poetry, but what about other and more modest houses, like the gentle Oxindens? And what of the traffic in poetry between town and country, as in the dispatching of books from London? All findings of this sort — some already scattered throughout the pertinent scholarship — should be drawn together into a synthesis, to help us plot the course of change between about 1580 and the 1660s.

Every item in my initial catalogue of daily doings and affairs touches a revelatory interest of the society's upper-class members. For instance, writing letters — how often, to whom, and in which style? — involved the critical relations pertaining to business, friendships, and family. Disbursements and expenditures indicated existential priorities. The use of household space also affirmed priorities, just as furnishings and decorations were code for group tastes and interests. Dress tracked aspects of social change and the evolution of group identities. Paying visits, like letter-writing, underlines the important relations of kin, friendship, and deference. The giving of a gold ring was a well-known gesture of friendship. Distance or proximity between the sexes was a measure of fear, prescribed roles, and even of property as a matter linked to marriage. The particulars of recreation, such as music, dancing, and oral recitation delineated some of the chief uses of privilege. Sexuality was a commentary on social roles, on the breaking of taboos, the lessons of restraint, marriage, and the boundaries of property. Relations with superiors and underlings echoed the animations, tone, or callousness of the social hierarchy. Church-going chronicled the society's allegiance (or lip service) to the transcendent order that was meant to justify or validate its material bases and moral guidelines. All these, and other like points of conduct, engaged the main values or energies of the society's privileged. And it is by these matters *too* that we may know them, for I take it as given that such knowledge must rest, in turn, on a detailed understanding of the primary realities (pp. 142—43).

As envisaged above, a history of everyday life is not the lunatic enterprise of 'total history'. It is the selective effort to study the points of daily importance — the everyday vitalities — in the life of an upper class. The aim is to build a model of that life, the changing model of a life process.

Notes

These notes are designed for use in strict tandem with the bibliography. References have been scaled down to last names of authors and page or chapter numbers where needed. When a note refers to an author with two or more entries in the bibliography, the year of publication will immediately follow the author's name. *Example* Marotti (1982).

CHAPTER 1   THEORY

1 Carr, ch. 2.
2 A stunning example in Forster, pp. 122—4.
3 Even his simple epigrams are likely to turn into multi-layered affairs. See E. Partridge, pp. 153—98.
4 E.g., A. F. Doni's *I Mondi,* Erasmus's *In Praise of Folly,* and More's *Utopia.*
5 Yet 'how negligible are the differences between the imagery of Donne's prose and that of his poetry.' Rugoff, p. 238.
6 Thus in poetry 'the emptiness of words' *vis-à-vis* the world, as in Krieger (1979), p. 25; or the movement from 'mimesis' to 'semiosis' (from meaning to an in-turned 'semantic unit') in Riffaterre, p. 4. In 'deconstruction' and one strain of semiology, language includes all meaning and signification, with the result that there seems to be no human reality outside the verbal system of signs. Thus, we evidently convert even such matters as war and famine into signs, and we react not to events as such but to their signs. See Derrida; Norris; Culler (1983); Belsey.
7 'A social reality (or a "culture") is itself an edifice of meanings — a semiotic construct.' Halliday, p. 2.
8 The distinction in this paragraph sins against Derrida's deconstruction of 'the metaphysics of presence'. I see no way for historians 'to privilege' language over events.

9 Dubrow, pp. 153—79. On genre and social hierarchy, Waddington, 'Milton', p. 343.

CHAPTER 2 STRATEGIES: FROM POEM TO WORLD

1 Sinfield (1974), pp. 341—55; and more generally, Ewbank, pp. 19—44; Javitch. On conventionality in the sonnets, Kennedy, pp. 68—9.
2 Bush (2nd edn , 1962), p. 112.
3 Kernan (1979), p. 30.
4 Waddington (1974), p. 13.
5 Wasserman, ch. 3; McClung; Turner; McGuire; Dubrow.
6 Heinemann, pp. 40—3.
7 Spriet, p. 324.
8 Cf. Marotti (1982); Matthews; Evans (1977), pp. xiv—xv; Neely, p. 383.
9 E.g., in *The Revenger's Tragedy* (by Middleton or Tourneur) and Marston's *The Malcontent.* But see the 'thematist' approach indicted in R. Levin (1979), ch. 4.
10 Gardner (1959), p. 4.
11 Colie (1973), p. 7, notes that 'decorum' is 'a social dimension' in the Aristotelian notion of mimesis; also Hall, pp. 211—13.
12 Tuve, p. 195, paraphrasing Puttenham.
13 Groom, p. 54.
14 Gill, 'Musa', pp. 66—7, citing Quintilian, *Institutio Oratoria, VI,* iii, 17.
15 Peterson, p. 88; Finkelpearl; and R. B. Gill, pp. 408—18.
16 Sinfield (1974), on words such as enjoy, touch, rent, gem, joy, ride, open, melt, die.
17 Kermode, p. 133.
18 On the Saussurean language—speech distinction, cf. Barthes (1964), ch. 1.
19 Martines, p. 37.
20 Vickers, pp. 132—3.
21 Though Donne assails the monarchy more boldly than many of his contemporaries: Lecocq, p. 66. Jonson's satiric vehemence sometimes verged on a dangerous loss of control: Newton, pp. 105—16. But Donne naturally varied language and style, best seen in the heightened tone of his verse letters to powerful patrons, on which Maurer (1976, 1980).
22 Evans (1955), pp. 23—4; more inclusively, Lever (1966), ch. 6; and Southall (1973), ch. 2.
23 Turner, pp. 101—6; Miner (1971), pp. 179—86, 283; C. J. Summers, p. 181.
24 Rostvig, I, 83, 195—6; Turner, pp. 38, 55, 85—7, and ch. 4.

25 A. J. Smith, 'Failure', p. 62.
26 Hornstein, pp. 638—53; and the rejoinder by Wentersdorf, pp. 231—59.
27 Rugoff, pp. 229—30; and the fine study by Carey, 'Coins', pp. 151—63. In Jonson's *Volpone,* the 'strong image-clusters' of 'feeding' and 'begetting' look out satirically both to economic and social matters: Knapp, p. 580.
28 Rugoff , p. 224.
29 My exemplary texts would be: Shakespeare's 'Being your slave, what should I do but tend', Spenser's 'Ye tradeful Merchants', the anonymous 'How often hath my pen, mine heart's solicitour' (from *Zepheria*), Drayton's 'Taking my Penne, with words to cast my Woe', and Spenser's 'This holy season fit to fast and pray'. My second numbered observation sides with Southall against Fowler, because though the latter rightly picks up the Biblical allusions and moral stress in Spenser's 'Ye tradeful Merchants', the imagery of precious stones from 'the Indias' makes for the poem's entire cargo of metaphor. A. Fowler, pp. 95—6.
30 Greenblatt (1980).
31 E. A. Armstrong, pp. 12—16.
32 Hendrickson, pp. 249—90.
33 Cicero, p. 101; and Halliday, pp. 31—2.
34 Cunningham (1966), p. xxiv.
35 Gentili, pp. 67—9.
36 Davie (1952), p. 140.
37 Gilbert; Lewis (1973), pp. 464—535; Peterson; Trimpi; Stein, pp. 306—16.
38 Peterson, pp. 350, 4—6, 9, 241.
39 That is, the 'middle style' in certain critical vocabularies, such as Gilbert, pp. 1—24. For a more cautious view, Hunter (in Brower), pp. 1—18.
40 Southall (1973), ch. 2; and cf. Wood, pp. 470—8.
41 Southall (1973), pp. 37, 44. This view accords with Croll, pp. 250—1, where style in Lyly's *Euphues* is seen as embodying both courtly and 'bourgeois' ideals.
42 Rarer because the spirit of hierarchy (aspiration) works upwards. Wherever rank and social degree pervade consciousness, people are more apt to try to copy their 'betters'.
43 My description of Donne's style relies on various works, including A. C. Partridge (1978); and Gilbert.
44 Love was one of the key conversational subjects in the princely courts of sixteenth-century Italy. As a literary topic, the passion in England was thought fit only for the nobility: e.g., Heinemann, pp. 181—3.
45 On the last point, Carey (1981), ch. 2; and Bewley, pp. 3—49.
46 Leavis, p. 36.

47 Walton (1955), p. vii.
48 *Ibid.,* p. 14.
49 *Ibid.,* p. 26.
50 Weidhorn, p. 145. More broadly on this tone, J. H. Summers (1970); and Anselment, 'Men', pp. 17—32, very good on the 'speaker' in Suckling's verse.
51 Chernaik (1968), p. 61. Helgerson (1983), pp. 185—204, assigns the rise of the Cavalier style to the exhaustion of Elizabethan genres and the takeover by a new generation.
52 Martz (1969), pp. 109—10.
53 A. J. Smith, 'Failure', p. 51; also Wedgwood (1977) pp. 15—31.
54 Morris and Withington, pp. 1vii—1xvii.
55 Evans (1955), p. 161; also Ing, p. 9.
56 Rostvig, I, 225; and Sharrock, pp. 3—40.
57 Rostvig, I, 195—6; to be set beside Lewalski (1979), pp. ix, 283, with its 'internalist' claim that the Bible, in the wake of Protestantism, was the chief new stimulus to the imagination of religious poets.
58 Gill, 'Musa', p. 51; Waddington (1974), p. 11; and Young, pp. 137—52, linking genre, tone, style, urban despair, Roman mores, and the problem of transferring the classical pagan epigram, with its sociological undertow (hence form = meaning), to a Christian world setting. For Helgerson (1983), *par contre,* genre is rather more a function of 'the literary system' and is used by poets to define and present themselves.
59 Miner (1971), p. 289. Light is also God, but Crashaw reverses this in his Epiphany hymn by turning the light of day into man's credulous darkness: Murrin, p. 130.
60 *Paradise Lost,* V, 36.
61 Lever (1971), p. 3; also W. A. Armstrong, pp. 234—49.
62 Drayton, ed. Hebel, V, 186, 189; and Newdigate, pp. 58—60.

CHAPTER 3 STRATEGIES: FROM WORLD TO POEM

1 McGowan, p. 218; Hardison, pp. 56, 108; Lewalski (1973), ch. 1; and the three studies by Maurer.
2 E.g., Danby, Thomson (1952, 1972), Helgerson (1983), Saunders, Maurer (all), McGuire, Marotti (1981).
3 Helgerson (1983). His laureate catagory gets at 'the literary system', 'authorial roles', and an aspect of the social function of genres.
4 Saunders, p. 257.
5 Horner, pp. 197—213.

6 Freeman, pp. 226—36.
7 Rostvig, I, 190. On another example of close affinities between patron and client, Maurer (1980), pp. 205—34.
8 And the two, praise and blame, belonged to 'epideictic' rhetoric.
9 Miner (1971), pp. 265—7.
10 Especially Allison, Chernaik (1968), Miner (1971), Sadler, Squier, Walton (1955), and Weidhorn. See also Judkins, pp. 243—58.
11 Parfitt (1974), p. xiii; and Gilbert, pp. 104—5, on public poetry.
12 Weidhorn, pp. 72—3.
13 Chernaik (1968), pp. 41, 129.
14 On Donne, e.g., see Buxton (1963), pp. 317ff. But professionals like Daniel could also pick out their readers: Maurer (1977), pp. 418—44.
15 Chernaik (1968), p. 172.
16 Frye (1971), p. 40; also Bateson (1950), p. 78; and Dryden's views, in Manley, pp. 290ff.
17 Frye (1971), p. 27.
18 H. Smith, p. 138.
19 T. R. Edwards, p. 17.
20 Finkelpearl, p. 105.
21 Buxton (1963), p. 320; Novarr, p. 95.
22 Buxton (1963), p. 327.
23 Erskine-Hill, p. 277.
24 Harbage, p. 98.
25 *Ibid.*, p. 100.
26 See Wilcox; Peter; Finkelpearl; Kernan (1959); Seldon; Powers; and R. B. Gill.
27 Ellrodt (1960), III, 43ff.
28 Melchiori, pp. 20—1.
29 Danby, p. 36.
30 Melchiori, p. 21.
31 Danby, pp. 16, 31—46, although he deemphasizes the homogeneity of social class.
32 *Ibid.*, pp. 16, 18.
33 *Ibid.*, pp. 17, 31.
34 *Ibid.*, p. 36.
35 Williams, pp. 258, 264.
36 *Ibid.*, pp. 279, 281. Dryden sought 'a smoother, tighter, and more majestic couplet which would elevate the mean manner of the genre [satire] by lofty words and numbers', Kimmey, p. 411.
37 Nevo, p. 52.
38 Miner (1971), pp. 44, 49.

39 Weidhorn, p. 97.
40 Empson (1966), p. 78.
41 *Ibid.,* p. 82.
42 On financial London see Stone (1973); Upton; and Ingram.
43 Finkelpearl, p. 7; Clark (1977), ch. 9; Prest.
44 Finkelpearl, p. 71.
45 Keach, p. 32.
46 Hoskins, pp. 38—9.
47 Weidhorn, p. 17. On differing Cavalier milieux, Squier, pp. 136—48.
48 Between 1580 and 1642 more than 100 comedies 'explicitly use London as a setting'. Barton (1978), p. 160.
49 May, pp. 385—94; also H. Smith, p. 10.
50 Weidhorn, pp. 146—7.
51 *Loc. cit.;* and Squier, chs 5—6.
52 E. H. Miller, p. 49.
53 *Loc. cit.*
54 Wallace; another example, Hensley, pp. 5—16.
55 E.g., Raleigh's 'The Lie', in hitting at the Court and high place, is really an attack on 'the official models of conduct'. Lerner, p. 30.
56 Miner (1969), p. 46.
57 Hobsbaum, p. 157.
58 M. M. Ross, pp. 94, 96. The implied view of causation here runs counter to the biblical stress in Lewalski (1979).
59 Cruttwell (1954), p. 199; and Sharrock, pp. 3—40.
60 Cruttwell (1954), p. 113. See also Wilson, pp. 17—24, on differences between Elizabethan and Jacobean.
61 Knights (1965), pp. 80—2; also Caudwell, pp. 73—4.
62 H. Levin (1953), pp. 54—5, 86; and Ornstein, pp. 26—7, on the figure of the pseudo-Machiavel.
63 Thomson (1952), p. 274.
64 Dyson and Lovelock, p. 222; also Farmer, pp. 312—13.
65 Miner (1971), p. 188; and more generally, Korshin, chs 1—2, 5.

CHAPTER 4   RECONSIDERATIONS

1 Hardin, p. 78.
2 Bishop, pp. 52—6, though the attacks were disguised. Raleigh was known as 'Paulus'. On Lovelace and the answer poem, Wilkinson, pp. 78—9, 279—80.

3 Broadbent, chs 5—14; Richmond; Peterson; Marotti (1982). There was a marked social stance in Jonson's frank rejection of the love theme: Helgerson (1983), pp. 110—11.

4 Forster; John; Scott.

5 Peterson, p. 125; Southall (1964), ch. 4; Trotter, pp. 23—7. Even in pastoral 'the otiose love-talk of the shepherd masks the busy negotiation of the courtier', notes Montrose, p. 154.

6 Bradbrook (1957), p. 79.

7 E. Holmes, p. 15.

8 Melchiori, pp. 35—6. This work relies on Donow's computer study.

9 Southall (1972), pp. 362—80.

10 *Ibid.,* pp. 363—5, 367.

11 *Ibid.,* pp. 369, 373. Cf. Wood, pp. 470—8.

12 A. C. Partridge (1971), p. 88.

13 McGowan, p. 182.

14 Thynne, p. 59. *Lais,* a variation of *lace,* one meaning of which in the 1590s was net, noose, or snare: thus here, by metaphorical extension, a whore.

15 Bradbrook (1978), p. 95.

16 Mahood, pp. 164—5.

17 *Ibid.,* p. 166; also Hunter, 'Poem', pp. 34—6.

18 Leishman (1961), p. 112.

19 E.g., Jakobson and Jones, p. 30, on their trick deciphering of anagrams; R. Fowler, pp. 79—122, on sonnet 73; and Gurr, pp. 221—6.

20 Bradbrook (1978), p. 184.

21 Epilogue, *The Conquest of Granada,* Part II, 1—4, 25—6.

22 Saunders, p. 255.

23 Bateson (1950), p. 96.

24 Mulder.

25 *Ibid.,* p. 80.

26 Ruthven, pp. 9—12.

27 Ellrodt (1961), pp. 346—7. For legally 'conceited' sonnets, see Shakespeare's 134 and the anonymous *Zepheria* (1594), 20.

28 Wells, pp. 30—1, 92, 100—1.

29 Spurgeon, p. 48.

30 *Ibid.,* p. 296, n. 2.

31 E. A. Armstrong, pp. 12—16.

32 Spurgeon, p. 40.

33 *Ibid.,* p. 38.

34 Matthews, p. 132; Bateson (1950), pp. 141—6; and the splendid piece on the falcon, though in a political context, by Anselment (1971).

35 H. Smith, p. 191; Empson (1966), pp. 93ff.

36 As noted by Bateson (1950); also R. J. Ross, pp. 171—81; cf. Deming, pp. 37, 56—7; but oddly not commented on by Deneef, pp. 81—4.

37 Wells, p. 167.

38 Such as burn—freeze, war—peace, live—die. Forster, ch. 1; Ruthven, pp. 18ff.

39 Hunter (1962), p. 140.

40 Finkelpearl, p. 90.

41 Turner, pp. 96—8; Anselment (1971); and Rothstein, p. 5.

42 Cruttwell, 'Love Poetry', p. 35; Sharp, pp. 20—1; Gill, 'Musa', p. 65; H. Levin (1953), pp. 40—1.

43 From *Hamlet* of course and Shakespeare's sonnet 86. On the force of ambition, Esler.

44 Wells, pp. 70, 94, 117, 170; E. Holmes, pp. 3—4, 15, 19, 60; Vickers, p. 148; H. Levin (1953), pp. 54—5.

45 Clemen, p. 92.

46 Mack, pp. 11—12.

47 H. Levin (1953), p. 43.

48 E. Holmes, pp. 14—15.

49 H. Levin (1953), pp. 86, 188.

50 Weimann, pp. 229—30. Cf. also Bateson (1965), pp. 53—4; Kenyon, pp. 44—5.

51 Cruttwell, 'Love Poetry', p. 26.

52 Southall (1973), ch. 3; Melchiori, pp. 34—7.

53 See, for example, Wilson, p. 99; Lever (1956), p. 148; Vickers, p. 139; H. Smith, p. 176; Danby, pp. 38—9, 159—62; Richmond, p. 135; Thomson, 'Donne', pp. 311—13; Nowottny, ch. 3; and Culler (1981), pp. 188—209.

54 Groom, pp. 56, 60. Helgerson (1983), pp. 104—8, argues that this change in style issues from the exhaustion of genres and the succession of a new generation of poets.

55 Wilson, p. 26.

56 Cruttwell (1954), p. 39.

57 Southall (1973), pp. 45—6; and Neely, p. 383.

58 Peterson, pp. 170, 287; Weiss, pp. 44—6.

59 Cunningham (1976), pp. 311—24; Pooley, pp. 2—18. Though plain style too could lapse into conventionality: Ewbank, p. 24; and Hunter, 'Poem', pp. 35—6.

60 Rebholz, p. 67.

61 Cunningham (1966), p. xxxviii.

62 E. H. Miller, p. 216.

63 Leishman (1962), pp. 16—17; also Cruttwell (1977), pp. 25—6, 30.

64 Finkelpearl, p. 76.

65 Parfitt (1974), pp. xiii—xiv; and Gilbert, pp. 104—5.
66 Hoffman (1962), pp. 21—2; and Groom, pp. 96—7.
67 Alvarez, p. 37.
68 *Ibid.*, p. 60.
69 *Ibid.*, p. 26; and Cruttwell (1977).
70 Knights (1945), pp. 41—2. Cf. Bennett (1964), p. 70, again on Herbert's 'right tone' owing 'to his breeding and early intercourse'.
71 Cruttwell, 'Love Poetry', pp. 20—1.
72 Gransden, p. 20; and R. B. Gill.
73 Selden, pp. 53—4; also D. A. Carroll in Guilpin, p. 14.
74 Weidhorn, p. 167.
75 Sharp, pp. 114—15.
76 Miles (1965), pp. 81—2; also Allison, pp. 25—38.
77 Chernaik (1968), p. 54; cf. Miner (1971), p. 21.
78 Miner (1969), pp. 27, 29.
79 Gardner (1965), p. ix; and Goldberg (1983), pp. 66—7, on Donne, love and political imagery.
80 Hunter (1962), p. 11.
81 Cunningham (1976), pp. 322—3.
82 Cruttwell's well known epithet, which includes Metaphysical poetry.
83 Carey (1981), chs 1—2.
84 Bradbrook (1978), p. 181; Pearlman, pp. 364—93, has called him an outright sycophant and toady — too harsh a judgement in Jonson's historical context.
85 McGowan, p. 182. Her italics.
86 Miner (1969), p. 56; also Thomson, 'Donne', p. 314.
87 Colie (1974), p. 99; Leishman (1961), p. 112; and Kernan (1979), pp. 28—9, 32.
88 Danby, p. 73.
89 Groom, pp. 61—2. The clerical tone is also strong in Greville and Edward Herbert.
90 G. Williamson, pp. 230—1.
91 Nevo, pp. 61, 68—9.
92 *Loc. cit.*
93 T. R. Edwards, pp. 75, 81, 76; also Knights (1971), pp. 82—92; and Wallace, ch. 2.
94 Weidhorn, p. 65.
95 *Ibid.*, p. 64.
96 Forster, ch. 1; and Scott. Helgerson (1983), p. 50, sees the love lyric as the chief genre for upper-class (amateur) poets.
97 A. Fowler, pp. 1—2, 19; and Southall (1964), chs 2, 4.

98 Also Henry Constable, Barnabe Barnes, Thomas Lodge, Giles Fletcher, William Percy, Richard Barnfield, William Smith, Bartholomew Griffin, Richard Lynche, Robert Tofte, and Nicholas Breton, 'so many good bourgeois names now rightly forgotten'. Melchiori, p. 19.

99 Hunter (1962), p. 129; Montrose, pp. 153—82; and Goldberg (1982), p. 527.

100 Empson (1966), p. 47.

101 Cooper, p. 144.

102 Colie (1974), p. 249.

103 H. Smith, p. 10; also Dorangeon, pp. 12—18, 28.

104 Thomson (1967), p. 112.

105 Grundy.

106 *Ibid.*, pp. 77, 89—90; Dorangeon, pp. 331—400.

107 Nevo, pp. 10, 20.

108 Vickers, pp. 137—8.

109 Keach, pp. 28—32; Bradbrook (1957), ch. 4; and Lanham, pp. 83, 94.

110 Portraits, dress fashions, commentary in private letters, household decoration, 'prodigy houses', and satiric verse all point to the ostentation. But see Stone (1965), pp. 547—86; and Gillett, pp. 297—309.

CHAPTER 5   A NEW DISCOURSE: NEEDS AND PROSPECTS

1 Matthews, pp. 119—37; echoed in Neely, p. 383.

2 Matthews, p. 123. Italics his.

3 See Cruttwell (1954); Caudwell; Wilson; Ellis-Fermor; Weimann; Kenyon. Though the age was soon regarded nostalgically: Barton (1981).

4 Ellrodt (1960), III, 16—17.

5 Cruttwell (1954), pp. 2, 18, 26, 39, 113, 135; and on the satirical element, R. B. Gill, pp. 408—18.

6 Cunningham (1976), pp. 311—24.

7 E.g., Aers (et al.); Knights (1962); Melchiori; H. Levin (1953); Southall (1973); Weimann; and Wayne, p. 97.

8 Aers (et al.), chs 2—4.

9 See pp. 109—12.

10 Trotter, p. 21; and A. Cowley (ed. Pritchard).

11 Two notable exceptions: C. Hill and C. V. Wedgwood.

12 Aers (et al.), p. ix; and Belsey, pp. 1—54; Eastman, chs 1—2; Hawkes, pp. 11—58.

13 Though for a spirited representation see Kress and Hodge; also Aers (et al.); Eastman; and Belsey.
14 Melchiori, p. 13, relying on Donow's computer print-outs.
15 Sidney, Shakespeare, Drayton, Daniel. Tallies in Donow.
16 Melchiori, pp. 13, 21.
17 *Ibid.*, p. 29.
18 F. Berry, p. 40.
19 A. C. Partridge (1971), pp. 239—40; also F. Berry, p. 103, for the effects of 'social etiquette' on John Fletcher's use of *thou* and *you.*
20 Melchiori, pp. 16—17.
21 *Ibid.*, p. 57; also cf. Booth (1977), pp. 305—9.
22 Miles (1965).
23 *Ibid.*, pp. 8, 59.
24 The paradigmatic example of such research: Donow.
25 Miles (1965), p. 67. On Jonson's ideological use of event, deed, and fact, see Wayne, pp. 79—103.
26 Aers (et al.), ch. 4.
27 Kress and Hodge, pp. 71—6. But I disagree that an anti-language 'is not a language to think in, but a language in which to escape from thought'. Much very odd thinking goes on in utopia. See also Halliday, pp. 164—82. and Goldberg (1983), pp. 66—7, on Donne's handling of love in the language of politics.
28 Empson (1951), chs 1—2; and of course (1930).
29 Forster, p. 52.
30 For a remarkable parallel in the Italian poetry of Dante's time, also connected with basic social and economic change, see Martines, pp. 79—86.
31 E.g., studies by Wells; E. Holmes; Spurgeon; Wentersdorf; Brandenburg; Rugoff; Clemen; and Mackenzie.
32 Martines, pp. 87—93.
33 But we could look at *Timon of Athens,* where betrayed generosity is somersaulted into hatred and self-destruction. Cf. Burke, pp. 115—24.
34 See pp. 24, 104. Jonson's 'Epistle to a Friend, to Persuade Him to the Wars' (*c.* 1620?) verges on turning lust into a catch-all sin.
35 Turner.
36 Pooley, p. 4.
37 Cf. E. Holmes.
38 E.g., Stagg. On metaphor as a search for new expression or 'a leap into the unknown', see Hirsch, pp. 105—6.
39 Regarding poverty, Empson (1979), on 'rogue' and 'dog', pp. 158ff.
40 My use of 'metaphor' is broad and would include much metonymy. See Culler (1981), pp. 188—209.

41 Though on its 'verisimilitude' see Powers.

42 Elliott, p. 139.

43 On which see Stone (1973); Upton; and Ingram.

44 On this and the following paragraphs see, as listed in my bibliography: Barthes, Derrida, Norris, Belsey, Culler, Eastman, and Hawkes.

CHAPTER 6   AGAINST SPECIALIZATION: HISTORY, POETRY, MILIEU

1 One professional historian of the English Civil War period has told me that apart from that which goes into his own writing, all his working time is spent in keeping up with scholarship on that twenty-year period.

2 As in some of the academic exercises, for example, in the otherwise outstanding book by Wrigley and Schofield.

3 See, e.g., Bercé, Muir, and Le Roy Ladurie.

4 In his *Love, Death and Money in the Pays d'Oc,* p. 511.

5 Cf. my review of the English translation, in 'Book World', *Washington Post* (19 December, 1982), p. 6.

6 Sabean, p. 96.

7 The word 'interplay' reveals the spatial and hence metaphorical aspects of this binary formulation. Translated into semiotic terms, the interplay would center on relations between two different codes or systems of signification.

8 Though even a pure imitation may belong to its time, as would be apparent in answers to the questions, why exactly has X done such an imitation? What of his tastes, education, and the possible encouragement of his contemporaries?

9 The exception lies with the isolated scholars whose work is a search for this unity, now most evident in studies of popular culture.

10 Cited in Davenport, p. 128. The point about 'transcoding' is touched on in Hawkes, pp. 121—2.

11 See, e.g., Cressy; Machin; Power (two items); Clark and Slack. But the 'classic' in the English quantitative mode is now the book by Wrigley and Schofield.

12 See the books by Clark; Cliffe; Fletcher; James; Morrill; Blackwood; and Watts.

13 On agriculture, Kerridge; Thirsk.

14 For a sharp critique of the county—community line, see C. Holmes.

15 Seen in the work of, e.g., Thomas, Stone, Manning, Clark, and James.

16 Not the recipe in Macfarlane's study of the Puritan clergyman, Josselin, though pp. 183—96 are noteworthy.

17 E.g., Dollimore, Heinemann, Greenblatt (1982), Goldberg (1983), Sinfield (1983), Chernaik (1983).

18 A start has been made of course in some of these matters, such as on household space by James (pp. 13—16), on friendship by Fletcher (pp. 44—53), on family and kinship by Macfarlane (pp. 105—60), on sexuality by Stone (1977), and — though moving down socially — on illicit sex among Somerset peasants by Quaife.

19 Thomas, p. 204.

Bibliography

Abbreviations used in the bibliography

EC — *Essays in Criticism*

ELH — *Journal of English Literary History*

ELR — *English Literary Renaissance*

HLQ — *Huntington Library Quarterly*

JEGP — *Journal of English and Germanic Philology*

MLQ — *Modern Language Quarterly*

MLR — *Modern Language Review*

PMLA — *Publications of the Modern Language Association of America*

PQ — *Philological Quarterly*

RES — *Review of English Studies*

SEL — *Studies in English Literature*

SP — *Studies in Philology*

SQ — *Shakespeare Quarterly*

TSLL — *Texas Studies in Literature and Language*

Aers, D., Hodge, Bob and Kress, Gunther. *Literature, Language and Society in England 1580—1680*. Dublin and Toronto, 1981.

Alden, R. M. 'The Lyrical Conceit of the Elizabethans', *SP*, XIV (1917), 129—52.

—— 'The Lyrical Conceit of the "Metaphysical Poets"', *SP*, XVII (1920), 183—98.

Allen, D. C. *Image and Meaning: Metaphoric Traditions in Renaissance Poetry*. Rev. edn. Baltimore, 1968.

Allison, Alexander Ward. *Toward an Augustan Poetic: Edmund Waller's 'Reform' of English Poetry*. Lexington, 1962.

Alvarez, A. *The School of Donne.* London, 1961.

Anselment, Raymond A. ' "Griefe Triumphant" and "Victorious Sorrow": A Reading of Richard Lovelace's "The Falcon" ', *JEGP,* LXX, 3 (1971), 404—17.

_____ ' "Men Most of All Enjoy, When Least They do": The Love Poetry of John Suckling', *TSLL,* XIV, 1 (1972), 17—32.

Armstrong, Edward A. *Shakespeare's Imagination: A Study in the Psychology of Association and Inspiration.* London, 1946.

Armstrong, William A. 'The Audience of the Elizabethan Private Theatres', *RES,* 10 (1959), 234—49.

Atkins, J. W. H. *Literary Criticism in Antiquity.* London, 1952.

Auerbach, Erich. *Mimesis: The Representation of Reality in Western Literature.* New York, 1957.

Barfield, Owen. *Poetic Diction: A Study in Meaning.* 2nd edn , London, 1951.

Barthes, Roland. *Éléments de Sémiologie.* Paris, 1964.

_____ *A Barthes Reader,* ed. Susan Sontag. London, 1982.

Barton, Anne. 'Harking Back to Elizabeth: Ben Jonson and Caroline Nostalgia', *ELH,* 48 (1981), 706—31.

_____ 'London Comedy and the Ethos of the City', *The London Journal: A Review of Metropolitan Society Past and Present,* 4, 2, (1978), 158—80.

Bateson, F. W. *English Poetry: A Critical Introduction.* London, 1950.

_____ *A Guide to English Literature.* Chicago, 1965.

Belsey, Catherine. *Critical Practice.* London and New York, 1980.

Bennett, Joan. *Five Metaphysical Poets.* Cambridge, 1964.

_____ 'The Love Poetry of John Donne: A Reply to Mr. C. S. Lewis', in *Seventeenth-Century English Poetry: Modern Essays in Criticism,* ed. Keast.

Bercé, Yves-Marie. *Fête et Révolte: Des Mentalités populaires du XVIe au XVIIIe siècle.* Paris, 1976.

Berry, Francis. *Poet's Grammar: Person, Time and Mood in Poetry.* London, 1958.

Berry, Ralph. *The Shakesperian Metaphor: Studies in Language and Form.* London, 1978.

Bewley, Marius. *Masks and Mirrors: Essays in Criticism.* London, 1970.

Bishop, C. J. 'Raleigh Satirized by Harington and Davies', *RES,* 23 (1972), 52—6.

Blackwood, B. G. *The Lancashire Gentry and the Great Rebellion, 1640—60.* Manchester, 1978.

Booth, Stephen. *An Essay on Shakespeare's Sonnets.* New Haven and London, 1969.

_____ (ed.) *Shakespeare's Sonnets.* New Haven and London, 1977.

Bradbrook, M. C. 'Herbert's Ground', *Essays and Studies,* 2nd ser., 34 (1982), 66—87.

—— 'No Room at the Top: Spenser's Pursuit of Fame', in *Elizabethan Poetry,* ed. Brown and Harris.

—— *Shakespeare and Elizabethan Poetry.* London, 1957.

—— *Shakespeare: The Poet in his World.* London, 1978.

Bradbury, M. and Palmer, D. (eds) *Metaphysical Poetry.* Stratford-Upon-Avon Studies 11, New York, 1970.

Brandenburg, A. S. 'The Dynamic Image in Metaphysical Poetry', *PMLA,* 57 (1942), 1039—45.

Broadbent, J. B. *Poetic Love.* London, 1964.

Brockbank, Philip. 'The Politics of Paradise: "Bermudas" ', in *Approaches to Marvell,* ed. Patrides.

Brower, R. A. (ed.) *Forms of Lyric.* New York, 1970.

Brown, Arthur, 'Citizen Comedy and Domestic Drama', in *Jacobean Theatre,* ed. Brown and Harris.

Brown, J. R. and Harris, B. (eds) *Elizabethan Poetry.* Stratford-Upon-Avon Studies 2, New York, 1960.

—— (eds) *Jacobean Theatre.* Stratford-Upon-Avon Studies 1, New York, 1960.

Brown, Stephen, J. *The World of Imagery: Metaphor and Kindred Imagery.* London, 1927.

Bullough, Geoffrey (ed.) *Poems and Dramas of Fulke Greville.* 2 vols, Edinburgh, 1938.

Burke, Kenneth. *Language as Symbolic Action.* Berkeley and Los Angeles, 1968.

Bush, Douglas. *English Literature in the Earlier Seventeenth Century, 1600—1660.* 2nd edn (rev.) Oxford, 1962.

Buxton, John. *A Tradition of Poetry.* London and New York, 1967.

—— *Elizabethan Taste.* London, 1963.

Canfield, J. Douglas. 'Religious Language and Religious Meaning in Restoration Comedy', *SEL,* XX, 3 (1980), 385—406.

Carey, John. 'Donne and Coins', in *English Renaissance Studies Presented to Dame Helen Gardner,* ed. J. Carey.

—— (ed.) *English Renaissance Studies Presented to Dame Helen Gardner in Honour of her Seventieth Birthday.* Oxford, 1980.

—— *John Donne: Life, Mind and Art.* London and Boston, 1981.

Carr, E. H. *What is History?* New York, 1961.

Carver, Larry. 'The Restoration Poets and their Father King', *HLQ,* XL (1977), 333—51.

Caudwell, Christopher. *Illusion and Reality: A Study of the Sources of Poetry.* New York, 1947.

Chernaik, Warren L. *The Poetry of Limitation: A Study of Edmund Waller.* New Haven and London, 1968.

____ *The Poet's Time: Politics and Religion in the Work of Andrew Marvell.* Cambridge, London and New York, 1983.

Cicero, *Orator,* ed. H. M. Hubbell, Loeb Classical Library Series. 1971 edn. London and Cambridge, Mass.

Clark, Peter. *English Provincial Society from the Reformation to the Revolution: Religion, Politics and Society in Kent 1500—1640.* Hassocks, 1977.

Clark, Peter and Slack, Paul. *English Towns in Transition, 1500—1700.* Oxford, 1976.

Clemen, W. H. *The Development of Shakespeare's Imagery.* London, 1951.

Cleveland, John. *The Poems of John Cleveland,* ed. B. Morris and E. Withington. Oxford, 1967.

Cliffe, J. T. *The Yorkshire Gentry from the Reformation to the Civil War.* London, 1969.

Colie, Rosalie L. *Shakespeare's Living Art.* Princeton, 1974.

____ *The Resources of Kind: Genre-Theory in the Renaissance,* ed. B. K. Lewalski. Berkeley, 1973.

Cooper, Helen. *Pastoral, Medieval into Renaissance.* Ipswich and Totowa, 1977.

Cowley, Abraham. *The Civil War,* ed. A. Pritchard. Toronto and Buffalo, 1973.

Cressy, David. *Literacy and the Social Order: Reading and Writing in Tudor and Stuart England.* Cambridge, 1980.

Croll, Morris W. *Style, Rhetoric and Rhythm,* ed. J. M. Patrick, R. D. Evans and J. M. Wallace. Princeton, 1966.

Cross, Claire. *Church and People 1450—1660.* London, 1976.

Cruttwell, Patrick. 'The Love Poetry of John Donne: Pedantique Weeds or Fresh Invention?', in *Metaphysical Poetry,* ed. Bradbury and Palmer.

____ 'The Metaphysical Poets and their Readers', *The Humanities Association Review,* 28 (1977), 20—41.

____ *The Shakespearean Moment and its Place in the Poetry of the Seventeenth Century.* London, 1954.

Culler, Jonathan. *The Pursuit of Signs: Semiotics, Literature Deconstruction.* London, Melbourne and Henley, 1981.

____ *On Deconstruction: Theory and Criticism after Structuralism.* London, Melbourne and Henley, 1983.

Cunningham, J. V. 'Lyric Style in the 1590s', pp. 311—24, in his *Collected Essays*. Chicago, 1976.

―――― (ed.) *The Renaissance in England*. New York, 1966.

Danby, J. F. *Poets on Fortune's Hill: Studies in Sidney, Shakespeare, Beaumont, and Fletcher*. London, 1952.

Davenport, A. 'The Quarrel of the Satirists', *MLR*, 37 (1942), 123—30.

Davie, Donald. 'A Reading of "The Ocean's Love to Cynthia" ', in *Elizabethan Poetry*, ed. Brown and Harris.

―――― *Purity of Diction in English Verse*. London, 1952.

Deming, Robert H. *Ceremony and Art: Robert Herrick's Poetry*. The Hague, Paris, 1974.

―――― 'Love and Knowledge in the Renaissance Lyric', *TSLL*, XVI,3 (1974), 389—410.

Deneef, A. L. *'This Poetick Liturgie: Robert Herrick's Ceremonial Mode*. Durham, 1974.

Derrida, Jacques. *Of Grammatology*. Trans. G. C. Spivak. Baltimore, 1977.

―――― *Writing and Difference*. Trans. A. Bass. London, 1978.

Dickey, F. 'Collections of Songs and Sonnets', in *Elizabethan Poetry*, ed. Brown and Harris.

Dollimore, Jonathan. *Radical Tragedy: Religion, Ideology and Power in the Drama of Shakespeare and His Contemporaries*. Chicago, 1984.

Donow, Herbert S. *A Concordance to the Sonnet Sequences of Daniel, Drayton, Shakespeare, Sidney, and Spenser*. Carbondale, Edwardsville, London and Amsterdam, 1969.

Dorangeon, Simone. *L'Églogue Anglaise de Spenser à Milton*. Paris, 1974.

Drayton, Michael. *The Works of Michael Drayton*, 5 vols, ed. J. W. Hebel. Oxford, 1931—41.

Dubrow, Heather. 'The Country-House Poem: A Study in Generic Development', *Genre*, 12 (1979), 153—79.

Dyson, A. E. and Lovelock, Julian. *Masterful Images: English Poetry from Metaphysicals to Romantics*. London, 1976.

Eastman, Antony. *Poetry as Discourse* London and New York, 1983.

Edwards, P., Ewbank, I.—S. and Hunter, G. K. eds. *Shakespeare's Styles*. Cambridge, 1980.

Edwards, T. R. *Imagination and Power: A Study of Poetry on Public Themes*. New York, 1971.

Elliott, Robert C. *The Power of Satire: Magic, Ritual, Art*. Princeton, 1960.

Ellis-Fermor, Una. *The Jacobean Drama, An Interpretation*. 5th edn, London, 1965.

Ellrodt, Robert. *L'inspiration personnelle at l'esprit du temps chez les poètes métaphysiques anglais.* Vol. 3, Paris, 1960.

—— 'La vogue de l'image scientifique dans la poésie anglaise du dix-septième siècle', *Études Anglaises,* 14, 4 (1961), 346—7.

Empson. William. *Seven Types of Ambiguity.* London, 1930.

—— *Some Versions of Pastoral: A Study of the Pastoral Form in Literature.* Harmondsworth, 1966.

—— *The Structure of Complex Worlds.* London, 1951; and new edn, 1979.

Erskine-Hill, Howard. 'Courtiers out of Horace', in *John Donne, Essays in Celebration,* ed. A. J. Smith.

Esler, Anthony. *The Aspiring Mind of the Elizabethan Younger Generation.* Durham, 1966.

Evans, Maurice (ed.) *Elizabethan Sonnets.* London, 1977.

—— *English Poetry in the Sixteenth Century.* London, 1955. Rev. edn, 1967.

—— *Spenser's Anatomy of Heroism.* Cambridge, 1970.

Everitt, Alan. *The Local Community and the Great Rebellion.* London, 1969.

Ewbank, Inga-Stina. 'Sincerity and the Sonnet', *Essays and Studies,* 34 (1981), 19—44.

Farmer, Norman K., Jr. 'A Theory of Genre for Seventeenth-Century Poetry', *Genre,* 3 (1970), 293—317.

Finkelpearl, Philip J. *John Marston of the Middle Temple: An Elizabethan Dramatist in His Social Setting.* Harvard, 1969.

Fletcher, Anthony. *A County Community in Peace and War: Sussex 1600—1660.* London and New York, 1975.

Forster, Leonard. *The Icy Fire: Five Studies in European Petrarchism.* Cambridge, 1969.

Fowler, Alastair. *Conceitful Thought: The Interpretation of English Renaissance Poems.* Edinburgh, 1975.

Fowler, Roger (ed.) *Style and Structure in Literature: Essays in the New Stylistics.* Oxford, 1975.

Freeman, A. 'An Epistle for Two', *Library,* 5th ser., XXV (1970), 226—36.

Freer, Coburn. *The Poetics of Jacobean Drama.* Baltimore and London, 1981.

Frye, Northrop. *The Critical Path: An Essay on the Social Context of Literary Criticism.* Bloomington and London, 1971.

—— *The Stubborn Structure: Essays on Criticism and Society.* London, 1970.

Gardner, Helen. *The Business of Criticism.* Oxford, 1959.

—— (ed.) *John Donne: The Elegies and the Songs and Sonnets.* Oxford, 1965.

—— 'The Metaphysical Poets', in *Seventeenth-Century English Poetry: Modern Essays in Criticism,* ed. Keast.

Gentili, Vanna. *Le figure della pazzia nel teatro elisabettiano.* Lecce, 1969.

Gibbons, Brian. *Jacobean City Comedy: A Study of Satiric Plays by Jonson, Marston and Middleton.* London, 1968.

Gilbert, A. J. *Literary Language from Chaucer to Jonson.* London, 1979.

Gill, R. B. 'A Purchase of Glory: The Persona of Late Elizabethan Satire', *SP,* LXXII, 4 (1975), 408—18.

Gill, Roma. 'Musa Iocosa Mea, Thoughts on the *Elegies',* in *John Donne, Essays in Celebration,* ed. A. J. Smith.

Gillett, Peter J. 'Me, U, and Non-U: Class Connotations of Two Shakespearean Idioms', *SQ,* XXV, 3 (1974), 297—309.

Goldberg, Jonathan. 'The Politics of Renaissance Literature: A Review Essay', *ELH,* 49 (1982), 514—42.

—— *James I and the Politics of Literature.* Baltimore and London, 1983.

Grandsen, K. W. (ed.) *Tudor Verse Satire.* London, 1970.

Greenblatt, Stephen (ed.) *The Power of Forms in the English Renaissance.* Norman, 1982.

—— *Renaissance Self-Fashioning: From More to Shakespeare.* Chicago, 1980.

Greene, R. L. 'A Carol of Anne Boleyn by Wyatt', *RES,* 25 (1974), 437—9.

Grierson, H. J. C. 'Metaphysical Poetry', in *Seventeenth-Century English Poetry: Modern Essays in Criticism,* ed. Keast.

Groom, Bernard. *The Diction of Poetry from Spenser to Bridges.* Toronto, 1955.

Grundy, Joan. *The Spenserian Poets.* London, 1969.

Guild, Nicholas. 'The Context of Marvell's Early "Royalist" Poems', *SEL,* XX, 1 (1980), 126—36.

Guilpin, Everard. *Skialetheia or A Shadow of Truth, in Certaine Epigrams and Satyres,* ed. D. Allen Carroll. Chapel Hill, 1974.

Gurr, Andrew. 'Shakespeare's First Poem: Sonnet 145', *EC,* XXI (1971), 221—6.

Hall, Vernon, Jr. *Renaissance Literary Criticism: A Study in Creative Sources.* New York, 1939.

Halliday, M. A. K. *Language as Social Semiotic: The Social Interpretation of Language and Meaning.* London, 1979.

Hamilton, K. G. *The Two Harmonies: Poetry and Prose in the Seventeenth Century.* Oxford, 1963.

Harbage, Alfred. *Shakespeare and the Rival Traditions.* 2nd edn. Bloomington and London, 1970.

Hardin, Richard F. *Michael Drayton and the Passing of Elizabethan England.* Lawrence, Manhattan, and Wichita, 1973.

Hardison, O. B., Jr. *The Enduring Moment: A Study of the Idea of Praise in Renaissance Literary Theory and Practice.* Chapel Hill, 1962.

Hawkes, Terence. *Structuralism and Semiotics.* London, 1983.

Heinemann, Margot. *Puritanism and the Theatre: Thomas Middleton and Opposition Drama Under the Early Stuarts.* Cambridge and London, 1980.

Helgerson, Richard. 'The Elizabethan Laureate: Self-Presentation and the Literary System', *ELH,* 46 (1979), 193—220.

_____ *Self-Crowned Laureates: Spenser, Jonson, Milton and the Literary System.* Berkeley, Los Angeles, and London, 1983.

Hendrickson, G. L. 'The Origin and Meaning of the Ancient Characters of Style', *American Journal of Philology,* XXVI, 3 (1905), 249—90.

Hensley, Charles S. 'Wither, Waller, and Marvell: Panegyrists for the Protector', *Ariel: A Review of International English Literature,* 3, 1 (1972), 5—16.

Hibbard, G. R. 'Love, Marriage, and Money in Shakespeare's Theatre and Shakespeare's England', in *Elizabethan Theatre VI,* ed. G. R. Hibbard. London, 1978.

Hill, Christopher. *Milton and the English Revolution.* New York, 1979.

Hirsch, E. D., Jr. *Validity in Interpretation.* New Haven and London, 1967.

Hobsbaum, Philip. *Tradition and Experiment in English Poetry.* London, 1979.

Hoffman, Arthur W. *John Dryden's Imagery.* Gainesville, 1962.

_____ 'Various John Dryden: "All, All of a Piece Throughout" ', in *Dryden: A Collection of Critical Essays,* ed. Schilling.

Hollander, John. *Vision and Resonance: Two Senses of Poetic Form.* New York, 1975.

Holmes, Clive. 'The County Community in Stuart Historiography', *Journal of British Studies,* XIX, 2 (1980), 54—73.

Holmes, Elizabeth. *Aspects of Elizabethan Imagery.* Oxford, 1929.

Honigmann, E. A. J. 'Shakespeare's "bombast" ', in *Shakespeare's Styles,* ed. Edwards, Ewbank and Hunter.

Horner, Joyce. 'The Large Landscape: A Study of Certain Images in Raleigh', *EC,* V (1955), 197—213.

Hornstein, L. H. 'Analysis of Imagery: A Critique of Literary Method', *PMLA,* 57 (1942), 638—53.

Hoskins, John. *Directions for Speech and Style,* ed. Hoyt H. Hudson. Princeton, 1935.

Howard, Clare (ed.) *The Poems of Sir John Davies.* New York, 1941.

Hulme, Hilda M. *Explorations in Shakespeare's Language: Some Problems of Lexical Meaning in the Dramatic Text.* London, 1962.

Hulse, S. Clark. 'Elizabethan Minor Epic: Toward a Definition of Genre', *SP,* LXXIII, 3 (1976). 302—19.

Hunter, G. K. 'Drab and Golden Lyrics of the Renaissance', in *Forms of Lyric,* ed. R. A. Brower.

—— *Dramatic Identities and Cultural Tradition: Studies in Shakespeare and His Contemporaries.* Liverpool, 1978.

—— 'English Folly and Italian Vice: The Moral Landscape of John Marston', in *Jacobean Theatre,* ed. Brown and Harris.

—— *John Lyly: The Humanist as Courtier.* London, 1962.

—— 'Poem and Context in *Love's Labour's Lost*', in *Shakespeare's Styles,* ed. Edwards, Ewbank, Hunter.

Ing, Catherine. *Elizabethan Lyrics: A Study in the Development of English Metres and their Relation to Poetic Effect.* London, 1951.

Inglis, Fred. *The Elizabethan Poets: The Making of English Poetry from Wyatt to Ben Jonson.* London, 1969.

Ingram, William. *A London Life in the Brazen Age: Francis Langley, 1548—1602.* Cambridge, Mass., 1978.

Ives, E. W., Knecht, R. J., and Scarisbrick, J. J. (eds) *Wealth and Power in Tudor England.* London, 1978.

Jakobson, Roman and Jones, Lawrence G. *Shakespeare's Verbal Art in* th'Expence of Spirit. The Hague, 1970.

James, Mervyn. *Family, Lineage, and Civil Society: A Study of Society, Politics, and Mentality in the Durham Region, 1500—1640.* Oxford, 1974.

Javitch, Daniel. *Poetry and Courtliness in Renaissance England.* Princeton, 1978.

John, L. C. *The Elizabethan Sonnet Sequences: Studies in Conventional Conceits.* New York, 1938.

Judkins, D. C. 'Recent Studies in the Cavalier Poets: Thomas Carew, Richard Lovelace, John Suckling, and Edmund Waller', *ELR,* 7 (1977), 243—58.

Keach, William. *The Elizabethan Erotic Narratives: Irony and Pathos in the Ovidian Poetry of Shakespeare, Marlowe, and their Contemporaries.* New Brunswick, 1977.

Kearney, Hugh. *Scholars and Gentlemen: Universities and Society in Pre-Industrial Britain, 1500—1700.* London, 1970.

Keast, William R. (ed.) *Seventeenth-Century English Poetry: Modern Essays in Criticism.* New York, 1962.

Kennedy, William J. *Rhetorical Norms in Renaissance Literature.* New Haven and London, 1978.

Bibliography

Kenyon, J. P. *Stuart England.* New York, 1978.

Kermode, Frank. *Shakespeare, Spenser, Donne: Renaissance Essays.* London, 1971.

Kernan, Alvin B. *The Cankered Muse: Satire of the English Renaissance.* New Haven, 1959.

—— *The Playwright as Magician: Shakespeare's Image of the Poet in the English Public Theater.* New Haven and London, 1979.

—— *The Plot of Satire.* New Haven and London, 1965.

Kerridge, Eric. *The Agricultural Revolution.* London, 1967.

Kettle, A. (ed.) *Shakespeare in a Changing World.* London, 1964.

Kimmey, John Lansing. 'John Cleveland and the Satiric Couplet in the Restoration', *PQ,* XXXVII, 3 (1958), 410—23.

King, Bruce. 'Green Ice and a Breast of Proof', *College English,* 26 (1965), 511—15.

—— *Marvell's Allegorical Poetry.* New York and Cambridge, 1979.

Knapp, Peggy. 'Ben Jonson and the Publicke Riot', *ELH,* 46 (1979), 577—94.

Knights, L. C. *Drama and Society in the Age of Jonson.* London, 1962.

—— 'On the Social Background of Metaphysical Poetry', *Scrutiny,* XIII, 1 (1945), 37—52.

—— *Public Voices: Literature and Politics with Special Reference to the Seventeenth Century.* London, 1971.

—— 'The Strange Case of Christopher Marlowe', *Further Explorations.* London, 1965.

Korshin, P. J. *From Concord to Dissent: Major Themes in English Poetic Theory, 1640—1700.* Menston, 1973.

Kress, Gunther and Hodge, Robert. *Language as Idealogy.* London and Boston, 1979.

Krieger, Murray. *A Window to Criticism: Shakespeare's* Sonnets *and Modern Poetics.* Princeton, 1964.

—— *Poetic Presence and Illusion.* Baltimore and London, 1979.

Ladurie, E. Le Roy. *Love, Death and Money in the Pays d'Oc.* New York, 1982.

Lanham, Richard A. *The Motives of Eloquence: Literary Rhetoric in the Renaissance.* New Haven, 1976.

Leavis, F. R. 'The Line of Wit', in *Seventeenth-Century English Poetry: Modern Essays in Criticism,* ed. Keast.

Lecocq, Louis. *La satire en Angleterre de 1588 à 1603.* Paris, 1969.

Leishman, J. B. *The Monarch of Wit.* 5th edn, London, 1962.

—— *Themes and Variations in Shakespeare's Sonnets.* London, 1961.

Lerner, L. *An Introduction to English Poetry: Fifteen Poems Discussed.* London, 1975.

Lever, J. W. *The Elizabethan Love Sonnet.* London, 1956. 2nd edn, 1966.

—— *The Tragedy of State.* London, 1971.

Levin, Harry. *The Myth of the Golden Age in the Renaissance*. New York, 1972.

—— *The Overreacher: A Study of Christopher Marlowe*. London, 1953.

Levin, Richard. *New Readings vs. Old Plays: Recent Trends in the Reinterpretation of English Renaissance Drama*. Chicago and London, 1979.

—— 'Some Second Thoughts on Central Themes', *MLR*, 67 (1972), 1—10.

Lewalski, B. K. *Donne's* Anniversaries *and the Poetry of Praise*. Princeton, 1973.

—— 'Donne's Poetry of Compliment: The Speaker's Stance and the Topos of Praise', in *Seventeenth-Century Imagery*, ed. Miner.

—— *Protestant Poetics and the Seventeenth-Century Religious Lyric*. Princeton, 1979.

Lewis, C. S. 'Donne and Love Poetry in the Seventeenth Century', in *Seventeenth-Century English Poetry: Modern Essays in Criticism*, ed. Keast.

—— *English Literature in the Sixteenth Century*. London, 1973.

—— *Studies in Words*. Cambridge, 1960.

Lovelace, Richard. *The Poems of Richard Lovelace*, ed. C. H. Wilkinson. Oxford, 1930.

Lytle, Guy Fitch and Orgel, Stephen (eds) *Patronage in the Renaissance*. Princeton, 1981.

Macfarlane, Alan. *The Family Life of Ralph Josselin: A Seventeenth-Century Clergyman*. Cambridge, 1970.

Machin, R. 'The Great Rebuilding: A reassessment', *Past and Present*, 77 (1977), 33—56.

Mack, Maynard. 'The Jacobean Shakespeare: Some Observations on the Construction of the Tragedies', in *Jacobean Theatre*, ed. Brown and Harris. Harris.

Mackenzie, Elizabeth. 'The Growth of Plants: A Seventeenth-Century Metaphor', in *English Renaissance Studies Presented to Dame Helen Gardner*, ed. Carey.

MacLure, Millar. *George Chapman: A Critical Study*. Toronto, 1966.

McClung, W. A. *The Country House in English Renaissance Poetry*. Berkeley, Los Angeles, and London, 1977.

McGowan, Margaret M. ' "As through a looking-glass", Donne's Epithalamia and their Courtly Context', in *John Donne, Essays in Celebration*, ed. A. J. Smith.

McGuire, Mary Ann C. 'The Cavalier Country-House Poem: Mutations on a Jonsonian Tradition', *SEL*, XIX, 1 (1979), 93—108.

McKeon, Michael. *Politics and Poetry in Restoration England: The Case of Dryden's 'Annus Mirabilis'*. Cambridge, Mass., and London, 1975.

McLane, P. E. *Spenser's Shepheardes Calendar*. Notre Dame, 1961.

Mahood, M. M. *Shakespeare's Wordplay.* London, 1957.

Manley, Lawrence. *Convention 1500—1750.* Cambridge, Mass., and London, 1980.

Manlove, C. N. *Literature and Reality, 1600—1800.* London, 1978.

Manning, Roger B. *Religion and Society in Elizabethan Sussex: A study of the enforcement of the religious settlement, 1558—1603.* Leicester, 1969.

Mannucci, Loretta Valtz. *Ideali e classi nella poesia di Milton: La nascita dell 'eroe borghese puritano in 'Paradise Lost' e in 'Paradise Regained'.* Milan, 1976.

Marlborough, Helen. 'Herrick's Epigrams of Praise', in *'Trust to Good Verses': Herrick Tercentenary Essays,* ed. Rollin and Patrick.

Marotti, Arthur F. 'All About Jonson's Poetry', *ELH,* 39 (1972), 208—37.

———— 'John Donne and the Rewards of Patronage', in *Patronage in the Renaisssance,* ed. Lytle and Orgel.

———— ' "Love is Not Love": Elizabethan Sonnet Sequences and the Social Order', *ELH,* 49 (1982), 396—428.

Martines, Lauro. *Power and Imagination: City-States in Renaissance Italy.* New York, 1979.

Martz, Louis L. 'The Action of the Self: Devotional Poetry in the Seventeenth Century', in *Metaphysical Poetry,* ed. Bradbury and Palmer.

———— *The Poetry of Meditation: A Study in English Religious Literature of the Seventeenth Century.* Rev. edn, New Haven and London, 1972.

———— *The Wit of Love.* Notre Dame, Indiana, 1969.

Matthews, G. M. 'Sex and the Sonnet', *EC,* II (1952), 119—37.

Maurer, Margaret. 'John Donne's Verse Letters', *MLQ,* 37, 3 (1976), 234—59.

———— 'Samuel Daniel's Poetical Epistles, Especially those to Sir Thomas Egerton and Lucy, Countess of Bedford', *SP,* LXXIV, 4 (1977), 418—44.

———— 'The Real Presence of Lucy Russell, Countess of Bedford, and the Terms of John Donne's "Honour Is So Sublime Perfection",' *ELH,* 47 (1980), 205—34.

May, Steven W. 'The Authorship of "My Mind to Me a Kingdom is" ', *RES,* 26 (1975), 385—94.

Melchiori, Giorgio. *L'Uomo e il potere: indagine sulle strutture profonde dei Sonetti di Shakespeare.* Torino, 1973.

Miles, Josephine. *Eras and Modes in English Poetry.* Berkeley and Los Angeles, 1957.

———— *The Continuity of Poetic Language: The Primary Language of Poetry, 1540's—1940's.* New York, 1965.

Miller, David L. 'Abandoning the Quest', *ELH,* 46 (1979), 173—92.

Miller, Edwin Haviland. *The Professional Writer in Elizabethan England.* Cambridge, Mass., 1959.

Miller, J. T. ' "Love doth hold my hand": Writing and Wooing in the Sonnets of Sidney and Spenser', *ELH,* 46 (1979), 541—58.

Miner, Earl. *The Cavalier Mode from Jonson to Cotton.* Princeton, 1971.

_____ *The Metaphysical Mode from Donne to Cowley.* Princeton, 1969.

Molesworth, Charles. 'Property and Virtues: The Genre of the Country-House Poem in the Seventeenth Century', *Genre,* 1 (1968), 141—57.

Montrose, Louis Adrian. ' "Eliza, Queen of Shepeardes", and the Pastoral of Power', *ELR,* 10 (1980), 153—82.

Morrill, J. S. *Cheshire 1630—1660: County Government and Society During the English Revolution.* Oxford, 1974.

Morris, Brian. 'Satire from Donne to Marvell', in *Metaphysical Poetry,* ed. Bradbury and Palmer.

Morris, Brian and Withington, Eleanor (eds) *The Poems of John Cleveland.* Oxford, 1967.

Muir, Edward. *Civic Ritual in Renaissance Venice.* Princeton, 1981.

Mulder, J. R. *The Temple of the Mind: Education and Literary Taste in Seventeenth—Century England.* New York, 1969.

Murrin, Michael. *The Veil of Allegory: Some Notes Toward a Theory of Allegorical Rhetoric in the English Renaissance.* Chicago and London, 1969.

Neely, C. T. 'The Structure of English Renaissance Sonnet Sequences', *ELH,* 45 (1978), 359—89.

Nevo, Ruth. *The Dial of Virtue: A Study of Poems on Affairs of State in the Seventeenth Century.* Princeton, 1963.

Newdigate, B. H. *Michael Drayton and His Circle.* Oxford, 1961.

Newton, R. C. ' "Goe, quit 'hem all": Ben Jonson and Formal Verse Satire', *SEL,* XVI, 1 (1976), 105—16.

Norris, Christopher. *Deconstruction: Theory and Practice.* London and New York, 1982.

Novarr, David. *The Disinterested Muse: Donne's Texts and Contexts.* Ithaca and London, 1980.

Nowottny, Winifred. *The Language Poets Use.* London, 1962.

O'Connell, Michael. *Mirror and Veil: The Historical Dimension of Spenser's Faerie Queene.* Chapel Hill, 1977.

Orgel, Stephen. *The Illusion of Power: Political Theater in the English Renaissance.* Berkeley, Los Angeles, and London, 1975.

_____ *The Jonsonian Masque.* Cambridge, Mass., 1965.

Orgel, Stephen and Strong, Roy. *Inigo Jones, The Theatre of the Stuart Court.* Berkeley, 1973.

Ornstein, Robert. *The Moral Vision of Jacobean Tragedy.* Madison, 1960.

Parfitt, George A. E. *Ben Jonson: Public Poet and Private Man.* London, 1976.

—— 'Donne, Herbert, and the Matter of Schools', *EC,* XXII (1972), 381—95.

—— (ed.) *Silver Poets of the Seventeenth Century.* London, 1974.

—— 'The Poetry of Ben Jonson', *EC,* XVIII (1968), 19—31.

Partridge, A. C. *John Donne: Language and Style.* London, 1978.

—— *The Language of Renaissance Poetry: Spenser, Shakespeare, Donne, Milton.* London, 1971.

Partridge, E. 'Jonson's *Epigrammes:* The Named and the Nameless', *Studies in the Literary Imagination,* 4 (1973), 153—98.

Patrick, J. Max, Evans, R. D. and Wallace, John M. (eds) *Style, Rhetoric, and Rhythm: Essays by Morris W. Croll.* Princeton, 1966.

Patrides, C. A. (ed.) *Approaches to Marvell.* London, 1978.

Patrides, C. A. and Waddington, R. B. (eds) *The Age of Milton: Backgrounds to Seventeenth-Century Literature.* Manchester and Totowa, 1980.

Pearlman, E. 'Ben Jonson: An Anatomy', *ELR,* 9 (1979), 364—94.

Peter, John. *Complaint and Satire in Early English Literature.* Oxford, 1956.

Peterson, Douglas L. *The English Lyric from Wyatt to Donne: A History of the Plain and Eloquent Styles.* Princeton, 1967.

Pooley, Roger. 'Language and Loyalty: Plain Style at the Restoration', *Literature and History,* 6, 1 (1980), 2—18.

Power, Michael. 'Shadwell: The Development of a London Suburban Community in the Seventeenth Century', *The London Journal,* 4,1 (1978), 29—46.

—— 'The East and West in Early-Modern London', in *Wealth and Power in Tudor England,* ed. Ives (et al.).

Powers, Doris C. *English Formal Satire: Elizabethan to Augustan.* The Hague, 1971.

Prest, W. R. *The Inns of Court Under Elizabeth I and the Early Stuarts.* London, 1972.

Prince, F. T. 'The Sonnet from Wyatt to Shakespeare', in *Elizabethan Poetry,* ed. Brown and Harris.

Quaife, G. R. *Wanton Wenches and Wayward Wives: Peasants and Illicit Sex in Early Seventeenth-Century England.* London, 1979.

Quintilian, *Institutio Oratoria,* trans. H. E. Butler. 4 vols. London and New York, 1920—22.

Raleigh, Sir Walter. *Poems,* ed. Agnes Latham. London, 1951.

Rauber, D. F. 'Carew Redivivus', *TSLL,* XIII, 1 (1971), 17—28.

Rebholz, Ronald A. *The Life of Fulke Greville: First Lord Brooke.* Oxford, 1971.

Ribner, Irving. *Jacobean Tragedy: The Quest for Moral Order.* London, 1962.

Richmond, H. M. *The School of Love, The Evolution of the Stuart Love Lyric.* Princeton, 1964.

Ricks, Christopher. ' "It's own resemblance" ', in *Approaches to Marvell,* ed. Patrides.

Riffaterre, Michael. *Semiotics of Poetry.* London, 1978.

Rivers, Isabel. *The Poetry of Conservatism, 1600—1745: A Study of Poets and Public Affairs from Jonson to Pope.* Cambridge, 1973.

Rollin, Roger B. 'Sweet Numbers and Sour Readers: Trends and Perspectives in Herrick Criticism', in *Herrick Tercentenary Essays,* ed. Rollin and Patrick.

Rollin, Roger B. and Patrick, J. Max (eds) *'Trust to Good Verses': Herrick Tercentenary Essays.* Pittsburgh, 1978.

Ross, M. M. *Poetry and Dogma: The Transfiguration of Eucharistic Symbols in Seventeenth-Century English Poetry.* New Brunswick, 1954.

Ross, Richard J. 'Herrick's Julia in Silks', *EC,* XV (1965), 171—81.

Roston, Murray. *The Soul of Wit: A Study of John Donne.* Oxford, 1974.

Rostvig, Maren-Sofie. *The Happy Man: Studies in the Metamorphoses of a Classical Ideal,* 2 vols. Oslo, 1962.

Rothstein, Eric. *Restoration and Eighteenth-Century Poetry, 1660—1780.* Boston, London and Henley, 1981.

Rubel, Vere L. *Poetic Diction in the English Renaissance: from Skelton through Spenser.* New York and London, 1941.

Ruff, L. M. and Wilson, D. Arnold. 'The Madrigal, The Lute, and Elizabethan Politics', *Past and Present,* 44 (1969), 3—51.

Rugoff, M. A. *Donne's Imagery: A Study in Creative Sources.* New York, 1939.

Ruthven, K. K. *The Conceit.* London, 1969.

Sabean, David. 'Communion and Community', in the Festschrift for Rudolf Vierhaus, *Mentalitäten und Lebensverhältnisse.* Göttingen, 1982.

Sadler, Lynn. *Thomas Carew.* Boston, 1979.

Sargent, Ralph M. *At the Court of Queen Elizabeth, The Life and Lyrics of Sir Edward Dyer.* London, 1935.

Saunders, J. W. 'The Social Situation of Seventeenth-Century Poetry', pp. 237—59, in *Metaphysical Poetry,* ed. Bradbury and Palmer.

Schilling, Bernard N. (ed.) *Dryden: A Collection of Critical Essays.* Englewood Cliffs, 1963.

Scott, Janet G. *Les Sonnets Élizabéthains.* Paris, 1929.

Selden, Raman. *English Verse Satire 1590—1765.* London, 1978.

Seronsy, Cecil C. 'Well-Languaged Daniel: A Reconsideration', *MLR,* 52 (1957), 481—97.

Shakespeare, William. *Shakespeare's Sonnets,* ed. S. Booth.

Shapiro, I. A. 'The "Mermaid Club" ', *MLR,* 45 (1950), 6—17.

Sharp, R. L. *From Donne to Dryden, The Revolt Against Metaphysical Poetry.* Chapel Hill, 1940.

Sharrock, Roger. 'Marvell's Poetry of Evasion and Marvell's Times', *English,* XXVIII, 130 (1979), 3—40.

Simon, Joan. *Education and Society in Tudor England.* Cambridge, 1966.

Sinfield, Alan. 'Sexual Puns in *Astrophel and Stella',* *EC,* XXIV (1974), 341—55.

—— *Literature in Protestant England 1560—1660.* London and Totowa, 1983.

Sloan, Thomas O. 'Rhetoric, "Logic" and Poetry: The Formal Cause', in *The Age of Milton: Backgrounds to Seventeenth-Century Literature,* ed. Patrides and Waddington.

Smith, A. J. (ed.) *John Donne, Essays in Celebration.* London, 1972.

—— 'Marvell's Metaphysical Wit', in *Approaches to Marvell,* ed. Patrides.

—— 'The Failure of Love: Love Lyrics after Donne', in *Metaphysical Poetry,* ed. Bradbury and Palmer.

—— 'The Metaphysic of Love', *RES,* 9 (1958), 362—75.

Smith, Hallet. *Elizabethan Poetry: A Study in Conventions, Meaning, and Expression.* Cambridge, Mass., 1952.

Southall, Raymond. *Literature and the Rise of Capitalism: Critical Essays Mainly on the Sixteenth and Seventeenth Centuries.* London, 1973.

—— 'Love Poetry in the Sixteenth Century', *EC,* XXII (1972), 362—80.

—— *The Courtly Maker.* Oxford, 1964.

Spitzer, L. 'Marvell's "Nymph" ', in *Seventeenth-Century English Poetry: Modern Essays in Criticism,* ed. Keast.

Spriet, Pierre. *Samuel Daniel (1563—1619): sa vie, son oeuvre.* Paris, 1968.

Spurgeon, Caroline F. E. *Shakespeare's Imagery and What It Tells Us.* Cambridge, 1935.

Squier, Charles L. *Sir John Suckling.* Boston, 1978.

Stagg, L. C. *An Index to the Figurative Language of George Chapman's Tragedies.* Charlottesville, 1970.

Stavig, Mark. *John Ford and the Traditional Moral Order.* Madison, 1968.

Stein, Arnold. 'Plain Style, Plain Criticism, Plain Dealing, and Ben Jonson', *ELH,* 30 (1963), 306—16.

Stone, Lawrence. *The Causes of the English Revolution, 1529—1642.* London and Henley, 1972.

—— *The Crisis of the Aristocracy 1558—1641.* Oxford, 1965.

___ 'The Educational Revolution in England 1560—1640', *Past and Present,* 28 (1964), 41—80.

___ *Family and Fortune: studies in aristocratic finance in the sixteenth and seventeenth centuries.* Oxford, 1973.

___ *The Family, Sex and Marriage in England 1500—1800.* London, 1977.

Strong, Roy. *Splendour at Court: Renaissance Spectacle and Illusion.* London, 1973.

Summers, Claude J. 'Herrick's Political Poetry: The Strategies of His Art', in *Herrick Tercentenary Essays,* ed. Rollin and Patrick.

Summers, J. H. 'Andrew Marvell: Private Taste and Public Judgment', in *Metaphysical Poetry,* ed. Bradbury and Palmer.

___ *The Heirs of Donne and Jonson.* New York and London, 1970.

Tennenhouse, Leonard. 'Sir Walter Raleigh and the Literature of Clientage', in *Patronage in the Renaissance,* ed. Lytle and Orgel.

Thirsk, Joan (ed.) *The Agrarian History of England and Wales, 1500—1640.* Vol. 4, Cambridge, 1967.

Thomas, Keith. *Religion and the Decline of Magic.* Harmondsworth, 1978.

Thomson, Patricia. 'Donne and the Poetry of Patronage, the *Verse Letters*', in *John Donne, Essays in Celebration,* ed. A. J. Smith.

___ (ed.) *Elizabethan Lyrical Poets.* London, 1967.

___ *Sir Thomas Wyatt and His Background.* London, 1964.

___ 'The Literature of Patronage, 1580—1630', *EC,* II (1952), 267—84.

Thynne, Francis. *Emblemes and Epigrames,* ed. F. J. Furnivall. London, 1876.

Tillman, James S. 'Herrick's Georgic Encomia', in *Herrick Tercentenary Essays,* ed. Rollin and Patrick.

Trimpi, Wesley. *Ben Jonson's Poems: A Study of the Plain Style.* Stanford, 1962.

Trotter, David. *The Poetry of Abraham Cowley.* London, 1979.

Turner, James. *The Politics of Landscape: Rural Scenery and Society in English Poetry 1630—1660.* Oxford, 1979.

Tuve, Rosemond. *Elizabethan and Metaphysical Imagery: Renaissance Poetic and Twentieth-Century Critics.* Chicago, 1947.

Upton, A. F. *Sir Arthur Ingram c. 1565—1642.* Oxford, 1961.

van Dorsten, Jan. 'Literary Patronage in Elizabethan England: The Early Phase', in *Patronage in the Renaissance,* ed. Lytle and Orgel.

Vendler, Helen. *The Poetry of George Herbert.* Cambridge, Mass., and London, 1975.

Vickers, Brian. 'The "Songs and Sonnets" and the Rhetoric of Hyperbole', in *John Donne, Essays in Celebration,* ed. A. J. Smith.

Waddington, Raymond B. 'Milton among the Carolines', in *The Age of Milton: Backgrounds to Seventeenth-Century Literature*, ed. Patrides and Waddington.

___ *The Mind's Empire: Myth and Form in George Chapman's Narrative Poems.* Baltimore and London, 1974.

Wadsworth, R. L., Jr. 'On "The Snayl" by Richard Lovelace', *MLR*, 65 (1970), 750–60.

Walker, R. S. 'Ben Jonson's Lyric Poetry', in *Seventeenth-Century English Poetry: Modern Essays in Criticism*, ed. Keast.

Wallace, John M. *Destiny His Choice: The Loyalty of Andrew Marvell.* Cambridge, 1968.

Walton, Geoffrey. *Metaphysical to Augustan: Studies in Tone and Sensibility in the Seventeenth Century.* London, 1955.

___ 'The Tone of Ben Jonson's Poetry', in *Seventeenth-Century English Poetry: Modern Essays in Criticism*, ed. Keast.

Wasserman, Earl R. *The Subtler Language: Critical Readings of Neoclassic and Romantic Poems.* Baltimore, 1968.

Waswo, Richard. *The Fatal Mirror: Themes and Techniques in the Poetry of Fulke Greville.* Charlottesville, 1972.

Watts, S. J. (with Susan J. Watts). *From Border to Middle Shire: Northumberland, 1586–1625.* Leicester, 1975.

Wayne, Don E. 'Poetry and Power in Ben Jonson's *Epigrammes:* The Naming of "Facts" or the Figuring of Social Relations?', *Renaissance and Modern Studies*, XXIII (1979), 79-103.

Wedgewood, C. V. 'Cavalier Poetry and Cavalier Politics'. *Velvet Studies.* London, 1977.

___ *Poetry and Politics under the Stuarts.* Cambridge, 1960.

Weidhorn, Manfred. *Richard Lovelace.* New York, 1970.

Weimann, Robert. *Structure and Society in Literary History: Studies in the History and Theory of Historical Criticism.* London, 1977.

Weiss, Wolfgang. *Die Elizabethanische Lyrik.* Darmstadt, 1976.

Wells, H. W. *Poetic Imagery: Illustrated from Elizabethan Literature.* New York, 1924.

Wentersdorf, K. P. 'Imagery as a Criterion of Authenticity: A Reconsideration of the Problem', *SQ*, XXIII, 3 (1972), 231–59.

Wilcox, John. 'Informal Publication of Late Sixteenth-Century Verse Satire', *HLQ*, XIII (1950), 191–200.

Wilkinson, C. H. (ed.) *The Poems of Richard Lovelace.* Oxford, 1930.

Williams, Raymond. *The Long Revolution.* London, 1961.

Williamson, Colin. 'Structure and Syntax in *Astrophil and Stella*', *RES*, 31 (1980), 271–84.

Williamson, George. *The Donne Tradition: A Study in English Poetry from Donne to the Death of Cowley.* Cambridge, Mass., 1930.

Wilson, F. P. *Elizabethan and Jacobean.* Oxford, 1945.

Wood, D. N. C. 'Decorum and Decoration in the Language of Elizabethan Poetry.' *Revue de l'Université d'Ottowa,* 42, 3 (1972), 470—8.

Wortham, C. J. 'Richard Lovelace's "To Lucasta, Going to the Warres": Which Wars?', *Notes and Queries,* 224, (1979), 430—1.

Wrigley, E. A. and Schofield, R. S. *The Population History of England, 1541—1871.* London, 1981.

Young, R. V., Jr. 'Jonson, Crashaw, and the Development of the English Epigram.' *Genre,* 12 (1979), 137—52.

Index

Aers, D. 112
allegory 22, 47, 69, 106
Alvarez, A. 87—8
Anselment, R. A. 156n34
answer poems, mocking 57—8, 74,
  155n2
Armstrong, E. A. 82
Aston family 148
audience *see* readers

Bacon, Francis 7, 90
ballad 14, 58, 92, 135
Barnes, Barnabe 31, 159n98
Barnfield, Richard 159n98
Bateson, F. W. 80
Berry, Frances 110
Bible 152n29, 153n57
biography 33, 37, 48—9, 61, 82, 142
blank verse 64
Bradbrook, M. C. 77
Breton, Nicholas 159n98
Browne, William 41, 95
Bucke, George 135
Buckingham, George Villiers, 1st Duke
  of 20, 21
Burke, Kenneth 58, 115
Butler, Samuel 46

C., E.: 'My heart is like a ship' 35
Carew, Thomas 42, 43, 44, 89, 111, 122
  'To Saxham' 73; masques 56; readers
  59, 66, 89, 93
Cartwright, William 66

Cary, Sir Lucius 20
Cavalier poetry 3, 31—2, 42, 57, 64,
  122—3, 140
  language 48, 83; readers 58, 59, 67;
  style 41, 89—91, 122, 153n51;
  themes 24, 49, 57, 72; tone 43—4
Cavaliers 32, 36, 44, 64, 89, 122, 140,
  148
Cecil family 147
Cecil, Robert 74
censorship 21, 69, 118
Chapman, George 21, 22, 55, 62
  Eastward Ho 21; language 28, 82,
  104, 114
Charles I, King of England 21, 58, 95
Chernaik, Warren L. 122
Cicero 38
Civil War 44, 46, 71, 106—7, 136—7,
  140
classics 114, 135
  Greek 135; Latin 40, 41, 79, 81, 90,
  92, 135; influence 40, 41, 43, 83,
  95
Cleveland, John 20, 44, 46, 111
  'The Hue and Cry after Sir John
  Presbyter' 92
Congreve, William 80
Constable, Henry 159n98
Cotton, Charles 66, 67
country 24, 32, 166
  houses 66, 159n110; *see also* retire-
  ment
couplet 15, 50, 64, 72, 154n36

Court 15, 26, 41, 72, 83, 90, 93
  attacked 93−4, 95, 102, 111, 118,
    122, 155n55; corruption 89, 103,
    104, 106; influence 19, 26, 27, 29,
    35, 38, 43, 66−7, 69, 100; as
    patron 27, 29, 30, 54, 56, 64, 78
courtly love *see* love poetry, courtly
Cowley, Abraham 21, 46, 111, 122
  Civil War 106−7; style 43, 87
Crashaw, Richard 122, 153n59
Cromwell, Oliver 22, 58, 68, 70, 92
culture 134
  high 27, 43, 131, 133, 134, 141, 142,
    146−7; popular 27, 125, 131, 133,
    134, 135, 142, 161n9; *see also*
    folklore
Cunningham, J. V. 87

Daniel, Samuel 21, 55, 75
  'Panegyricke Congratulatorie' 21;
    diction 81; readers 59, 61, 154n14;
    sonnets 94, 160n15; verse letters
    15, 45, 56
Dante Alighieri 27, 160n30
Davies, Sir John 62, 69, 90
  Gulling Sonnets 49, 65, 93; *Nosce
    Teipsum* 87; diction 26; style 86, 87
Day, John 21
deconstruction 73, 126, 127, 150n6,
  150n8
decorative arts 118, 140, 147, 148,
  159n110
decorum 25, 38, 42, 45, 54, 61, 91, 93,
  151n11
deep structures 109, 111, 112, 141
Dekker, Thomas 82
Denham, Sir John 87
  'Cooper's Hill' 20, 73
Derrida, Jacques 150n8
dialect 25, 26, 27
diction 25, 30, 76, 81, 105, 111, 123
  allusions 49; associations 2, 6, 18, 36,
    48, 77, 82; courtly 30, 39, 77;
    learned 40; and patronage 27; plain
    26, 28, 29, 30, 40; poetic 25−6,

  27, 28; sonnet 39, 80, 81; *see also*
    imagery; language
display 66, 103, 118, 146, 147, 159n110
Donne, John 14, 16, 29−30, 37, 42, 45,
  62, 63, 69, 123−4
  Anniversaries 27, 42, 55; *Elegies* 26,
    40; 'Letter to Sir Henry Wotton'
    110; *Satyres* 40; *Songs and Sonnets*
    40; friends 87−8, 148; imagery 23,
    33, 36, 72, 84, 88, 92, 104, 114,
    124, 150n5; language 26, 27, 28,
    29, 40, 78, 81, 110, 111, 113, 114,
    151n21, 160n27; love poetry 7, 36,
    69, 70, 72, 88; patrons 4, 54, 55,
    56; readers 42, 59, 60−1, 87, 88;
    religious poetry 36, 72; secular
    poetry 40; sonnets 93; style 40−1,
    61, 86, 87, 88, 104, 121, 124,
    151n21; tone 90, 91; verse letters
    15, 27, 40, 45, 54, 55, 56, 151n21
Donow, Herbert 110
Drayton, Michael 21, 54, 60, 75
  Idea 91; *Ideas Mirrour* 54; *The Owl*
    47, 74; 'Taking my Penne' 152n29;
    eclogues 49; masques 56; readers
    59, 61; sonnets 27, 31, 74, 81, 93,
    94, 160n15; view of poetry 41, 55,
    95
dress 83, 140, 146, 147, 148, 159n110
Drummond, William 78
Dryden, John 16, 46, 58, 72, 80, 108
  Absalom and Achitophel 20; *The
    Conquest of Granada* 156n21;
    circle 69, 148; style 87, 154n36
Dudley family 55, 147
Dyer, John 59, 78, 86
  'Coridon to his Phyllis' 78

economy 102, 123
  expansion 71, 77, 78, 103, 113−14,
    120, 160n30
editing 5−6
education 15, 56, 76, 79, 80−1, 92,
  96, 135

Inns of Court 26, 90—1, 103;
university 61—2, 103, 146
Egerton family 55
elegy 45, 106, 107
Elizabeth I, Queen of England 4, 21, 27,
48, 55, 66, 83, 101, 146
emblems 47, 140
Empson, William 64—5, 94, 113
epic 14, 15, 16, 45, 60, 106—7, 138
mock-heroic 46, 50; readers 59, 60;
vocabulary 25
epigram 2, 44, 45, 50, 59, 62, 74, 104,
153n58
epitaph 45
epithalamion 14, 45
escapism 3, 67
Essex, Robert Devereux, 2nd Earl of 48,
66
Everitt, Alan 144

Fabre, J. -B. Castor 132
Fairfax, Thomas, 3rd Lord 56
Fairfax, William 135
fashion 66, 96, 114, 118, 146
attacked 93; influence 31, 35; in
language 78, 79, 114
Filmer, Sir Robert 3
flattery 54, 56
Fletcher, Giles 41, 95, 159n98
Fletcher, John 160n19
Fletcher, Phineas 41, 95
folklore 132, 133—4
form *see* genre
Fowler, Alastair 152n29
furnishing 146, 147, 148

Gardner, Dame Helen 25
genre 14—15, 44, 153n58
changes 15, 16, 34, 46, 50, 93;
conventions 2, 13, 15, 16, 31, 34,
45, 96, 99; hierarchy 14, 44; and
society 15, 45, 46, 93, 96, 107
Gill, Roma 26
Godolphin, Sidney 58

Goodere, Anne *see* Rainsford, Anne,
Lady
Greene, Robert 62, 78, 87
Greville, Fulke, Lord Brooke 21, 48, 59,
86, 90, 158n89
Griffin, Bartholomew 159n98
Grundy, Joan 148
Guilpin, Everard 26, 62, 86, 90, 141

Habington, William 44
Hall, John 135
Hall, Joseph 60, 62, 86
Hammond, William 135
Harington, Sir John 55, 62
Harvey, Gabriel 62
Helgerson, Richard 153n58, 157n54
Henrietta Maria, Queen 67
Herbert family 148
Herbert, Edward, 1st Baron Herbert of
Cherbury 42, 59, 88, 158n89
Autobiography 7
Herbert, George 42, 59, 88, 122,
158n70
Herrick, Robert 83, 92, 111, 122
Hill, Christopher 145
Hill, George 135
history 125, 128—45
everyday 146—9; local 144—5;
quantitative 125, 131, 144, 145,
161n11; and language 76, 77, 127;
and literature 16, 71, 108, 128,
139, 141, 143, 145; and poetry 5,
8, 10, 12—13, 18, 22, 37, 48, 51,
52, 74, 97, 98, 99, 105, 107, 108,
120—4, 134, 136, 137, 138, 140,
142, 143, 145; and prose 7, 9, 11,
12, 97, 134, 145; and reality 28,
97, 132, 133, 134, 137; method
131, 135, 136, 137—8; relevance
128, 129; specialization 123,
129—30, 131, 134, 136—7,
141—2; writing in Britain 143—5
Hobbes, Thomas 3, 104
Hoby, Lady Margaret 147
Hodge, Bob 112

Holmes, Elizabeth 77, 114
Horace 14, 24, 45, 46, 61, 67
Hoskins, John 66, 81
hymn 14
hyperbole 30, 32, 41, 84

imagery 2, 30—1, 81, 113—17, 123,
    125
  and biography 33, 37, 82; Cavalier
    31—2, 83; commercial 113—14,
    115, 117; Elizabethan 84—5; eyes
    116; fetishistic 32, 83; Jacobean
    84—5; learned 33, 81, 83; legal 35,
    81, 116, 156n27; metaphysical 82,
    83—4; nautical 35, 82, 115;
    religious 36; Restoration 84; rural
    32, 116—17; scientific 33, 81,
    118; seasonal 31, 32, 114—15;
    sexual 115—16; sonnet 83; and
    social background 32—3, 37, 82,
    83; sources 34—6, 48, 81, 82, 105,
    113, 114, 115; urban 31, 32, 118
Inns of Court *see* London
interpretation 5, 98, 99, 105, 106
inversion 47
irony 32, 35, 47, 95

James I, King of England 21, 95
James, Mervyn 144
Jonson, Ben 16, 21, 30, 62, 90, 156n3,
    158n94
  Eastward Ho 21; 'Epistle to a Friend'
    160n34; *Sejanus* 48; 'To Penshurst'
    4, 19, 54, 73; *Volpone* 113,
    119—20, 152n27; language 26,
    28, 29, 30, 54, 80, 82, 111—12,
    114; masques 56, 91; patrons 54,
    56, 59, 91; plays 80, 91; poetry 6,
    11, 55, 69; readers 59, 61, 87, 88,
    148; style 41, 43, 86, 87, 122,
    151n21; tone 43, 91; verse letters
    15, 45, 56
Juvenal 14, 67

King, Henry 66

Kress, Gunther 112

Ladurie, E. Le Roy 132, 133
language x, 27, 109, 111, 126—7,
    150n6—7
  ambiguity 2, 18, 77, 111, 113; anti-
    language 113, 160n27; associations
    2, 18, 48, 76, 77, 78, 99, 113;
    choice 26, 27, 29, 40, 109—10;
    colloquial 26, 27, 28, 104, 110,
    118; fashion 79, 81; figurative *see*
    imagery; history 5, 76, 77, 81; as
    social criticism 29, 30, 90; and
    society 109, 124—5; urban 26, 27,
    67; usage 27—8, 29, 78, 81, 104,
    109; adjectives 111; articles 105,
    109, 112; nouns 111; pronouns 62,
    105, 109, 110, 112, 160n19; verbs
    78, 111; *see also* diction
Laud, William, Archbishop of
    Canterbury 20, 58
Levin, Harry 83
linguistics 123, 125
literature x, 2, 13, 97
  and history 108, 128, 129, 132, 139,
    141, 143, 145; and society 15—16,
    38, 95, 99
Locke, John 3
  Second Treatise of Civil Government
    22
Lodge, Thomas 45, 62, 78, 159n98
London 21, 32, 65, 67, 76, 90, 100,
    120, 155n48
  Gray's Inn 65; influence 26, 27, 66,
    72; Inns of Court 26, 29, 35, 40,
    49, 50, 65, 66, 69, 76, 89, 90, 102,
    103; St Paul's 58
love poetry 19, 20, 23—4, 32, 60, 98
  anti-courtly 69, 70, 75; Cavalier 89;
    conventions 45, 49, 69; courtly 2,
    3, 26, 29, 39, 42, 45, 49, 69, 75,
    85, 93, 152n44, 158n96; erotic 56,
    66, 95—6; fashion 66, 69, 93;
    imagery 34—6, 75, 82, 113;
    language 48, 75, 77—8; as

metaphor 4, 23, 32, 98, 106; as
parody 4, 35, 49, 50, 69, 104;
readers 59
Lovelace, Richard 43, 66, 111, 122,
135, 155n2
'The Grasshopper' 48; 'To Althea' 64;
readers 89, 93
Luther, Martin: *The Babylonian
Captivity* 98
Lyly, John 78
Euphues 152n41
Lynche, Richard 159n98
'Weary with serving' 35
lyric 45, 93, 102, 124
style 38, 86, 99, 101, 104, 105,
121—2

Machiavelli, Niccolò 7, 104, 112
The Prince 22, 107, 125
Marlowe, Christopher 60, 61, 71
The Jew of Malta 84—5, 103; 'The
Passionate Shepherd' 74, 83;
imagery 84—5, 114; language 77,
82, 114; patrons 96; plays 71, 85
marriage 100, 101, 108, 140
Marston, John 21, 62, 90
Eastward Ho 21; *The Metamorphosis
of Pigmalions Image* 60; *The
Scourge of Villanie* 119; language
26, 78; satires 26, 60, 86, 119
Martial 14
Marvell, Andrew 22, 46, 49, 108, 122
'An Horatian Ode upon Cromwell's
Return from Ireland' 22, 68, 70,
92; 'The Last Instructions to a
Painter' 22; 'The Nymph Complain-
ing for the Death of her Faun' 23;
'To His Coy Mistress' 49; 'Upon
Appleton House' 20, 56, 68, 73;
political verse 42, 58, 68
masques 56, 78
May, Thomas 135
Melchiori, Giorgio 77, 109—10, 111,
112

metaphor 30, 31, 32, 50, 81—2, 114,
117—18, 127, 160n38, 160n40
associations 2, 36—7, 47, 85, 105,
106
Metaphysical poetry 70, 72, 92, 140
language 82, 83—4; style 88; tone
42, 90
Middleton, Thomas 62
Miles, Josephine 111
milieu 1, 11—12, 65—8, 91, 140, 143
construction 51—2, 105, 136, 137,
138—9, 141—2
Milton, John 22, 48, 58, 70, 122
Paradise Lost 138
Miner, E. 70
Montaigne, Michel de 7
Morrill, John 144
Mulder, J. R. 80
music 78, 140, 148
mythology, classical 33, 40, 83

Nashe, Thomas 62
*The Choice of Valentine's or Nashe's
Dildo* 80
Niccols, Richard 68
nostalgia 76, 78, 159n3

occasional verse 21, 22, 45, 56—8, 93,
98
ode 15, 46
Ovid 45, 66, 81, 95
Oxinden family 148

panegyric 14, 22, 57, 93, 95, 98
parody 14, 35, 49, 58, 93, 95
Partridge, A. C. 78
Pascal, Blaise 7
pastoral 14, 45, 67, 94—5, 156n5
conventions 2, 15; language 79;
parodied 74, 95
patronage 5, 27, 30, 53—6, 61, 73,
102, 103, 123

Court 27, 29, 30, 56, 62, 64, 78;
    female 27, 90, 94, 101; poetry 4,
    19, 20, 24, 27, 35, 44, 45, 46, 53,
    54, 55, 56, 57, 58, 62, 63, 69, 75,
    96
Peele, George 62
Percy, William 159n98
Persius 67
personification 30, 32, 67, 81, 83
Petrarch, Francesco 14, 23, 26, 35
    influence 40, 45, 50, 75, 91, 93, 101
Phillips, John: 'Satyr against Hypocrites'
    92
Pindar 14
Plato 23
plays 54—5, 63, 102
    city comedy 67; comedy 31, 48;
    Elizabethan 38, 48, 64, 80, 108;
    Jacobean 24, 80, 108, 120;
    Restoration 64, 72; tragedy 64;
    verse 55, 64, 72, 80
poetry 135—6
    dramatic 55, 56, 72, 80; Elizabethan
    45, 60, 71, 78, 91; Jacobean 4, 23,
    71; personal 93, 104, 148; public
    22, 72, 81, 87, 93; Restoration 84,
    89; as action 19, 20, 53, 58, 73;
    and history 5, 6, 7, 8, 10, 12—13,
    18, 22, 48, 52, 105—6, 107, 120,
    123—4, 125, 135, 136, 137, 138,
    140, 142; and prose 6—7, 11, 38;
    and reality 7, 8, 9, 47—8, 102,
    137; and social background ix, x, 1,
    2—3, 4, 7, 9, 11—12, 14—15,
    18—19, 20, 21, 31, 33—4, 43, 45,
    46, 50—2, 62—3, 94, 99, 104,
    126, 136, 146, 148; as transformed
    experience 3, 6, 7—8, 10, 11, 12,
    13, 15, 16—17, 60, 91, 106;
    prestige 24, 44, 62, 63, 94; status
    54, 55, 63, 95, 100, 112; traffic in
    19, 55, 59, 148; uses 8, 10, 14, 15,
    19—20, 44, 56—7, 71, 72; *see also*
    the names of individual kinds or
    schools

'poetry of address' 57
poets 2, 3, 4, 8, 11, 39, 51, 64, 135
    amateur 55, 59, 158n96; and patrons
    24, 27, 54, 55—6, 57, 59, 61, 75,
    91, 95; professional 55, 59, 95,
    102, 153n3; and readers 58—61,
    122; royalist 72; social background
    1, 5, 10, 15, 24, 33, 37, 39, 61, 80,
    87, 91; social position 50, 57, 63,
    64, 95, 104; Spenserian 41, 94,
    148
political poetry 4, 6, 20, 21, 22, 50, 68,
    69, 70, 73
    Civil War 44, 46, 70, 92, 137;
    imagery 48, 98; Royalist 57—8, 64
politics 3, 31—2, 68—70, 108, 137,
    142
    corruption 66, 69
Pope, Alexander 44, 80
portraits 56, 140, 147, 159n110
poverty 118, 141, 160n39
Powell, Edward 135
prose ix, 6
    best-selling 13—14; diaries 29, 145,
    147; and history 7, 9, 12, 97, 134,
    145; letters 29, 145, 148, 159n110;
    and poetry 6—7, 11, 38
publishing 55, 103, 118, 148
puns 26, 47, 78—9, 156n14
Puritans 43, 71, 83, 92, 96, 122, 140
Puttenham, George 26, 38, 58
    The Arte of English Poesie 39

Quintilian 26

Rainsford, Anne, Lady 27
Raleigh, Sir Walter 55, 66, 69, 73, 74,
    155n2
    'If all the world and love were young'
    74; 'The Lie' 155n55; language 28;
    patrons 27, 55—6, 75; readers 45,
    59; style 86
Randolph, Thomas 66

readers 5, 9, 14, 16, 34, 58—60, 64, 120, 122
  Cavalier 67, 89; coterie 26, 66, 78, 79, 87, 135, 148; educated 26, 39, 42, 61, 79, 82, 87, 89, 102; Elizabethan 67—8; influence 26, 57, 59—60; as patrons 27, 45, 59, 66; and style 45, 61, 87, 89, 104; urban 67, 89; women 89, 102, 148
recitation 146, 148
reference
  direct 20—1, 22, 24, 73, 74, 97—8; indirect 46—7, 48, 74
register 38
religion 41, 69, 71, 72, 96, 102, 123, 145, 147
  church-going 146, 147, 148; and imagery 36, 118
religious poetry 70, 92, 98, 108, 122—3, 153n57
  and profane love 4, 36
Restoration 72
retirement 3, 24, 31, 44, 46, 67, 70, 72, 106
rhetoric 6, 8, 18, 19, 34, 38, 58, 81, 92, 135
Rich, Penelope (née Devereux) 19, 26
Riffaterre, M. 132, 150n6
Rochester, John Wilmot, 2nd Earl of 80, 148
royalists 32, 43, 46, 48, 58, 92, 140
Russell family 147
Russell, Conrad: *Parliaments and English Politics* 143

Sandys, George 111
satire 30, 46, 62, 69, 91, 118—19, 161n41
  content 22, 45, 67, 74, 98, 103, 104, 106, 118, 119, 159n110; language 26, 29, 31; readers 59; style 86, 88—9, 92; tone 42
science 23, 33, 72, 81, 92, 102, 118
semiotics x, 4, 123, 125, 126—7, 132, 146, 147, 150n6, 161n7

sexuality 24, 100, 101, 104, 106, 115—16, 148, 160n34, 162n18
Shakespeare, William 14, 23, 45, 54, 60, 63
  As You Like It 79; *Cymbeline* 82; *Hamlet* 157n43; *Henry IV, Part II* 82; *King Lear* 112; *Love's Labours Lost* 79; *Lucrece* 68; *Midsummer Night's Dream* 38; *Romeo and Juliet* 85, 96; *Sonnets* 2, 42, 54, 69, 73, 77, 80, 81, 91, 93, 94, 98—9, 110, 111, 152n29, 160n15; sonnet 86, 157n43; sonnet 94, 64—5, 82—3, 111; sonnet 134, 156n27; *Timon of Athens* 160n33; *Titus Andronicus* ix; *Venus and Adonis* 68; language 27, 35, 36, 38, 77, 79, 80, 81, 82—3, 84, 99, 114; patrons 96; readers 61; style 86; tragedies 90
Sherburne, Edward 135
Shirley, James 111, 135
Sidney family 19, 55, 148
Sidney, Lady Dorothy 90
Sidney, Sir Philip 62, 63
  Arcadia 91; *Astrophel and Stella* 7, 19, 26, 39, 59, 83, 92, 101, 109; language 28, 78, 109; readers 59, 61; sonnets 160n15; style 39, 86
simile 2, 30
Smith, William 159n98
social analysis ix, x, 3, 14, 23, 36—7, 51—2, 142
  of individuals 10, 33, 50, 61, 145; and language 124—5, 126; method 1, 123; of poetry 4, 5, 23, 34, 53, 62, 63, 71, 97, 99, 104—6, 107—8, 109, 121—4, 125; of satire 118—19
social class 34, 38, 45, 54, 61—5, 83, 91, 146, 152n42
  aristocratic 35, 38, 40, 41, 42, 62, 63, 82—3, 90, 99—100, 147, 148; gentry 40, 41, 43, 44, 45, 55, 62,

89, 94, 100, 140, 146, 147, 148; lower 38, 40, 61, 62; middle 35, 38, 89, 103; mobility 62, 84, 85, 94, 146; privilege 141, 148
society 62, 123, 140, 141, 146—9
and art 15—16, 51; changes 41, 42—3, 76, 84—5, 99, 102—3, 106, 109, 144—5; cohesiveness 14, 31; criticism 90, 118—19; identity 34, 43, 99, 103, 107, 125—6; and literature 38, 46, 50—1, 91, 95, 126
Song of Roland, The 138
sonnet 2, 14, 15, 19, 34, 39—40, 49, 100—1, 110—11
attacked 50, 94, 101; changes 31, 93—4; language 80, 81, 83, 101, 109—11; love theme 2, 23, 26, 34—6, 39, 93, 100; parody 93—4, 95, 101; Petrarchan 60, 91, 93, 100, 101
Southall, Raymond 77, 78, 152n29
Southampton, Henry Wriothesley, 3rd Earl of 68, 79, 80
Southwell, Robert 86
speech 104
and class 27, 38; colloquial 26, 27, 94, 133; educated 27, 40, 94; usage 27, 28, 118
Spenser, Edmund 54, 55, 60, 62, 63, 109—10, 111, 112
Amoretti 62, 94, 109, 112; *Epithalamion* 39, 78; *The Faerie Queene* 47, 63; 'This holy season fit to fast and pray' 152n29; 'Ye Tradeful Merchants' 152n29; allegory 22, 63; conservatism 29, 69; followers 41, 94, 148; language 28, 30, 35, 40, 78, 109; readers 61; style 39, 41
Spurgeon, Caroline 82, 114
Squier, Charles L. 122
Stanley, Thomas 44, 135
Poems and Translations 135
Stone, Lawrence 137, 145

style 18, 37—9, 42, 86—90
Cavalier 89—90, 122; changes 16, 41, 104, 109, 121—2; grand 38—9, 41, 86, 89, 90, 104; high 25, 38, 46; low 25, 38, 46; middle 38, 152n39; plain 38, 86, 88, 89, 90, 102—3, 104; and readers 87—8, 102, 103; satirical 88—9, 92, 103, 104; and social background 34, 37—9, 40, 41, 42, 43, 86—7, 99, 123
Suckling, Sir John 43, 66, 89, 93, 122
Summers, J. H. 122
Swift, Jonathan 80
symbolism 2, 47, 48, 82, 106, 113—17, 133, 134

tapinosis 25
taste 13, 14, 56
aristocratic 40; changes 31, 50; educated 56; popular 38, 104; Restoration 64
theatres 54—5, 96, 103
private 55, 64; Restoration 64
themes 10, 18, 21—2, 23, 34, 74—5, 76, 104, 105, 106, 139
Cavalier 24, 31, 57; Jacobean 24; non-political 42; pagan 96, 147; satirical 45, 74, 118, 119
Thomas, Keith 145
Religion and the Decline of Magic 145
Thynne, Francis: 'A Puritane' 79
Tofte, Robert 159n98
tone 34, 42, 43—4, 91, 92, 105, 119, 123
topography 20, 22, 73
town 66
imagery 31; setting 26, 67, 118, 155n48
Traherne, Thomas 70, 122
Tucker, Francis 135

university wits 62, 66, 102

Vaughan, Henry 46, 70, 122

vers de société see occasional verse
verse letter 14, 15, 19, 45—6, 56, 57, 80
  for ladies 59
viewpoint 42, 91, 109, 123
Virgil 14

Wallace, J. M. 22
Waller, Edmund 21, 58, 64, 66, 122
  'Upon His Majesty's Repairing of St Paul's' 58; language 28; style 42, 43, 87, 89—90
Walton, Geoffrey 122
Webbe, William 58

Weever, John 90, 141
Weidhorn, Manfred 122
Wells, H. W. 81—2, 114
wit 29, 35, 43, 83
Wither, George 21, 41, 60, 95
wooing 4, 55, 94, 101
word counts 109, 110, 111, 112
wordplay 2, 78—9, 85 *see also* puns
writers, professional 95, 102, 103
Wyatt, Thomas 77—8, 111
  'Who so list to hount' 82

Zepheria 152n29, 156n27